STUDIES IN HISTORY, ECONOMICS AND PUBLIC LAW

Edited by the

FACULTY OF POLITICAL SCIENCE

OF COLUMBIA UNIVERSITY

NUMBER 493

THE HOUSE COMMITTEE ON FOREIGN AFFAIRS

BY

ALBERT C. F. WESTPHAL

THE HOUSE COMMITTEE ON FOREIGN AFFAIRS

BY

ALBERT C. F. WESTPHAL

AMS PRESS
NEW YORK

Reprinted with the permission of Columbia University Press
From the edition of 1942, New York
First AMS EDITION published, 1968
Manufactured in the United States of America

AMS PRESS, INC.
New York, N.Y. 10003

PREFACE

On December 7, 1941, while Japanese bombers were attacking American territory, I was preparing the preface to this monograph which I had revised and completed some seven weeks previous. In the face of this aggression there resulted a characteristic unity of purpose between the executive and legislative branches of our government in order to prosecute the war to a successful conclusion. Until such success has been achieved any discussion of congressional efforts to shape and determine American foreign policy must necessarily be academic. Because I believe that a return to a period of peace will revive the contest between the President and Congress on matters of foreign policy, I have not been dissuaded from setting forth my findings on one fragment of this large subject. This monograph, originally intended to be a full length study of the role of the House of Representatives in foreign policy, has been whittled down to an analysis of the Committee on Foreign Affairs. As a predoctoral fellow of the Social Science Research Council, I was able to spend a year in Washington, studying the issues at first hand. For this privilege and encouragement I record my indebtedness to the Council.

Much of my labor in Washington would have been futile had it not been for the kindness and generosity of the late Sam D. McReynolds, chairman of the Committee, who placed at my disposal the extant records of that Committee. I drew exhaustively from them as well as from the wide personal knowledge of Mr. McReynolds who often was able to supplement the Committee's records by reference to his personal correspondence and his own recollection of events as he saw them in his sixteen years on the Committee. His secretaries, Mr. P. Lincoln White and Mrs. Lucille Schilling, cooperated with me to make my research easier. The former clerk of the Committee, Mr. I. R. Barnes, was more than generous with his time. Only his intimate acquaintance with Committee procedure and details could

5

save me from the many errors I would otherwise have committed. Other members of the Committee and of Congress have been of assistance to me. I especially want to thank Representative James A. Shanley of Connecticut for the many hours of stimulating conversation and discussion on the complexities that lie beneath congressional attention to, and action on, foreign affairs. To gain an understanding of the executive viewpoint, I discussed many aspects of this subject with members of the State Department. Only their passion for anonymity prevents my making a more detailed acknowledgment of my debt to them. The archivist of the State Department, Mrs. Natalie Summers, made my explorations of the Department's archives a lighter and more pleasant task. Finally, I want to thank Professors Charles C. Hyde, Philip C. Jessup, Lindsay Rogers and Schuyler Wallace of Columbia University for their friendly criticisms and suggestions. I alone, of course, assume all responsibility for any errors and misstatements that may appear in this book.

A. C. F. W.

New York City, N. Y.
December 7, 1941

Since the above was written, I have been called to active duty as an Officer in the United States Naval Reserve. The views expressed in this book are those of the author and do not necessarily reflect the opinions of the Navy Department.

TABLE OF CONTENTS

CHAPTER VII

CHAPTER VIII

CHAPTER I
INTRODUCTION

1. THE PROBLEM STATED

THE Supreme Court, in the Curtiss-Wright case, narrowed the area of doubt that remained regarding the President's power to act in the " vast external realm " of international affairs when it declared categorically that " the President alone has the power to speak or listen as a representative of the nation." [1] The exercise of this " plenary and exclusive power," the Court held, was checked only by its " subordination to the applicable provisions of the Constitution." In essence, it reaffirmed what writers on the subject have often maintained and Presidents have insisted upon—freedom to conduct the foreign affairs of the nation. This assertion has been associated in the lay mind with the idea that policy so enunciated has been arrived at independently by the President (possibly in collaboration with a group of advisers) without regard to the other agencies of government or that fluid force that passes as public opinion. In other words, not only is the President free to deal with foreign nations whenever adjustments in our relations with them are necessary, but the formulation of the policy to be pursued is within his exclusive domain.

Presidential practices and precedents notwithstanding, our congressional system does not permit the executive the same unlimited freedom in the determination of foreign policy that he enjoys in the conduct of foreign affairs. [2] The years since

1 299 *U. S.* 319. *Cf. U. S. v. Pink* (1942), 62 *Sup. Ct.* 552.

2 The restrictions imposed upon the executive in the neutrality acts passed since 1935 are a case in point. Even executive agreements, entered into without the approval of the Senate, may be the subjects of congressional action. Postal conventions and reciprocal trade agreements are based upon the prior consent of Congress. Secretary Olney, in 1896, entered into an agreement with the British Ambassador providing for the expulsion of the Canadian Cree Indians from the United States. The appropriation necessary to carry out this agreement was subsequently voted by Congress. *Cf.* John B. Moore, " Treaties and Executive Agreements," *Pol. Sci. Quar.*, XX (Sept., 1905), p. 385 ff.

1900 have witnessed an increasing participation by Congress in this field. This participation may be found not only in the usual legislative questions handled by Congress since the inception of the government—for example, tariff and appropriations—but in the extension of the legislative process to newer spheres. Illustrative of this are the arms embargo and neutrality measures, the Silver Purchase Act, the Gold Reserve Act and the Exchange Stabilization Fund. In other matters, as the growth of the merchant marine and the control of immigration, there has been a quickening of congressional interest.[3] The concern of Congress in foreign affairs, however, does not stop with legislation.[4] Through resolutions, hearings and investigations, conducted or guided by its committees, as well as by extended debates, it has been able to exert an influence. In 1938, the furor created in Congress by discussions between a member of the Navy Department and the British Admiralty led Secretary Hull to deny the accusation that an Anglo-American naval pact was under consideration.[5] A hearing before the House

3 *Cf.* Charles A. Beard, *The Idea of National Interest* (New York, 1934), chap. IX, Foreign Implications of Domestic Affairs.

4 It is appropriate at this point to note that legislation may be the result either of a bill or of a joint resolution, introduced into either the Senate or the House of Representatives, subsequently passed by both Houses, and signed by the President. Both the processes of congressional action and the legal effect are the same for the joint resolution as for the bill. While the use of the former is said to be for "the incidental, unusual, or inferior purposes of legislating," no sharp line can be drawn in actual practice. One member remarked that his choice was determined by "whichever I happen to put my hand on first," referring to the form used by congressmen in offering a bill or resolution. Note, for example, that measures dealing with neutrality have been introduced into the House in both forms.

"Concurrent resolutions have been developed as a means of expressing fact, principles, opinions, and purposes of the two Houses" and are not sent to the President for approval. *Jefferson's Manual and Rules of the House of Representatives*, sec. 396 (1934 ed.).

A simple resolution performs the same functions for one of the two Houses. It, too, does not need the President's approval. In addition, simple resolutions, called resolutions of inquiry, may call on the President or members of the cabinet for information. *Ibid.*, sec. 857.

5 75th Cong., 3rd Sess. (1938). *Cong. Record*, February 8, 1938, pp. 1621-1622.

Military Affairs Committee on the location of frontier air bases
was the occasion for a sharp rebuke by President Franklin D.
Roosevelt when the Committee indiscreetly published confidential military information pertinent to relations with Canada.[6]
The Senate Finance Committee, starting with an investigation
into the sale of foreign bonds in the United States, examined
the whole post-war structure of capital exports.[7]

National elections seldom reflect public sentiment on foreign
policy. In the first place, personalities and domestic issues, often
sectional, occupy public attention. Secondly, the fixed intervals
between elections prevent the immediate testing of public reaction to policy changes, whether on domestic or foreign questions.
If foreign policy is to be put to the voters' judgment, therefore,
it must be capable of sustaining public attention over a long
period—such as a major foreign conflict—or must " break " as
election time nears; otherwise interest lags. Within the last forty
years only four presidential campaigns have presented elements
of foreign policy as paramount issues—in 1900, the question of
imperialism; in 1916, the neutrality policy of President Wilson;
in 1920, the relations of the United States to the League of
Nations; and, in 1940, the question of aid to Britain. In each
instance, however, they never attained the rank of exclusive
issues and had to be weighed by the electorate along with a
complex array of domestic questions.

This inability to single out foreign policy for public determination at the polls throws upon Congress the responsibility for
expressing what it believes to be the aspirations of its constituents. Congress becomes at once both a forum and a sounding
board. But unable to ascertain the executive's views as directly
and openly as the House of Commons does through the question
hour, Congress uses the committees to accomplish this purpose.

6 74th Cong., 1st Sess. (1935). Hearings on the *Location of Air Defense
Bases*, H. R. 6621 and H. R. 4130. Chairman McSwain subsequently ordered
that the printed copies of the hearings be destroyed. This was done; but not
before some of them had been distributed. Private information.

7 72nd Cong., 1st Sess. (1931-1932). Senate Committee on Finance, *Sale of
Foreign Bonds or Securities in the United States.*

They are liaisons between the legislature and the executive. As will be shown, this permits a more intimate discussion than debates on the floor of the House. Today the powerful Committee on Appropriations only considers bills designed to carry out a previous legislative enactment. This means that, in the first instance, another committee must have deliberated upon and approved the policy contained in that legislation. The Committee on Naval Affairs examines measures determining the strength and composition of the navy. The Committee on Military Affairs performs a similar function for the army. They may follow the suggestions of the President as revealed either in budgetary requests or in special messages to Congress or heed the requests of the appropriate cabinet officers sent to them in an open letter or suggested in a less formal manner to the chairman; but theirs is the responsibility for presenting the bill around which congressional policy will be built. Only after enactment of these measures into law does the Committee on Appropriations enter the picture. Similarly, the House Committees on Immigration, Ways and Means, Interstate and Foreign Commerce, Coinage, Weights and Measures, Insular Affairs, and Territories, each within its respective field, handle proposed legislation and weigh problems which may affect American foreign relations. In the Senate, analogous committees perform a similar function. Even the House Committee on Rules, through its ability to report a special order providing both the time and method of debate, may influence the outcome of pending legislation.[8] For a thorough study of the role of Congress

8 The resolution providing for the annexation of Hawaii was reported favorably by a majority of the Foreign Affairs Committee and was certain, if brought to a vote, to pass the House. " The one obstacle was Speaker Reed, implacable opponent of annexation, who as chairman of the Committee on Rules could prevent the consideration of the resolution. For three weeks he held out against pressure from the Administration and his fellow-Republicans in Congress, but there was a limit beyond which even he would not go in opposing the wishes of his party, and he finally gave his consent to tactics which would bring the resolution before the House without a special rule." Julius W. Pratt, *Expansionists of 1898* (Baltimore, 1936), pp. 320-321. Also, William A. Robinson, *Thomas B. Reed* (New York, 1930), pp. 366-367.

in foreign affairs, therefore, one must inquire into many of the forty-seven standing committees of the House and the thirty-three of the Senate. This monograph, however, has only one purpose: to study functionally, primarily since 1898, the work of the one committee in the lower House that embraces within its jurisdiction those matters which bear most directly and immediately on our international relations, that is, the Committee on Foreign Affairs.

2. The History and Development of the Committee on Foreign Affairs

Historically, legislative interest in foreign affairs in the United States has followed a line of development different from that of other countries. European parliaments, in so far as they have any voice in the shaping of foreign policy, have gained

A vote on the McLemore resolution, warning Americans not to travel on armed ships, was welcomed by President Wilson because its lengthy preamble, so unsatisfactory to members of the House, would cause its defeat. Mr. McLemore, realizing the undesirable features of his resolution, "appeared before the Rules Committee and asked it to strike out all of his resolution except the warning feature of it, but the committee refused to do so," wrote Representative Kitchin to a constituent. Kitchin to Dr. H. Q. Alexander, March 9, 1916. *Kitchin Papers.* The same day he wrote to a friend, Mr. W. P. White: " The Rules Committee (and between us, the Administration) was afraid to give us a straight vote on a simple resolution warning Americans to stay off armed vessels of the belligerents." *Ibid.* On February 29, 1916, President Wilson wrote Mr. Pou, acting chairman of the Rules Committee, to urge an early vote on the McLemore resolution "in order that there may be afforded an immediate opportunity for full public discussion and action upon them and that all doubts and conjectures may be swept away and our foreign relations once more cleared of damaging misunderstandings." *Pou Papers.*

The Rules Committee, through its power to report on the creation of new committees, has undertaken to examine matters which ordinarily would have fallen within the jurisdiction of the Foreign Affairs Committee. Thus, in the first session of the Sixty-sixth Congress (1919) a joint resolution providing for the appointment of a committee to investigate the Mexican situation, led to the holding of hearings. It heard Ambassador Henry P. Fletcher as well as other individuals who might throw some light on the confused state of Mexican affairs. Its inquiry was concerned far more with the latter than with the narrow problem of the desirability of the creation of a new committee. The committee was never appointed.

that right by depriving the executive of what had been theretofore an exclusive domain. This transition in constitutional governments has been neither universal nor uniform and, in any
case, it has been unusually slow. Even so well established a
parliamentary system as that of Great Britain still makes little
provision for legislative participation in the shaping of foreign
policy.

The earliest conduct and control of foreign affairs in what
was to be the United States rested with popularly elected bodies.
This procedure was grounded as much on the heritage of col-
onial committees as it was on the absence of any executive
agency.[9] Even before the Declaration of Independence the
Continental Congress appointed a committee of five " for the
sole purpose of corresponding with our friends in Great Britain,
Ireland and other parts of the world." [10] The specialized character of its work was recognized by the spring of 1777 when
its title was changed from the Committee of Secret Correspondence to that of Committee for Foreign Affairs.[11] Partisanship
and personalities, frequent changes in personnel and the use of
special committees, impaired the efficient functioning of the
committee and made a coherent policy impossible. Through
these multiple channels the Congress appointed, instructed, and
recalled its agents; it communicated with foreign representatives
who came to these shores; and, in 1778, Congress itself ratified
the treaties with France.[12] Policy was further diffused by the
initiative taken by envoys abroad who were faced with the
necessity of making immediate decisions.[13] The presence in

9 Cf. Paul D. Hasbrouck, *Party Government in the House of Representa-*
tives (New York, 1927), chap. III, The Committees. George C. Wood,
Congressional Control of Foreign Relations during the American Revolution,
1774-1789 (Allentown, Pa., 1919), chap. I-III.

10 November 29, 1775. *Secret Journals of Congress,* II, p. 5.

11 April 17, 1777. *Journals of the Continental Congress, 1774-1789* (Washington, 1904-1934), VII, p. 274.

12 Hunter Miller, *Treaties and Other International Acts of the United*
States of America (Washington, 1931), II, p. 29.

13 Wood, chap. VII.

Europe of several agents, often representing different factions and working at variance with each other, made constructive efforts even more difficult. Weakness at home enabled Franklin in Paris to interpret generously the instructions Congress gave him in 1778.[14] Even after a Department of Foreign Affairs was set up Robert Livingston, the first Secretary, and a close friend of Franklin, allowed the latter a wide latitude in negotiations. Conduct and control of foreign affairs, at least for several years, passed to the hands of American agents in Europe.[15]

Recognizing " the fluctuation, the delay and indecision " of the existing system, but reluctant to surrender complete control, the Congress set up a Department of Foreign Affairs early in 1781.[16] The resolution setting up the new office attempted to provide legislative direction with a minimum of executive discretion. The Department was " to be kept always in the place where Congress shall reside." The information accumulated by the Secretary was " to be laid before Congress when required; " he was to transmit " such communications as Congress shall direct." Since he was to reflect the attitude of Congress, he was at " liberty to attend Congress that he may be better informed of the affairs of the United States, and have an opportunity of explaining his reports respecting his department." The limited powers conferred upon the Secretary were further restricted by the continued practice of appointing committees to deal with specific problems in foreign affairs.[17] Less than two years under this arrangement convinced Livingston of its impossibilities and he submitted his resignation, although he remained in office until the spring of 1783 when a successor was selected.[18]

14 *Ibid.* The instructions may be found in the *Secret Journals,* II, pp. 107-111.

15 Wood, chap. VII.

16 January 10, 1781. *Jour. of Cont. Cong.,* XIX, p. 43.

17 Wood, chap. VIII.

18 Livingston expressed himself at length on the shortcomings of the act of 1781. A committee of three, examining his objections, reported a measure to correct, in part, some of them. On February 22, 1782, the Congress passed a new act, thereby repealing that of 1781. While enlarging his powers and clarifying his duties, the Secretary was still an agent of the Congress. *Jour. of Cont. Cong.,* XXII, p. 87.

Pending boundary disputes and questions on the rights of navigation brought home to Congress the desirability of centralized direction. The new Secretary, John Jay, experienced and vigorous, moved boldly in his new office, but not without attempts—partly successful—on the part of some members of the Congress to check him and to resurrect the committee system of control. Throughout the balance of his incumbency which ended with the Continental Congress, there was a noticeable tendency, not uninterrupted, however, to give the Secretary a larger share in both the control and formulation of foreign policy.[19] Not only was he given power to negotiate with Spain in 1785, but he often made recommendations to the Congress which were favorably received. Initiative was shifting gradually from the legislative body to an executive officer. As one writer has pointed out, the weakness exhibited by the Congress in the handling of foreign relations was one of the factors that directed the attention of the Constitutional Convention to the need for a stronger executive.[20]

The theory of separation of powers under the Constitution had to be tempered by the necessities for harmonious action at least between the executive and legislative divisions. A bridge was needed to span the gap. The House standing committee, which today performs that service, was of undetermined merit and, indeed, distrusted. There was a partial reversion to the practices prevailing before 1789.

Custom had not begun to make it necessary that everything should be referred to small committees for examination and report. Bills often went through without being referred at all. If a proposition was referred, whether the subject had been introduced by petition or resolution, by message from the President or communication from the head of a department, the normal course was for

19 John Jay held the office of Acting Secretary of State from September 16, 1789, to March 22, 1790, when he was succeeded by Thomas Jefferson.

20 Wood, chap. IX. *Cf.* Gaillard Hunt, *The Department of State* (New Haven, 1914), p. 52.

the Committee of the Whole to control, not simply to approve or reject. When it made up its mind, then a committee would be appointed to draw up and bring in a bill according with specific direction.[21]

Thus, there was a continuation of the select committee idea. That such a loosely coordinated arrangement operated for twenty years was due to the vigorous role of the President and his agents, aided by a party caucus. Under such conditions House organization was retarded. But once the strong hand was removed, as it was during Madison's administration, confusion and ineffectiveness were the results. Under the stimulus of an aggressive leader, Henry Clay, the House not only righted the balance in the constitutional machine but even tipped it in its (the House's) favor. The rapid increase in House membership and in its business made the Committee of the Whole an unwieldy body for preliminary discussion. The main advance, therefore, was in the perfection of machinery within the House itself. One improvement lay in the augmentation of the standing committees that had slowly come into being. When Clay left the Speaker's chair in 1825, no fewer than twenty-five existed.[22]

Prior to the creation of the standing committee those portions of the President's message to Congress touching on foreign affairs or diplomatic and consular matters were referred to a select committee on foreign affairs.[23] Nominally an agent of the House, it reflected the views of the majority party and particularly those of the majority leaders. Henry Clay, as Speaker, appointed Peter B. Porter chairman and thereby brought added

21 Robert Luce, *Legislative Procedure* (Boston, 1922), p. 101.

22 Ralph V. Harlow, *The History of Legislative Methods in the Period before 1825* (New Haven, 1917), p. 216.

23 See, for example, the resolution of Mr. Dawson. "Resolved, that so much of the message of the President of the United States as relates to aggressions committed within our ports and waters by foreign armed vessels, to the violations of our jurisdiction, and the measures necessary for the protection of our ports and harbors, be referred to a select committee." 10th Cong., 1st Session, October 29, 1807. *Annals of Congress*, p. 795.

pressure on President Madison to adopt a strenuous course toward Great Britain. His message of April 1, 1812, recommending an embargo, was followed shortly by Porter's report to the House, admittedly " draughted according to the wishes and directions of the Secretary of the Treasury." [24] We have the word of John Quincy Adams that " the Chairman of the Committee on Foreign Relations has always been considered as a member in the confidence of the Executive, and Mr. Forsyth acted thus at the last session. The President has hitherto considered him as perfectly confidential, and directed me to communicate freely to him the documents concerning foreign affairs, particularly those with Spain, which I have done." On occasion reports of the Committee to the House were given first to the President for his scrutiny. [25]

When the Foreign Affairs Committee was established in 1822, it had seven members; today it has twenty-five. In size, it is exceeded only by Appropriations with forty and Judiciary with twenty-six. Eight other House committees also have twenty-five. Not only its numerical strength but the scope of its activities led Speaker Clark, in 1916, to refer to it as one of the

24 12th Cong., 1st Sess. *Annals of Congress, Supp. Jour.*; cited in Harlow, p. 241. President Madison's war message of June 1, 1812, was referred to the Committee on Foreign Relations. (Note that throughout this early period the committee was referred to either as the Committee on Foreign Affairs or the Committee on Foreign Relations.) Two days later Calhoun, the acting chairman, brought in the committee's report. Gaillard Hunt has presented strong evidence to show that Secretary of State Monroe prepared the report and passed it on to Calhoun for his use. Gaillard Hunt, " Joseph Gales on the War Manifesto of 1812," *Amer. Hist. Rev.*, January 1908, p. 303 ff.; cited in Frank A. Updyke, *The Diplomacy of the War of 1812* (Baltimore, 1915), pp. 128-129.

It should also be noted that the Secretary of War discussed questions of military policy with the Foreign Affairs Committee. Henry Adams, *History of the United States during the Administration of James Madison* (New York, 1930 ed.), Book VI, p. 129.

25 *Memoirs* (Philadelphia, 1874-1877), IV, p. 65. Other evidence of the close connection between the State Department and the chairman may be found on pages 183-184, 210, 212-214, 474-476, 478, and 505-506.

four most important committees of the House.[26] Like all committees, selection for membership is made with a view to geographical representation and personal preference. No special
qualifications attach to membership on it. Education through
travel or research on international affairs has not marked its
personnel, although several members have held appointments
to important conferences. Delegates to the Interparliamentary
Union often include some of its members. The knowledge of
foreign affairs which is brought to the Committee by the fresh-
men members is no greater, and may be even less, than that
possessed by other representatives. Active service over a span
of years is, therefore, the best instruction available. Although
there has been an improved stability in membership in the last
forty years, nevertheless the change in personnel has been high.
From the Fifty-fifth to the Seventy-fifth Congresses, inclusive,
one hundred and sixty members have been assigned to the Committee. Eighty-three of these have served two or less terms. In
other words, less than fifty percent of its members have served
for more than four years. So far as can be checked, no major
proposal on foreign affairs has emanated from those with less
than four years service. Nor have they participated to any degree in the hearings conducted by the Committee. The burden
of interrogation, one gathers from reading the hearings and
minutes, has been the work of relatively few men, usually those
with some years of service behind them. If the majority of its
members are passive, it is not necessarily from want of interest
in the Committee's activities. Rather, the problems handled by
it are in a field which, under the pressure of domestic issues, has
not come within their purview. Moreover, the relatively small
degree of political capital that can be extracted from issues of
foreign policy does not encourage Committee members to ex-

26 65th Cong., 2nd Sess. *Cong. Rec.*, p. 318. December 14, 1917. This
compliment was doubtless given to the Committee because of the prominence
it gained in the two previous years. The other three committees were Ways
and Means, Judiciary, and Appropriations. He added that Post Offices and
Interstate and Foreign Commerce were "forcing themselves into the same
class."

pend too much energy on the mastery of details of that subject.

The following analysis indicates the quantitative extent of the Committee's work during the Seventieth Congress (1927-1929) and the Seventy-fifth Congress (1937-1938).

Seventieth Congress: Bills and Joint Resolutions.

	Referred to CFA	Considered by CFA	Passed by House	Passed by Cong.	Enacted into law
Private	48	20	12	9	9
Claims (other than private)....	12	10	9	8	8
Neutrality, disarmament, embargo, peace measures, etc. ...	19	5	0	0	0
Measures pertaining to the State Department	10	8	1	1	1
International conferences, fairs expositions, etc.	40	27	15	9	9
Miscellaneous	28	12	5	4	4
Total..................	157	82	42	31	31

Seventy-fifth Congress: Bills and Joint Resolutions.

	Referred to CFA	Considered by CFA	Passed by House	Passed by Cong.	Enacted into law
Private	12	7	5	5	5
Claims (other than private)....	21	20	18	18	18
Neutrality, disarmament, embargo, peace measures, etc. ...	42	5	1	1	1
Measures pertaining to the State Department	12	5	2	2	2
International conferences, fairs expositions, etc.	44	31	19	18	17
Miscellaneous	25	22	9	8	8
Total..................	156	90	54	52	51

In addition, there were:

	70th Cong.	75th Cong.
House resolutions	14	12
House current resolutions	2	9
Senate bills and joint resolutions	12	18
Total	28	39

In the Seventieth Congress only one House resolution was considered as against three in the Seventy-fifth. Concurrent resolutions were not acted upon in either Congress. Four of the Senate bills and one of the Senate joint resolutions of the Seventieth Congress had counterparts in the House in contrast with three and eight respectively in the Seventy-fifth Congress. Reports by the Committee to the House were sixty-two and seventy-seven, respectively.[27]

The transformation of the Foreign Affairs Committee from a select to a standing committee made no apparent change either in its functions or its relations to the House. As new foreign situations arose, demanding congressional action or arresting the attention of the House by virtue of their importance, the Committee enlarged the scope of its activities. The *Notes and Annotations,* supplementing the rule which defines the Committee's jurisdiction, give some idea of its expansion. They read:[28]

It has a broad jurisdiction over foreign relations, including bills to establish boundary lines between the United States and foreign nations, to determine naval strength, and regulate bridges and dams on international waters, for the protection of American citizens abroad and expatriation, to maintain the treaty rights of American fishermen, for extradition with foreign nations, international arbitration, relating to violation of neutrality, international conferences and congresses, the incorporation of the American National Red Cross and protection of its insignia, immigration of Chinese and Japanese, intervention abroad and declarations of war, affairs of the consular service, including acquisition of land and buildings for legations in foreign capitals, creation of courts of the United States in foreign countries, treaty regulations as to protection of fur seals.

The committee has also considered measures for fostering commercial intercourse with foreign nations and for safeguarding

27 This study is based on the information contained in the *Calendar* of the Committee on Foreign Affairs for the Seventieth and the Seventy-fifth Congresses.

28 Jefferson's *Manual,* sec. 689.

American business interests abroad, and even the subjects of commercial treaties and reciprocal arrangements, although in later practice the Committee on Ways and Means has considered such matters. Foreign Affairs has exercised a general but not exclusive jurisdiction over legislation relating to claims having international relations. The committee also exercised a preliminary jurisdiction as to the canal between the Atlantic and Pacific Oceans.

In addition, from 1885, when the jurisdiction of the Committee on Appropriations was circumscribed by the House rules, until 1920, the Committee also had authority to report appropriations.

Bearing in mind that we are primarily concerned with the Committee's role, not that of the House, the above list would seem to indicate that the Committee was unusually active, if not influential, in shaping legislation and policy. The fragmentary records do not bear out this belief. The minute books are mere listings of measures referred to it with no indication of the discussions, if any, that took place. As pointed out below, most of the work was done by innumerable subcommittees rather than the whole Committee. Occasionally a debate on the floor, supplemented by outside material, throws some light on the inner workings. Thus, in 1868, Chairman Banks, discussing the appropriation measure to make possible the fulfillment of the treaty for the purchase of Alaska, revealed some of the Committee's discussion and general attitude and dwelt also on the role of the House in connection with treaties.[29] He assured the members that the bill was reported "from a sense of duty alone." The efforts of the chairman may be gleaned from correspondence with Secretary Seward, found in the State Department archives. Contemporary newspaper accounts, purporting to reveal the difficulties in the Committee, add something to our information.[30]

29 40th Cong., 2nd Sess. (1868). *Cong. Globe*, Appendix, p. 385.

30 *The New York Tribune*, February-July, 1868. I am indebted to Mr. Reinhard Luthin for calling this material to my attention.

In explanation of the Committee's comparatively unexciting career, several points may be noted. Foreign affairs throughout the last three-quarters of the nineteenth century were overshadowed by domestic issues; only intermittently, and then briefly, did they flash across the congressional arena. Underlying most issues, at least up to President Johnson's administration, was the conflict between the executive and Congress. Beginning with President Grant's administration there was a sharp reaction in the legislature against executive leadership. The House, turbulent and often in political disagreement with the executive, was unable or unwilling to assume command and the initiative passed to the Senate.[31] Moreover, members showed a preference for action in the Committee of the Whole or the House itself. Measures which today would first merit the judgment of the Committee usually were not referred to it. The lengthy debates on our relations with the newly established South American states were carried on, for the most part, in the Committe of the Whole.[32] Only after the House had unanimously condemned the French occupation of Mexico did the Committee study the question. Even then, it was the principle enunciated by President Lincoln in his explanation to the French Government rather than the immediate issue that stirred it to action.[33]

In foreign affairs more than in domestic the House was less willing to impress upon the President its claims to participation. The Committee itself seemed lacking in initiative. Part of this may be attributed to the rules which, until 1890, made difficult the introduction of public bills and resolutions. [34] Frequently a

31 See, *passim*, William E. Binkley, *The Powers of the President* (Garden City, 1937).

32 16th Cong., 2nd Sess. *Annals of Congress*, pp. 1042-1055. February 6, 1821.

33 38th Cong., 1st Sess. *Cong. Globe*, p. 1408. April 4, 1868.

34 "At first motions for leave to introduce a bill were not very common, the habits of the House inclining rather to let the committee draft the bill on jurisdiction conferred by the reference of a petition or by a resolution of

committee report also contained the bill upon which the House
was asked to act. Thus the Committee itself introduced bills.
Further, the Committee relied much more than it does today
upon the President's message to inform it of matters requiring
its attention. Typical of this dependence was the bill, enacted
into law, giving the President power to assure reciprocal commercial relations between the United States and Canada.[35]
Public opinion sometimes filtered into the inner sanctum and
forced action. Chairman Ingersoll was in a minority on his own
committee when he sought to report favorably on the annexation of Texas. But the elections of 1844 returned a majority
favoring annexation.[36]

Finally, the selection of committees by the Speaker gave to
one man an inordinate degree of power.[37] Amenability rather
than ability determined the choice. The effects were most marked

the House instructing them so to do. Later, from 1835 to 1850, it was a
more frequent practice for bills to be introduced on leave." Until 1880 the
introduction of bills was not permitted without notice or leave on Monday
mornings. Asher C. Hinds, *Precedents of the House of Representatives of
the United States* (Washington, 1907), sec. 3365.

35 52nd Cong., 1st Sess. (1892), H. R. 9324. For the debates, see *Cong.
Rec.*, p. 6350 ff. The immediate issue was that of passage of American vessels
on the St. Lawrence River, the Great Lakes, and waterways connecting them.
Where discrimination was practised by a government against American vessels
on those waters—obviously Canada—the President had discretion to suspend
the right of free passage through St. Mary Falls Canal of those vessels flying the flag of such government. The question of free passage was only one
of a series of vexatious questions that existed between the two governments.,
For a detailed discussion of these issues, see James M. Callahan, *American
Foreign Policy in Canadian Relations* (New York, 1937), chap. XVII.

36 " His (Ingersoll's) diary has shown that the annexationists had planned
to make an appeal to the people from the adverse Congress. In pursuance of
this plan, not only did he make his canvass as a thorough-going advocate
of immediate annexation, but he reminds us that Polk did the same thing,
and notes how, at the next session of Congress, the first vote on the subject
showed that the elections had changed many votes and had shifted the as-
cendancy in Congress." William M. Meigs, *The Life of Charles Jared
Ingersoll* (Philadelphia, 1897), pp. 268-269.

37 For a discussion on the selection of committees since the Speaker lost
that privilege, see Hasbrouck, *Party Government*, p. 41 f.

in the case of chairmen whose responsibilities for the efficient dispatch of business were—and still are—admittedly great. From 1822 to 1895, twenty-seven chairmen presided over the Committee on Foreign Affairs in thirty-nine Congresses. Chairman Ingersoll, jumping from Judiciary to the head of Foreign Affairs, found himself unfamiliar with the Committee's work and its personnel.[38] Two of his own party opposed him on the annexation of Texas. Nathaniel Banks, serving his first term in the Thirty-ninth Congress, was immediately appointed chairman. He was the only chairman during those years to serve for four terms. Previously, in the Thirty-seventh Congress, Mr. Crittenden assumed the office simultaneously with his election to the House. Mr. Everett, Mr. Curtin and Mr. McCreary each had one term to his credit when elevated to head the Committee. The same rapid change marked the membership as a body. Only one member who served on the Committee in the Forty-seventh Congress had served in the previous Congress. It was not uncommon for the entire membership to change with each Congress. This condition was checked when the Republicans gained and retained control of the House from 1895 to 1911. That an element of stability was introduced may be gathered from the fact that Mr. Hitt served as chairman for ten years under three Speakers—Reed, Henderson and Cannon—his control terminated only on his death. Similar evidence may be offered in connection with other committees, perhaps the most notable being the sixteen-year chairmanship of Mr. Hull of Iowa of the Committee on Military Affairs.

[38] "Dec. 25 (18)43. Mr. Adams having presented two petitions *against* the admission of Texas into the Union, and had them referred to the committee on foreign affairs, that, probably unwittingly on his part (I was mistaken; he understood the committee better than I did), gives me charge of this subject." Quoted from the notes of Mr. Ingersoll in Meigs, cited, p. 259.

CHAPTER II
THE COMMITTEE AT WORK

1. Introduction

ONE participant and observer has discerned the functions of a congressional committee as threefold: first, the acquiring of information and opinion from outside; next, the forming and formulating of judgment from within; third, the persuading of the House to adopt the conclusion reached.[1] Certainly the first of these functions has been exercised by the Foreign Affairs Committee with any degree of consistency only in comparatively recent decades. Whether it regarded the possession of information as futile is debatable. More important, little effort was made to acquire a broader view and more thorough comprehension of the subjects within its jurisdiction. This inertia may be checked from other angles—the hearings held and the reports made to the House. Here the yield of data confirms this.[2]

Historically, then, the Foreign Affairs Committee has performed the first of the three functions with reasonable thoroughness and effectiveness only during the last forty years. This is contemporaneous with the emergence of the United States as a world power. Even in the years immediately following 1898, the Committee's quest for information was restricted largely to an examination of the annual appropriation bill for

1 Robert Luce, *Legislative Assemblies* (New York, 1922), p. 129. Mr. Luce was a member of the House for twenty years. The first two of the three functions are discussed in this analysis.

2 This observation is based upon an examination of the *Checklist of United States Public Documents, 1789-1909* (1911) and the catalogs of the Library of Congress and the New York Public Library. Together they list available published hearings prior to the Sixtieth Congress. A search of the Committee files prior to that time does not disclose the existence of the manuscript copy of the hearings.

During the Fifty-fifth Congress, covering the Spanish-American War, the Committee on Foreign Affairs had sixty-seven bills and resolutions referred to it, forty of which touched on matters other than Spain and Cuba. Only two hearings were held, both on the Cuban question.

the diplomatic and the consular services. The expansion in size and functions of these two services, together with the method of appropriation by post instead of by grade, gave the members an opportunity to roam over the field of American foreign relations. They sought information why an increase in salary was justified in Cairo, why a secretary should be appointed to the legation at Haiti, what the International Joint Commission had done to warrant its appropriations. Theirs was primarily a pecuniary jaunt. Occasionally the Secretary of State would present a thumb-nail sketch of the more important activities of the Department during the previous year, as Secretary Knox did when he listed twenty major topics handled by his office.[3] The list included the Hukuang loan, Manchurian railway neutralization, Honduras debt funding negotiations, elimination of Zelaya (the Nicaraguan dictator), State Department reorganization, Liberia, and Argentine naval contracts. This was the knowledge with which the Committee fortified itself when it made its most important—and possibly only—appearance before the whole House in a congressional session.

The World War made more important the work of the Committee and, in part, changed its emphasis. In the first place it more readily accepted the increased appropriations requested for the foreign services as a natural concomitant of wartime conditions. The act of 1915 put into law the executive orders of Presidents Roosevelt and Taft, commissioning members of the services to offices rather than posts.[4] The Committee no longer was concerned with allocations of money to each of the many foreign service posts; its scrutiny was focused on the numerical strength and the efficient functioning of the services. Secondly, the quickening of public consciousness on international matters was reflected not only in discussions on the floor of the House, but also in the measures introduced and referred to the Foreign

3 Hearings on *Diplomatic and Consular Appropriation Bill*, 61st Cong., 2nd Sess. (1910).

4 38 *Stat.* 805. See, *infra*, pp. 122.

Affairs Committee. Some of these measures—those, for example, expressing sympathy with various European peoples and others touching on Irish independence—commanded the attention of diverse groups of citizens and hence affected, directly in some cases, in others, indirectly, the political fortunes of the representatives. The acquisition of information was often subordinated to the publicizing of a "cause."

No doubt popular revolt against " secret diplomacy " left its mark on the Committee's activities. During President Wilson's first Congress—the Sixty-third—only three hearings were held by the Committee; during his last—the Sixty-sixth—when the Committee was under Republican direction, no less than twenty-six hearings were held on as many measures, all of which were reported out.[5] As indicated below, hearings are not the only means of obtaining information. But so frequent are they today, and so easily reducible to quantitative designation, that they may serve as a fairly accurate indicator of the Committee's labors.

2. PURPOSES OF HEARINGS

The acquisition of information is not usually the ultimate objective of the hearing; curiosity is seldom the motive.[6] The Committee members may apply the information derived to a preconceived end, and like the medieval scholastics, seek to prove what they already believe; conversely, their judgment may be molded by the data placed before them. By the nature of the questioning and the vigor of the attack—not always detectable in the cold printed word—they may reveal not only their own sentiments but those of the House. Where the sentiments of a

5 The incompleteness of the Committee files for the Sixty-sixth Congress (1919-1921) prevents any accurate estimate of hearings on measure not reported out.

6 Neither the rules nor the precedents of the House instruct congressional committees on their internal conduct. *Cf.* Rule XI which lays down the jurisdiction of the various committees. Rule XII, par. 49, reads: " The rules of the House are hereby made the rules of the standing committees so far as applicable ... " See, also, Hinds, *Precedents*, secs. 4558-4564.

substantial portion of the Committee differ from those of the executive branch, the hearings may constitute a form of legislative pressure on the latter. As one representative observed: " Hearings bring a certain pressure upon the Departments and frequently in that way result in compliance with our wishes." [7]

Partisans of an important measure that has been heard in open session are able to garner much ammunition for the verbal barrage that may ensue on the floor. Even beyond the legislative halls the attendant publicity may be used by congressmen to bring pressure on their colleagues—in and out of the Committee. It is not possible to ascertain how effective this pressure has been in determining the vote of each member; but its existence is evidenced by the mail that comes to the Committee.[6]

The beneficent effects of hearings have been appreciated by the Committee where it is working substantially as a unit in behalf of a particular bill. In the course of hearings on Representative Burton's resolution prohibiting the exportation of arms and munitions, one member remarked:[9]

Mr. Burton's resolution relates to a very important matter, and I think hearings would help very materially in securing its passage through the House and Senate, and even help with the general public. It is my experience . . . that on matters of importance like that where we go into hearings quite extensively, the hearings are read much more freely than we think they are . . .

Because the Committee, especially the supporters of the administration, understands the dangers inherent in a resolution of inquiry calling on the Secretary of State for data in his possession, it usually prefers the more cautious expedient of executive session hearings if, indeed, any hearings are to be held.[10] By this practice it frequently can secure for the author

---

7 66th Cong. (1919-1921). Files, C. F. A.

8 Cf. Charles Warren, "Congress and Neutrality," p. 141, in *Neutrality and Collective Security*, edited by Quincy Wright (Chicago, 1936).

9 70th Cong. (1927-1929). Minutes, C. F. A.

10 For the resolution of inquiry, see, *infra*, p. 90.

of the resolution the information he desires without publicity or without debate on the floor of the House, information which would not be forthcoming if the hearings were open.[11] In the Sixty-sixth Congress several resolutions of inquiry asking for information on the retention of American troops in Siberia were referred to the Committee. The following colloquy took place:[12]

If we get that information preliminary to determining whether we are going to pass a resolution asking for it, I would not see any reason for then asking for it.

Would that not be a pretty good plan? Suppose we get all the information we can, and save the House the trouble of passing this resolution?

I think we should do everything we can to avoid long discussions and debates in the House. It will be well to accomplish everything we can here in the committee. . . .

In a later session of the same Congress a similar resolution elicited this observation:[13]

. . . It has been my policy, when a resolution of this kind is before the Committee, to try to ascertain the facts to the satisfaction of those who have introduced the resolution, and perhaps avoid a debate on the floor of the House upon the question. These matters are always of more or less delicacy, and the less inquiry there is on the floor of the House, the better for the country . . .

On a less controversial subject, the protection of fur seals, the Committee anticipated difficulties in the House because of the technical character of the subject. The bill therefore was considered section by section " in order to make it very clear, not

11 Secretary Bryan, testifying on President Wilson's Mexican policy, felt free to speak at length because the chairman made it clear that the testimony would not be made public. 63rd Cong. (1913-1915). Files, C. F. A.

12 66th Cong. (1919-1921). Files, C. F. A.

13 *Ibid.*

only to members of the Committee, but also to members of the House." [14]

Behind the neutrality hearings of recent years runs a farrago of cross-purposes, least important of which has been the search for information. Technicians from the government departments could have supplied any specialized details the Committee wanted. Yet for days it heard testimony, repetitious, rambling, and often irrelevant, to forestall criticism that no opportunity was afforded for public statements in the subject.[15] Among some members there was a feeling that without hearings the Senate Foreign Relations Committee would steal the show. Because the objective was legislation, this was one of the few occasions when the House Committee could assume a position of equality on a basic point of foreign policy. Lastly, the reduction of the Democratic majority in 1938, at the very time when foreign affairs loomed largest in the national life, made the Democrats less reluctant to open themselves to criticism for denying hearings and, coincidentally, gave the Republicans a chance to press for full and complete consideration. While none professed partisanship, Republican critics of the administration used the hearings as another means of attack, and conversely, Democratic members found themselves defending the President with varied degrees of vigor.

The hearing as a corrective to the spread of misinformation is best illustrated by reference to those held on the Burton resolution to prohibit the exportation of arms.[16] Representative

14 62nd Cong., 2nd Sess. (1912). Hearings on H. R. 1657, *Protection of Fur Seals and Seal Otters*, p. 12.

15 The printed record of the hearings does not show the members present at each session. But it may be stated authoritatively that frequently less than half the Committee has been present during the open sessions. The burden of cross-examination was carried by a small number of members. The hearings on the Lend-Lease bill, early in 1941, were among the best attended. Doubtless the parade of distinguished witnesses explains the phenomenon.

16 70th Cong., 1st Session. (1928). H. J. Res. 183.

Andrews, a member of the Naval Affairs Committee, wrote the Navy Department for its views on the pending resolution. A reply, "prepared by the General Board" and "drafted" by Admiral Schofield, was sent Mr. Andrews.[17] Chairman Butler of the Naval Affairs Committee, learning of this, requested that the communication be addressed to his Committee in order that it might receive public notice. His request was dated March 15, 1928. Secretary Wilbur's reply came the following day, simultaneously with its publication in the press. This was the first intimation that the Foreign Affairs Committee had of the attitude of the Navy Department. So irritated was the Committee by this procedure that the Secretary found it desirable to request to be heard and appeared on March 17. No effort was spared to show Mr. Wilbur that the contents of his letter were thoroughly misleading to congressmen and his tactics incorrect. Chairman Porter called his attention to the position in which he placed the Committee " which was directly in charge of the bill. Your statement goes out. We do not hear of it for four or five days, and the War Department statement goes out. I have never seen a copy of that. The result is that a great many men on the floor have been misled by this statement." [18] He remarked that he " could not understand where all this propaganda was coming from on the floor." [19] Though the Secretary considered his own letter " a fair statement and easily understandable," he expressed a willingness to write a second one " in which you may, perhaps, eliminate some of the suggestions you gentlemen have in mind." With this the chairman could not agree. " If you put in another letter it would create greater confusion." [20]

17 *Ibid.*, p. 50.

18 *Ibid.*, p. 115.

19 *Ibid.*

20 *Ibid.*, p. 118. During the hearings on *Conditions in Russia* the chairman observed that "there appears to be an impression abroad that the State Department prohibits American citizens from trading with Russian citizens or with the Soviet government. We desire to know the facts in regard to that matter." The hearings continued in order to allow Under Secretary Davis ample opportunity to refute this idea. 66th Cong., 3rd Sess. (1921). P. 215 ff.

3. Sources of Committee Information

Seldom has the Committee on Foreign Affairs proceeded to the discussion of an international question with no other material before it than that contained in newspapers or magazines.[21] For one thing such discussions are inclined to be purposeless and often unnecessary. Major developments, and even minor ones, in foreign affairs are invariably followed by the introduction of at least one bill or resolution of inquiry, providing the Committee with a point of departure for its discussions.[22] However much members of Congress may rely on the press as their guide, members of the Committee—majority and minority—have at their disposal, should they wish to use it, more complete and authoritative sources of information.

Informal " off-the-record " talks, as distinct from hearings, given by officials and private citizens, acquaint the Committee

21 Many of the questions asked of Acting Secretary of State Davis during the hearings on *Conditions in Russia* were based upon news accounts. 66th Cong., 3rd Sess. (1921). H. Res. 635, p. 215 ff.

In discussing a measure *Further Regulating the Granting of Visés* a point of order was made that no bill had yet been introduced on that subject; the Committee, to save time, was studying only a draft of a bill. Further consideration was deferred until a bill had been referred to the Committee. 66th Cong., 3rd Sess. (1921). H. R. 15857 and H. R. 15953, pp. 3-6.

During the hearing on *Conditions in Nicaragua and Mexico* Representative Fairchild, to forestall the calling of the Secretary of State, offered President Coolidge's message to Congress in lieu thereof, pointing out that it " contains complete and accurate information." 69th Cong., 2nd Sess. (1927). H. Res. 373 *et al.*, p. 53.

22 *Cf.* 63rd Cong., 2nd Sess. (1914). H. Res. 561, introduced by Mr. Kahn, called on the Secretary of State " to transmit forthwith to the House of Representatives for its information, if not incompatible with the public interest, such letters or documents or instructions given or sent to the Hon. John Lind, special representative of the President of the United States in Mexico, in relation to assurances given by the said John Lind to Capt. S. G. Hopkins, of Washington, D. C., or any other person " regarding the transportation of war materials to Mexico via Cuba.

In explaining his resolution to the Committee, Mr. Kahn stated that " there appeared in *The New York Herald* and in the newspapers of this country, beginning in the latter part of June and running through the early days of July, a number of communications that purported to be letters emanating from Captain Sherbourne G. Hopkins ... in relation to the Mexican situation." Files, C. F. A.

with contemporary developments. The tempo is more casual, the tone more conversational, than the formal hearings. Thus Ambassador Bullitt appeared to explain economic conditions as he found them in Russia.[23] Several members of the foreign service have discussed conditions in other European countries. An invitation to talk with the Committee is regarded by most State Department officials as a means of placing before responsible individuals not only important background material but also a synopsis of contemporary events. Private citizens qualified by experience and education have enlightened the Committee on the repercussions of American foreign relations abroad, especially in the Far East.

Because the Foreign Affairs Committee does not and cannot operate *in vacuo,* it tends to look to the corresponding division within the executive sphere for information and collaboration. This is not to suggest that it is dependent solely upon the Department or that its decisions represent the Department's views. But there is a sufficient mutuality of interest, and frequently in foreign affairs a harmony of outlook, that encourages an unusual degree of interdependence. The aura of patriotism that surrounds debates on foreign policy as well as the canalizing of information on foreign affairs in the executive's hands reduces the points of friction that enliven debates on domestic issues. Most Committee members work upon the assumption that the direction taken by the executive in the conduct of foreign affairs is predicated upon data gathered through the facilities of the State Department and interpreted by the accumulated experience of its personnel, political shifts notwithstanding. Observations, criticisms, even prejudices must therefore have some basis in facts. The use to which these may be put after presentation to the Committee is the responsibility of the individual members and the collective obligation of the Committee. It invites members of the Department to appear before it, it receives memoranda prepared by Department officials, and through the use of

23 74th Cong. (1935-1937). Minutes, C. F. A.

the resolution of inquiry, circumscribed by rules and precedents, it requests specific information " if not incompatible with the public interest." [24]

The relations between members of the Department and the Committee have generally been cordial. In the first place, the functions of the Department do not readily lend themselves to partisan approaches; and secondly, even where they do, the large personal interest of the President in foreign affairs deflects the attacks from the Department toward the President. Both former and present members of the Committee are generally agreed that there has been an increasing degree of cooperation with the Department and even with the President in foreign affairs. Some members attribute it to the difficulties experienced by President Wilson; others, to the enlarged public interest in international events as reflected in congressional debates and remarks and the consequent efforts to legislate on foreign policy. Whatever the cause, the Department has shown a willingness to cooperate. The evidence of these interrelationships will be examined below. For the moment it is sufficient to observe that contacts are not confined to formal written communications, but are supplemented by an interchange of personal and informal meetings that smooth the way.[25]

That pleasant mixture of business and pleasure—the congressional junket—is not capable of application by the Committee on Foreign Affairs. Apart from the cost of transporting a committee of twenty-five to the farthest portions of the world, the intrusion by a legislative committee in the sovereign

24 *Infra*, p. 90.

25 It is not unusual for the Department to invite members to examine confidential materials in the Department. Mr. Carter, assistant in the Russian Division, stated that there was " a large quantity of documentary evidence . . . open to your inspection." 66th Cong., 3rd Sess. (1921). H. Res. 635, *Conditions in Russia*, p. 195.

Secretary Hull has met a select group of members of both parties in his home to examine neutrality legislation. *The New York Times*, May 27, 1939. *Cf.* letter of Secretary Hull to Senator Pittman and to Representative Bloom, May 27, 1939. Department of State *Press Releases*, June 3, 1939, pp. 475-477.

sphere of the several nations would raise grave problems of propriety. From the viewpoint of the individual members, with their cardinal obligations to their constituents and constituencies, it would be impractical. Only one instance is recorded of a junket by the Committee. That was a visit in 1916 to the Niagara River region in connection with a bill for the control and regulation of the waters of that river.[26]

4. WHAT MEASURES RECEIVE A HEARING

No single rule or line of conduct determines whether the Committee will grant a hearing on a bill.[27] Sometimes the content

<hr>

26 64th Cong. (1915-1917). Minutes, C. F. A. In 1927, Senator Borah introduced a resolution authorizing the Committee on Foreign Relations or a subcommittee thereof " to investigate and study conditions and policies bearing upon the relationship between the Central American countries, Mexico, and the United States." The Committee was authorized "to visit such countries." As reported out by that Committee, the Committee was empowered to conduct such investigations only "within the United States." 69th Cong., 2nd Sess. (1927). S. Res. 366; S. Rep. 1647. In January, 1941, Representative Van Zandt introduced a concurrent resolution, setting up a joint committee of ten members, five from each House, "to ascertain at first hand all possible information concerning the financial, economic, and social conditions and their effect upon the people of the United Kingdom resulting from the war with the Axis Powers, and to study the measures taken to safeguard the lives and health and to preserve the morale of said people." 77th Cong., 1st Sess. H. Con. Res. 14. See Mr. Van Zandt's statement, *Cong. Rec.*, January 29, 1941, app., pp. 316-317.

27 Hearings are characterized by the presence of witnesses and are customarily recorded by official stenographers. But there are instances where official stenographic notes have been made of informal discussions. The usual procedure, however, is for the clerk of the Committee to prepare a summary of the proceedings at the end of each meeting. Some clerks, able to take shorthand, have left verbatim minutes of the informal sessions.

The distinction between hearing and discussion may be illustrated by reference to the *Calendar*, prepared at the end of each Congress since the Sixty-eighth Congress. Under the heading "action" on Mr. Fish's resolution favoring the ratification by the United States Senate of the Kellogg Peace Pact the following notations appear:

Jan. 4, 1929—Hearings before committee.
Jan. 5, 1929—Considered by committee, action postponed until Jan. 15, 1929.
Jan. 15, 1929—Considered by committee.
70th Cong. (1927-1929), *Calendar*, C. F. A., p. 22.

itself may be a sufficient guide. The numerous bills, for example, authorizing acceptance of foreign decorations, incorporate the same general phraseology and on the floor of the House follow a routine path. Most bills of a private or non-controversial character are based upon facts gathered by the State Department and submitted by the President in a message to Congress. A hearing would elicit no new data that could not be more expeditiously obtained by a written communication from the Department.[28]

In analyzing the line of reasoning by which the Committee reaches its decisions one has only fragmentary remarks and restricted observations as a guide; the records give little insight into the varied forces that influence it. But some generalizations may be advanced. No committee will venture upon hearings without some attention to the relative chance of passage by the House if the measure is favorably reported. At this point a committee must weigh several imponderables: the general sentiment of the House toward a particular bill, the committee's place on the Calendar Wednesday schedule or the possibility of getting a rule from the Committee on Rules, and the relative importance of the measure itself as compared with others that are pending. Nor will a measure, liable to produce prolonged controversy, be given a hearing as adjournment approaches. The spirit of the House on such occasions is to give preference to bills whose enactment is necessary for the continued functioning of the Government, such as deficiency appropriation bills, or to measures that have priority on the Calendar. The aim is to clean up the House Calendar, not to lengthen it. Should the bill require hearings, the committee's report will thereby be delayed and action by the House will be more remote. Rather than begin the consideration of a measure so late in a congressional session, a committee will usually defer action until the following session.

28 See, for example, 75th Cong. (1937-1938), H. J. Res. 349, *Authorizing Certain Retired Officers or Employees of the United States to Accept such Decorations, Orders, Medals, or Presents as Have Been Tendered Them by Foreign Governments. Calendar*, C. F. A., p. 19.

Time, together with content, may also determine the advisability of holding hearings. As early as the Sixty-eighth Congress a resolution prohibiting the sale of arms abroad was introduced by Mr. Fairchild, a member of the Committee. This and kindred resolutions were the forerunners of the neutrality proposals of the last ten years. Yet opinion had not crystallized to the point where the Committee even discussed these measures. By 1928, at the very time the multilateral peace pact was holding the world's attention, Congress took under advisement means to control the arms traffic as a step toward the curtailment of war. The revelation of Mr. Shearer's role at the Geneva Conference, the failure of the Preparatory Disarmament Conference and the exposé of munitions manufacturers followed in quick succession. Then came the beginnings of rearmament in programs abroad. Starting with the Seventieth Congress successive Congresses saw the introduction of bills and resolutions designed to correct the dangers of the munitions traffic and to maintain the neutrality of the United States. Public restlessness, reflected by the introduction of these drafts, was stimulated by the interest taken by the administration on these questions. To allay the critics and to meet the demands for statutory regulation every Congress, from the Seventieth to the present, except the Seventy-first, has studied measures relating to munitions control or neutrality and the Foreign Affairs Committee has held hearings on them.[29]

A " fishing expedition " sponsored by a minority member and calculated to embarrass the administration received no sympathetic support from the majority. In discussing the desirability of a hearing on a minority measure calling for withdrawal of

[29] Two members of the Committee on Foreign Affairs, Mr. Porter and Mr. Fish, reintroduced resolutions in the Seventy-first Congress dealing with the control of arms shipments. The Committee held no hearings on them; the minutes do not indicate that they were even considered. See *infra*, chap. VI, VII.

Hearings to examine bills and resolutions designed to assist oppressed peoples have been frequent, due largely to their humanitarian effect and political appeal.

recognition of a particular Power, apart from the question of congressional control in matters pertaining to recognition, the majority opposed a hearing without a prior knowledge of the character of the witnesses to be presented and the relevancy of the questions to be propounded.[30]

Prior consultation with the State Department to determine its attitude toward a hearing on a particular measure has been the exception rather than the rule. The chairman opened a hearing on a resolution to restrict the sale of munitions abroad with the comment that " the State Department say they have no objection to the hearing and any action that this committee may see proper to take." In view of the Committee's insistence that the proposed legislation was domestic rather than international in character it may be doubted that the Department's opposition would have forestalled a hearing.[31] During the strained relations with Mexico in the Coolidge administration one of the many resolutions referred to the Committee on the subject *authorized* the Secretary of State to furnish certain data regarding the expulsion of American citizens from Mexico. The faulty factual premise annoyed the Committee; hearings, it was felt, would only increase the tension between the two countries. To dispose of it " gracefully," the chairman was instructed " to confer with the State Department before a hearing was granted."[32] After consultation with the Secretary of State, the chairman was able to furnish the congressman with a copy of the Department's report. This was regarded by the Committee as sufficient justification for withholding hearings.

Bills and resolutions on technical subjects or those anticipating a change in existing policy or administration of the State Department usually receive hearings. There is a hesitation to urge their passage by the House without an adequate under-

30 74th Cong. (1935-1936). Minutes, C. F. A.

31 72nd Cong., 1st Sess. (1931-1933). H. J. Res. 282, *To Propose a Multilateral Agreement Renouncing the Sale or Export of Arms.*

32 69th Cong. (1925-1927). Minutes, C. F. A.

standing of the contents, especially where the bill has been drafted in, or with the assistance of, a governmental department.[33] For the new members, lacking a grasp of the details and background, these hearings prove valuable. Although the Committee was relieved of the authority to report appropriations in 1920, it has not relaxed its scrutiny of bills authorizing appropriations.[34] Passage of the authorization bill is the first, and very often the most important, legislative hurdle. To facilitate the passage of a subsequent appropriation bill the Foreign Affairs Committee has undertaken a survey not only of the objectives of the appropriation, whose merits it alone is competent to judge, but of the proposed expenditures under the bill.[35] A general exception to this statement may be found in the cases of authorization of funds for the payment of small claims of foreign governments acting on behalf of their nationals. A report from the State Department to the Foreign Affairs Committee

33 See, for example, 68th Cong., 1st Sess. (1924). H. J. Res. 201, *Chinese Indemnity*. This observation is applicable to other committees.

34 From 1885 to 1920, the Foreign Affairs Committee was one of ten House committees having power to report appropriations directly to the House. Since the latter date it considers all measures pertaining to foreign affairs which authorize appropriations. The appropriations pursuant to such bills are handled by the Committee on Appropriations.

About the turn of the century the Committee discontinued its practice of turning over to a subcommittee the annual appropriation bill for the diplomatic and consular services. In its stead the full Committee held hearings which ultimately were made available in printed form.

35 *Cf.* 70th Cong., 2nd Sess. (1929). H. J. Res. 355, *Inter-American Highway*.

72nd Cong., 1st Sess. (1932). H. J. Res. 163, *General Disarmament Conference*. The draft, submitted by the State Department, read " that so much as may be necessary is hereby authorized to be appropriated." The chairman objected to this. " I told (Mr. Carr) I did not think it would stand in the House or before the committee, and that there would have to be some specific sum mentioned." P. 1. After examining the proposed expenditure in detail, the Committee reported out the resolution with an amendment specifying $450,000. *Ibid.*, H. Rep. 30.

72nd Cong., 2nd Sess. (1933). H. J. Res. 536, *International Monetary and Economic Conference*.

detailing the incidents which warrant financial responsibility on the part of the United States has usually been sufficient.

When other devices prove ineffective, an appeal to congressional courtesy may move a Committee to action. Congressmen whose pet projects have lain untouched on the calendar approach a member, usually the chairman whose experience and position weigh heavily with his colleagues, with a request for a hearing. The chairman himself may take the responsibility of suggesting that hearings be held, subject to reversal by the members. But if he feels that there is opposition in the Committee or prefers to have a refusal come from the Committee rather than himself, he refers it to the whole membership for decision. A member of the House, anxious to have a hearing on his resolution *directing* the President to call an international conference to revise a particular treaty, was held off with the statement that the Committee wanted a respite from its continuous meetings. Early the following session the request was renewed and the chairman stated that he would turn the matter over to the Committee. There is no evidence that he did. When one considers the tenor of the preamble of the resolution, its encroachment on the executive sphere, and the policy pursued by the administration, it is apparent that the chairman's action—more properly, inaction—would have had the approval at least of the majority.[36] As a rule a request from another committee for consideration or a hearing is not denied, although there is only one instance where such a request has been made of the Foreign Affairs Committee. That was by the Military Affairs Committee on a measure to prohibit the exportation of arms. Perhaps the degree of courtesy in this case may be better appreciated when it is realized that the resolution had already been reported out before a hearing was asked.[37]

36 70th Cong. (1927-1929). Files, C. F. A.

37 70th Cong., 1st Sess. (1928). H. J. Res. 183. Chairman McSwain of the Military Affairs Committee said: "When the matter was called to the attention of the Military Affairs Committee, that the possible effects ... of the enactment into law of House Joint Resolution 183, might be such as

5. THE PRINTING OF HEARINGS

The Committee has no predetermined attitude toward the publication of its hearings. If any principles guide it in its judgments, they may be said to be the degree of public and congressional interest in the question and the nature of the testimony offered. Where public interest is evident and the testimony is neither indiscreet nor irrelevant, the Committee has shown no hesitation in publishing its hearings.[38]

to impair the preparedness program and might impinge upon the national defense, it was suggested that the Committee on Military Affairs itself ascertain that fact, but upon reconsideration, in the spirit of comity and of courtesy that should prevail between coordinate committees of the House, and especially, in consideration of the high esteem in which the members of the Committee on Military Affairs held the individual membership of this committee, it was decided, rather, to memorialize this committee as to the significance that appeared to the majority of our committee to be involved in House Joint Resolution 183, and for that reason to ask this committee to hear the facts that might be presented by such persons as might desire to appear and to make statements with reference to the consequences of the enactment of the House resolution into law ..." P. 1.

The resolution was reported to the House on January 26, 1928. (H. Rep. 492). Hearings started on March 15, 1928. *Cf.* 70th Cong., *Calendar*, C. F. A., p. 15.

During the hearing Chairman Porter observed that "it is not customary unless people ask to be heard to request them to be heard. The committee realizes that we are going out of the usual course by fixing this hearing, but we are anxious to hear anybody that desires to be heard on this or any other measure." Hearings, p. 3.

The Committee turned down a suggestion that it seek an invitation to sit with the Senate Foreign Relations Committee to hear testimony on Mexico and Nicaragua. The rejection was occasioned, in part, by the knowledge that the Secretary of State would be present before the Senate Committee, a course to which most of the Republican majority of the House Committee objected. *Cf.* 69th Cong., 2nd Sess. (1927). Hearings on *Conditions in Nicaragua and Mexico*, p. 61.

38 See, e. g., 67th Cong., 2nd Session. (1922). Hearings on H. Con. Res. 52, *The Establishment of a National Home in Palestine*; 72nd Cong., 1st Sess. (1932). Hearings on H. Res. 378, *Permanent Court of International Justice.*

"There is always a considerable body of public opinion that wants everything made public but diplomatic negotiations with other countries are of a delicate nature," one member commented. 69th Cong. (1925-1927). Files, C. F. A.

If testimony of a confidential or critical character is anticipated, whether from government officials or private citizens, the precaution of an executive session is followed. Even the official stenographer may be excused.[39] Where a stenographic record has been kept of executive session meetings, the Committee, or an ad hoc subcommittee, may determine what portions, if any, shall be printed.[40] Fourteen hearings on H. J. Res. 422—concerning American neutrality policy—were held during the Seventy-fourth Congress. Nine were in executive session and five in open session. The printed copy contains the hearings of two of the meetings in executive session in addition to the five held in open session.[41] On a similar measure in the Seventy-fifth

Witnesses in executive sessions, and sometimes in open sessions, may ask the stenographer to "raise his pen" in order to speak "off-the-record." No notation of these interruptions appears in the published hearings.

During hearings on the improvement of the foreign service Mr. Linthicum digressed to query Acting Secretary Huntington Wilson about a constituent who had been dropped from the service. The notation reads: "(Mr. Wilson explained at length the circumstances of Mr. Carter's resignation, but suggested that his statement be not made of public record, but be given Mr. Linthicum for his private information and for the private information of Mr. Linthicum's constituent, Mr. Carter, if desired.)" 62nd Cong., 2nd Sess. (1912). H. R. 20044, p. 80.

39 Cf. 72nd Cong., 2nd Sess. (1933). Hearings on H. J. Res. 580, *Exportation of Arms*, p. 25, where it is noted that Secretary Stimson testified in executive session.

40 Cf. 66th Cong., 3rd Sess. (1921). Hearings on H. Res. 635, *Conditions in Russia*. The title-page bears the notation "Transcript compiled by Subcommittee of the House Committee on Foreign Affairs..." The subcommittee was empowered to exclude irrelevant or immaterial matter. P. 231.

Also, 62nd Cong., 2nd Sess. (1912). Hearings on S. J. Res. 152, *Exportation of Pulp Wood from Canada to the United States*, p. 4.

A subcommittee of three examined the testimony given on H. R. 3404, *To Provide the Salary for a Minister to Ireland*, 66th Cong., 2nd Sess. (1920). It reported that "only a small part of the material can fairly be said to be relevant to the bill under discussion; some of it does not belong in the hearing." The published text, however, contains few variations from the transcript copy. The Committee adopted a resolution that "all members of Congress requesting the same be permitted to have their remarks included in the hearings." This is a usual congressional courtesy.

41 74th Cong., 2nd Sess. (1936). Hearings on H. J. Res. 422, *American Neutrality Policy*, p. 1. Cf. *Calendar*, C. F. A., *ibid.*, p. 20.

Congress three of the five sessions were executive, but all the testimony may be found in the final copy.[42]

The smooth rhetorical flow that participants in the Committee hearings maintain is due, in part, to the generosity of the Committee. Transcript copies are forwarded each of them for correction and perfection. In the course of reviewing his testimony, a witness may request the deletion of portions of it. Where the request comes from an official of the Government, or a witness invited by the Committee to appear before it, the Committee has shown a disposition to comply. It is understood that the Senate Committee on Foreign Relations has refused, on at least one occasion, to grant the request of a Secretary of State that only the deleted copy be printed. It insisted upon the right to print the unedited copy.[43]

The feasibility of printing testimony presented by voluntary witnesses, promoting a " cause " and hoping to publicize it, has been deliberated by the Committee. One Committee minute reads:

Mr. * * * brought up the subject of printing the hearings on . . . (Several members) expressed their indifference or reluctance in doing so. It was their impression that many statements were made in the hearings that were unethical and nothing could be gained by making the testimony public in the way of a printed hearing for general distribution to the public. Mr. * * * asked if the hearings could not be carefully edited and such parts be excluded which appeared objectionable, and it was finally decided that a subcommittee should peruse the hearings for such purpose . . .[44]

There is no indication that the subcommittee submitted a report; the hearings were never published.

In a hearing on a bill restricting passport visas in certain cases the Committee weighed the possibility of retaliatory ac-

42 75th Cong., 1st Sess. (1937). Hearings on H. J. Res. 147 and H. J. Res. 242, *American Neutrality Policy*. Cf. *Calendar*, C. F. A., *ibid.*, p. 17.

43 Private information.

44 69th Cong. (1925-1927). Minutes, C. F. A.

tion because of discrimination practiced especially by Great Britain in barring American musicians. Testimony offered by an American orchestra leader, corroborated by various documents, was anti-British and anti-French in tone. Before the hearing was sent to the printer, some of the more extreme statements and comments were deleted.[45]

Contending that the transcript copy of a particular hearing should not be handed to the printer because the State Department had not been heard, one member stated:

. . . There were a number of resolutions before the Committee, some of them opposing the attitude of the administration and criticising it . . . Now, it is proposed to print a record which will contain only an attack upon the administration without any opportunity to have the opposite side appear in the hearing. It is unfair and improper . . .

To this another replied:

. . . At least some members of the committee were anxious to hear the other side of the matter and someone made a motion that we ask the Secretary of State to come down here that we might hear the other side of the matter and that was voted down by two votes . . . It is a peculiar situation for the gentleman from * * * to object to printing the hearings on the * * * situation because we did not hear witnesses on the other side when he was one of those who voted that we should not hear the principal witness on the other side, who is the Secretary of State.

By a vote that cut across party lines the Committee ordered the hearings printed.[46]

The records show few cases where publication has been deferred because of the intercession of the State Department. As the hearings on the retention of American troops in Siberia

45 69th Cong., 1st Sess. (1926). H. R. 8307. The Committee agreed that "considerable has to be stricken from the record should it be decided to print the hearings." Minutes, C. F. A.

46 69th Cong. (1926). Files, C. F. A.

drew to a close, some members raised the issue of publication. There was general agreement that the testimony showed a " gross breach of faith " on the part of another Power, a knowledge of which " would only inflame the feeling that already exists between the two nations." The State Department official who had supplied the information pointed out that on a related matter this same Power had " placed an interpretation . . . which changes the whole complexion of the agreement and nullifies the agreement . . ." It is apparent from the record that this confirmative statement reinforced the Committee's reluctance to make public the hearing, despite wide public interest.[47]

In 1926, the Committee held very extended hearings on the circumstances surrounding the murder of Vice Consul Imbrie in Persia and the subsequent settlement made by the Persian Government. Satisfied neither with the settlement nor the conduct of the Department, the Committee decided to publish the hearings while further negotiations with the Persian Government were in progress. The Department made known to the Committee its wish that publication be withheld because of " the impropriety and embarrassment the printing of the hearings might bring about." The Committee showed an appreciation of the difficulties involved and, accordingly, reversed its previous action.[48] The hearings have never been published.

6. WITNESSES

Although the President is charged with the conduct of foreign affairs, the Committee has never invited him to appear before it. The only motion put to it on this question was defeated without a record vote.[49] The burden of presenting firsthand information rests with the Secretary of State and his subordinates. From the days of Secretary Root to 1920, when

47 66th Cong. (1919-1921). Files, C. F. A.

48 69th Cong. (1925-1927). Files, C. F. A. See, infra, pp. 78-79.

49 The subject was "the claim of Ireland to the right of self-determination." 65th Cong. (1917-1919). Minutes, C. F. A.

the Committee lost control of the diplomatic and consular appropriations, the Secretary usually put in an appearance to explain and justify the appropriations for the foreign services. Apart from those bills, measures dealing with the reorganization and improvement of the Department and the foreign service have always been discussed by the Secretary before the Committee.[50] Since 1920 the secretaries have made few personal calls. Secretary Hull has shown up at a few meetings. On one occasion he expressed a willingness to appear only after the Committee had " formulated " a neutrality bill.[51]

The less frequent attendance of the Secretary at Committee hearings may be attributed, in part, to the high degree of specialization that has developed in the Department in the last quarter century. Even when testifying on matters of appropriation during the war years, the Secretary contented himself with

50 Among the examples that may be cited are:

59th Cong., 1st Sess. (1906). Secretary Root appeared in behalf of a bill to reorganize the consular service.

62nd Cong., 2nd Sess. (1912). Secretary Knox spoke in behalf of H. R. 20044, on the improvement of the foreign service.

66th Cong., 2nd Sess. (1920). Secretary Lansing presented an elaborate plan for the reorganization of the State Department.

68th Cong., 1st Sess. (1924). Secretary Hughes discussed H. R. 17 and 6357, providing for the reorganization of the foreign service.

In the absence of Secretary Kellogg, Assistant Secretary Olds analyzed at length the need for reorganization of the State Department. 70th Cong., 1st Session. (1928). H. R. 13179.

51 75th Cong., 1st Sess. (1937). Hearings on H. J. Res. 147 and 242, *To Maintain the Neutrality of the United States.* Chairman McReynolds stated: " He (the Secretary) was asked to come up here today.... He said that he didn't want to appear in the attitude of suggesting anything that the State Department desired put in this bill. He wanted this bill to be the bill of this Committee and he thought after we had formulated our bill and gotten it in some shape if the Committee then wanted him as Secretary of State to come up here, and if we wanted to ask him about it—whether he found anything objectionable in it or whether he approved it—he could then state his reasons..." P. 34.

More recently Mr. Hull made known his position on a pending bill by a public letter to the acting chairman, followed by a conference with some members at his home. *The New York Times,* May 27, 28, 1939.

a general statement on the needs of the Department and allowed his subordinates, headed by Mr. Carr, to supply the details. The Committee itself has come to recognize this specialization by not pressing for the appearance of the Secretary, but rather, asking that " someone " from the Department come up to explain or elaborate on particular matters before it. Thus the legal adviser, the economic adviser, chiefs of the geographical divisions as well as lesser officials have presented the Department's —and the administration's—point of view. On the other hand, the Department has recognized the desirability of having pending legislative matters concentrated in the hands of a ranking officer of the Department to relieve the Secretary of this work. Among the duties of the Assistant Secretary charged with administration is that of presenting and explaining the Department's views on matters before the various congressional committees or arranging for other officers within the Department to present themselves for examination. It may be safely presumed, however, that if the Committee by a majority vote were insistent that the Secretary testify on a legislative proposal of importance, refusal would be difficult and possibly embarrassing.[52]

52 When the Committee is considering, not holding a hearing on, a bill observations are frequently forwarded over the signature of the Secretary, usually upon the request of the chairman acting either on his own initiative or in response to the Committee's direction. These informative comments guide the Committee in its deliberations and sometimes are incorporated in its report to the House. See, e. g., 75th Cong., 1st Sess. (1937). H. Rep. 1434, to accompany H. J. Res. 473, *Regulating the Use of Public Streets and Sidewalks within the District of Columbia.*

Secretary Kellogg acknowledged a request to appear by presenting himself for examination on a joint resolution to prohibit the exportation of arms and munitions from the United States to certain countries. 70th Cong., 2nd Sess. (1929). Hearings on H. J. Res. 416, p. 8.

In opening the testimony on the Lend-Lease Bill, Secretary Hull stated: " I shall not discuss the technical details of the proposed measure, since that will be done by other departments of the Government more directly concerned with these matters. I shall place before you briefly the controlling facts relating to the manner in which the dangers that now confront this hemisphere and, therefore, this Nation, have arisen..." 77th Cong., 1st Sess. Hearings on H. R. 1776, *Lend-Lease Bill*, January 15, 1941, p. 2.

A friendly majority has precluded the Secretary from testifying on a subject fraught with political dynamite and capable of creating widespread criticism of the administration. Early in 1927 the strained relations existing between the United States and Nicaragua and Mexico had evoked both denunciation and commendation in and out of Congress on President Coolidge's policy. In the Senate the attack was led by Senator Borah, chairman of the Foreign Relations Committee, and culminated in the much publicized defense of the administration by Secretary Kellogg before that Committee.[53] Simultaneously the Foreign Affairs Committee was holding hearings on a series of resolutions touching these subjects.[54] In the belief that the Secretary could enlighten the House Committee, Mr. Moore (D., Va.) moved that he " or some of his subordinates " be invited to appear, a motion ultimately killed by the insistence of Mr. Fairchild (R., N. Y.) on his point of order that the House was in session.[55] " The effort seems to be to put blind bridles on this committee," charged Mr. Moore; to which Mr. Fairchild, defending administration policies, retorted: ". . . it does seem to me there is a constant effort to put our own Government on trial before this committee." [56] The following day Mr. Moore renewed his motion to invite the Secretary.[57]

Mr. Moore. . . . We are without the facts. A representative of the State Department went before the Senate committee yesterday

53 Cf. The New York Times, January 13, 1927, for an extended report of the Secretary's alleged remarks in executive session.

54 69th Cong., 2nd Sess. (1927). Hearings on H. Res. 373, 372, 368, 388, 389, 394, 376, 371, 357, Conditions in Nicaragua and Mexico. The resolutions were of two types—those expressing the sense of the House and those asking the Secretary to supply information. Until Mr. Fairchild brought up his resolution, the Committee was concerned primarily with the latter type. None of them contemplated concurrent action by the Senate or required the signature of the President.

55 Rule XI, par. 46, states: " No Committee, except the Committee on Rules, shall sit during the sitting of the House, without special leave."

56 Op. cit., pp. 33, 35.

57 Ibid., pp. 50-52.

and made a statement in secret that has not been given out and we are entitled to know the facts as fully as the Senate is, and I think this committee would be sacrificing its duty in the premises and also taking a very undignified position not to request the Secretary to come here and tell us his story as he told it to the Senate Committee on Foreign Relations.

Mr. Fish (R., N. Y.).   I second the motion . . . it is our right, and I regard it as the duty of this committee, to ask the Secretary of State to come here as soon as he can conveniently and give us information we are entitled to. I do not know who is in the confidence of the Secretary of State. I do not know that this committee knows any more than some other committee that has not had this referred to them. I do not believe that members of this committee know as much about it as newspaper reporters. . . .

.   .   .   .

Mr. Cooper (R., Wis.). . . . we are asked here now without having heard a solitary witness of any kind from the executive department . . . to declare that what has been done in this tremendously important affair by our officials, meets with our approval. . . . It may be a question of war. We, of this committee, are responsible for our acts, we should not rely as we are now asked to rely, upon a mere newspaper report of what a witness testified before the Senate committee. We are entitled to know the facts at first hand from the lips of witnesses who should know the truth, and we are entitled to examine and cross examine them.

.   .   .   .

Mr. Begg (R., Ohio). . . . I think there is no better way for the National Government to get into trouble than to have the Congress undertake to meddle before they are requested for advice or assistance. . . . It is the business of the Executive, as I see it; it is his business and responsibility; it is he who will answer to the country; and when the time comes, if it comes, where it gets to be a serious matter and he comes to Congress, then is the time he can show me. Let us not belittle our Nation; let us not jeopardize our interests by taking ill-advised action here in either way. . . . I have no disposition to delay votes or anything of the kind, but I do think and cannot say it too positively that I think we are too big men to try to embarrass the President of the United States in an international situation like this, even though he may not be doing the thing that agrees with our ideas. Let him work it out and he will get out without war.

Mr. Moore. Is it suggested that we are trying to embarrass the President?

Mr. Begg. Certainly a resolution calling for the withdrawal of troops or marines down in Nicaragua can have no other effect than embarrassment to the President and the country at large.

On two successive votes proponents of the administration were able to vote down the critics. A show of hands gave a 7-7 vote on the motion to invite the Secretary. The chairman, Mr. Porter, defeated the motion by voting in the negative. The second vote was on an amended motion, providing that the Committee meet the next day to continue its hearings. Nine Republicans lined up against four Democrats and one Progressive to defeat it. The call of the Committee then rested with the chairman.[58]

More than two weeks elapsed before the Committee met again. When it did, Mr. Fairchild immediately called up his resolution, endorsing the President's policy, and offered in support of it " only the message of the President of the United States on Nicaragua." [59] He immediately asked for a favorable report on his resolution.

[58] *Ibid.*, p. 53.

[59] The message referred to was that which President Coolidge sent to Congress on January 10, 1927. He concluded that it was his duty "to use the powers committed to me to insure the adequate protection of all American interests in Nicaragua, whether they be endangered by internal strife or by outside interference in the affairs of the Republic." 69th Cong., 2nd Sess. (1927), H. Doc. 633.

Mr. Fairchild's resolution, H. Res. 357, read: " Resolved, That the House of Representatives of the United States of America hereby expresses its full concurrence with the President, and pledges its support, in protecting the life and property of citizens of the United States in Mexico, and in protecting the rights and interests of the United States and its citizens in Nicaragua including the treaty rights of the United States to construct an interoceanic canal through Nicaraguan territory, with due regard to the protection of the Panama Canal, and also with due regard to the rights and obligations of the United States embodied in existing treaty with the Government,

. . . Without criticising the viewpoint of those who disagree with me, it has become self-evident that the course they have followed is to use the House and to use this committee for partisan propaganda purposes against the President of the United States in the Nicaraguan matter . . . One side here wishes to continue the hearings in order to continue use of the Foreign Affairs Committee for propaganda purposes. Our position is that that course is inexcusably wrong. I am one of those who believe that we should stop further discussion, that these hearings should stop, that the efforts to embarrass the President of the United States in international relations should cease, and that every one who believes with me, and I hope Democrats on this committee will listen to my appeal, will accord with the resolution I have offered to report the bill . . .[60]

Charges and counter-charges broke the usual calm and often obscured the main point—the invitation to the Secretary. Mr. Moore and Mr. Connally led the Democratic attack. The former felt " a sense of humiliation " over the refusal to ask the Secretary and the haste with which it was sought to push through the supporting resolution. To him it was apparent that the President had been misled " by somebody in regard to the facts." Without these facts the resolution would carry little weight with the country.[61] When the vote was taken, Mr. Connally was the only Democrat present; and he had remained only to raise the point of no quorum which the chairman upheld. At the following meeting, after adopting Mr. Fairchild's resolution, nine Republicans against five Democrats, Mr. Moore brought up a privileged resolution—H. Res. 388—calling on the Secretary of State for certain information pertaining to

which obligations, as well as the treaty rights of the United States, in the opinion of the House of Representatives, require the United States Government to support the constitutional government of Nicaragua, as recognized by the Government of the United States, against any aggression by any foreign power, whether such aggression be by direct action or indirectly through furnishing, or permitting to be furnished, arms, ammunition, or soldiers in aid of attacks upon the said constitutional government of Nicaragua."

60 *Op. cit.*
61 *Ibid.*, pp. 61-62.

American activities in Nicaragua. For the third time Mr. Moore presented his motion to call the Secretary, only to be defeated, 8 to 7.[62]

The hearings on Latin American affairs were interspersed with those on Mr. Porter's concurrent resolution requesting the President to negotiate with China for the replacement of the unequal and non-reciprocal treaties then in force.[63] A Republican member queried whether the Committee ought " to pass resolutions of this kind without, at least, hearing representatives of the State Department. Sound reasons may exist why it is not expedient." " You would put the Department in an embarrassing situation," replied a majority colleague, " to ask them to aid us in forming our opinions because the Department has nothing to do with this resolution." A Democrat was even more emphatic. " We bring the State Department down here and it tells us certain things and then it cannot act independently as it should act. We have a perfect right, and it is not only our right but our duty to express how we feel in reference to this situation." Although the subcommittee entrusted with the redrafting of the resolution was also given permission to call the Secretary, it failed to do so. The resolution as reported from the subcommittee was adopted by the full Committee, eleven members voting aye and three present.

In both instances the Committee decided not to request the Secretary to appear. But behind each of these decisions lay different lines of reasoning. In the case of the China resolution the Committee was only expressing a sentiment—and a sentiment that prevailed on both sides of the House. Testimony of private experts served to strengthen the prevailing attitude and enabled the Committee, and the House, to express its own opinion without reference to the executive branch. Moreover, the resolution was introduced by the chairman, a strong, if silent, supporter of the President. This, in itself, suggested that

62 *Ibid.*, p. 85.

63 69th Cong., 2nd Sess. (1927). H. Con. Res. 45 and 46.

the administration did not look with disapproval upon the measure.

The aggressive policy of the administration in Latin America did not meet with the approval of the minority and a small, but vociferous, part of the majority in both Houses. Secretary Kellogg's testimony before the Senate Foreign Relations Committee spurred his opponents on the House Committee to demand the Secretary's appearance, lest the newspapers regard its members " like a lot of schoolboys without any information at all," becoming " rubber stamps of either Secretary Kellogg or Mr. Fairchild." With the opposition the request for the Secretary's presence became almost a point of honor. The resolutions of inquiry and of censure, introduced by the administration's critics, were regarded as attempts to disparage further the handling of Latin American affairs. The resolutions of censure, offered during the most heated part of the controversy, had no chance of acceptance. The information sought by the resolutions of inquiry, if furnished, would have given the opposition additional ammunition with which to wage their fight. It was to forestall this that the Republicans blocked all minority resolutions and offered one of approval.

The Committee has had the opportunity to hear executive and ranking officers of agencies and departments other than the State Department.[64] Bills authorizing appropriations for international conferences and giving effect to treaties not self-executing have enabled it to explore government operations ordinarily not within its jurisdiction.[65] The Secretary of War

64 During the hearings on the Lend-Lease Bill in January, 1941, four cabinet officers testified—the Secretaries of State, Treasury, War, and Navy —as well as Mr. Knudsen, Director General of the Office of Production Management.

65 In the Seventy-fourth Congress (1936) Secretary of Agriculture Wallace testified on a joint resolution authorizing him to expend A. A. A. funds for participation by the United States in a World Poultry Congress.
Cf. 74th Cong., 2nd Sess. (1936). Hearings on S. 3413, *To Give Effect to the Convention Between the United States and Certain Other Countries for the Regulation of Whaling.* Also, 62nd Cong., 2nd Sess. (1912). Hearings

and members of the Engineering Corps of the Army have testified on pending legislation pertaining to the boundary waters
of the United States and their uses.[66] The Committee was seeking guidance not in the formulation of a policy so much as in
the detail of execution.

When President Coolidge requested additional funds for the
American delegation to the Geneva Preparatory Disarmament
Conference, the chairman invited the chief of naval operations
to discuss the whole question of submarines, a part of the conference agenda. Although several members doubted the perti-
nency of the testimony offered, the admiral was able to present
a sketch of comparative submarine strength for the Committee's
information.[67] Following the failure of the Conference, a bill
came before the Committee urging the abolition of the submarine as a weapon of warfare. Speaking for the Navy Department, the Assistant Secretary expressed a willingness to supply
information on " technical points," but refused to " express the
opinion of the Department as to the resolution, or the policy of
the Department as to the building of submarines." [68]

On two different occasions the Committee has considered it
proper to invite foreign diplomats to testify. Had they been unfavorably disposed toward the measures under consideration,
it is doubtful if their positions would have permitted them to
disclose their objections. But their testimony was of a corrobor-
ative character, interspersed with the usual diplomatic caution
and niceties.[69]

on H. R. 16571, *To Give Effect to the Convention ... for the Preservation
and Protection of the Fur Seals and Sea Otter.*

66 64th Cong., 2nd Sess. (1917). Hearings on H. R. 20115, *Diversion of
Water from the Niagara River*; 71st Cong., 3rd Sess. (1931). Hearings on
H. R. 5051, *Lake of the Woods.*

67 69th Cong., 2nd Sess. (1927). H. J. Res. 352.

68 70th Cong., 1st Sess. (1928). H. J. Res. 139 and 186.

69 In 1881, the Nicaraguan Minister to the United States expressed his
agreement with a joint resolution before the Committee on the subject of an
international canal to be built without European aid. To him the resolution
appeared "proper and just." Hearings, 46th Cong., 3rd Sess. (1881).

Representatives other than Committee members testify before the Foreign Affairs Committee, a practice predicated on the golden rule.[70] When a hearing on a bill has been agreed upon, it is expected that the sponsor will speak in its favor. Prosaic measures, such as that in behalf of the Armenians, or to carry into effect a treaty regulating the level of the Lake of the Woods, win little public acclaim even among a congressman's own constituents. Details of his testimony probably never reach the press; and if they do, the chances are that the multifarious activities of a typical congressional day will obscure them. But given a bill having a popular appeal or affecting the interests of his community, a congressman may capitalize in full on the advantage. He may enlist the support of his colleagues, take an active part in arranging for the appearance of interested outsiders, and stimulate the press to publicize the proceedings. Mr. Mason, a member of the Committee, played such a role in sponsoring a bill to provide for the salaries of a minister and consuls to the Republic of Ireland.[71] More recent examples may be found in the testimony on bills providing for federal participation in international expositions.[72]

The majority of private citizens coming before the Committee are invited by individual representatives; seldom does the

In 1928, the Committee heard representatives from Bolivia and Peru testify on the subject of a Pan American highway. Both considered the move to build such a highway a " friendly " act. 70th Cong., 1st Sess. (1928).

Mr. Vasili D. Dumbadze, General Diplomatic and Economic Representative of the Republic of Georgia, made a plea in behalf of a measure providing for the appointment of a diplomatic representative to the National Republic of Georgia. 69th Cong., 1st Sess. (1926).

70 Senators have appeared infrequently. In addition to the instances noted below, Senator Underwood spoke in favor of a resolution relative to the exportation of pulpwood from Canada to the United States, S. J. Res. 152, 66th Cong., 2nd Sess. (1920), and Senator Norbeck discussed the Whaling Treaty Act, S. 3413, 74th Cong., 2nd Sess. (1936).

71 66th Cong., 2nd Sess. (1920). Hearings on H. R. 3404.

72 See, for example, 75th Cong., 1st Sess. (1937). Hearings on H. J. Res. 234 and H. J. Res. 304, *Authorizing Federal Participation in the New York World's Fair, 1939*. Fifteen representatives and one senator were among those testifying.

Committee as a body solicit testimony.[73] This does not preclude individuals from requesting the right to speak. Invariably the requests are granted, though more in a spirit of impatient indulgence than a search for information. Jane Addams, heading a delegation to speak for a " commission for enduring peace," found the silence of the members " embarrassing," because " we seem to be instructing you."[74] Three members of a self-styled " hobo union " asked for, and received, a hearing on the question of a referendum on a declaration of war. When an attorney from Cleveland asked permission to speak for five minutes on the same subject, the chairman denied his request because he came " without any notice and without any invitation." The Committee subsequently gave him the five minutes over the chairman's protest.[75]

Over a period of forty years citizens from all walks of life have appeared—perhaps a more varied array of witnesses than before any other House committee. Intellectuals and labor leaders, newspapermen and doctors, spokesmen for religious groups and patriotic organizations, travelers, engineers, and businessmen as well as citizens of foreign countries have presented their viewpoints. Except for the labors of " peace " organizations, the Committee has not been subjected to the pressure of lobbyists.[76] Peihaps the most accurate generalization

73 Chairman Porter's observation that " it is not customary unless people ask to be heard to request them to be heard " refers to invitations extended by the Committee. 70th Cong., 1st Sess. (1928). Hearings on H. J. Res. 183, p. 3.

Mr. Fish, ranking minority member of the Committee, was responsible for the appearance of witnesses not in sympathy with the terms of the Lend-Lease Bill. They were regarded as his witnesses and he led in the examination of them. Chief among these individuals were Norman Thomas, national chairman of the Socialist Party, and Colonel Charles Lindbergh. 77th Cong., 1st Sess. (1941). Hearings on Lend-Lease Bill, pp. 317 f., 371 f.

74 64th Cong., 1st Sess. (1916). Hearings on H. R. 6921 and H. J. Res. 32.

75 Ibid., 2nd Sess. (1917). Hearings on H. Res. 492.

76 Chairman McReynolds to Miss Jeannette Rankin, representing the National Council for Prevention of War: " This committee has always tried to give everyone a hearing and tried to be fair, but we are somewhat amazed

of its attitude toward those who have presented themselves is that they have been accorded a respectful, if not always a sympathetic, hearing. Their influence is not easily determined. Against the weight of facts and emotional appeal is the intangible pull of politics and party loyalty. Legislative proposals fostered by an administration in political agreement with the majority start with a presumption in their favor. Witnesses in opposition find refutation difficult, if not impossible.

7. DELIBERATIONS

In forty years the processes by which the Foreign Affairs Committee has acquired information have not been altered fundamentally. The change has been one of degree, not of technique. In a study of its deliberative work the same conclusion is not valid. Most striking is the diminished role of the subcommittee.[77] In the 1890's ad hoc subcommittees of three, occasionally five, members were the repositories for all bills and petitions referred to the Committee. Measures on the same subject were sent to the same subcommittee. New items meant new subcommittees. Thus a member might find himself on ten or a dozen different subcommittees in one Congress. When and if they reported to the whole Committee, they had fulfilled their function and thereby relinquished any special interest they may have had in the particular subject. Wilson's observation that each standing committee had consigned to it " the entire direction of legislation upon those subjects which properly come to its consideration " and was thereby " entitled to the initiative,

when an effort is made to organize another committee by a lobbyist. We do not appreciate it and I think I speak the sentiments of the Committee when I say that." 75th Cong., 1st Sess. (1937). Hearings on H. J. Res. 147 and 242, *American Neutrality Policy*, p. 52.

Recent events in Spain and the Far East have brought numerous petitions, telegrams, and appeals to the Committee, many from "inspired" sources as evidenced by the uniformity of phraseology. They have had no effect on the members.

77 *Cf.* Burton French, " Subcommittees of Congress," *Amer. Pol. Sci. Rev.*, IX (1915), p. 68.

and all legislative action with regard to them " merits a modification when applied to the Foreign Affairs Committee.[78] The initiative and action stemmed from the subcommittee. In practice this meant the two, or three, majority members.[79]

Today the subcommittee is primarily an expedient to iron out the wrinkles that hearings expose. Seldom is it the burying ground.[80] Whenever created, it has a real function in the legislative process. In the last twenty years it has been used for polishing up and redrafting measures in accordance with the wishes of the whole Committee.[81] Claims bills and minute matters unfamiliar to the full membership have been referred to subcommittees for examination and report.[82] Legislative pro-

78 Woodrow Wilson, *Congressional Government* (Boston, 15th ed.), p. 70. In the Fifty-second Congress (1891-1893) all petitions were sent to a subcommittee. " The chairman suggested that it would greatly facilitate matters if all such (sub)committees would make their reports in writing." Minutes, C. F. A. The files of the Committee for that Congress contain no written reports by these subcommittees.

79 See, *infra*, chap. IV.

80 There is no record of a report by a subcommittee set up in the Seventy-second Congress to redraft H. J. Res. 317, pertaining to the Far East. Minutes, C. F. A. *Cf. Calendar*, C. F. A., p. 12.

81 68th Cong., 2nd Sess. (1925). H. Res. 426, *World Court*, was drafted by a subcommittee of four to take the place of H. Res. 258 and H. Res. 420. Minutes, C. F. A. 69th Cong., 2nd Sess. (1927). H. Con. Res. 45, *Treaty Revision with China*, was redrafted by a subcommittee of five. Minutes, C. F. A. In both instances the redrafted measure was characterized by a diminution of the many " whereas " clauses to a compact preamble and a correction of minor details in the body of the resolution. It may be added that redrafting is sometimes entrusted to the chairman or is undertaken by the whole Committee.

82 *Cf.* 74th Cong., 1st Sess. (1935). H. R. 6612, *Claims on Behalf of Foreign Governments and Their Nationals, Calendar*, C. F. A., p. 7. 75th Cong., 1st Sess. (1937). S. 1607, *Payment to Government of Japan for Proposed Deportation of Enemy Aliens from China during the World War, ibid.*, p. 34.

Also 68th Cong., 2nd Sess. (1925). H. J. Res. 294, *Status of Swains Island*. Mr. Moore was appointed a subcommittee of one to consult with the State Department and report back to the Committee. The details of his investigation appear in H. Rep. 1549.

posals which, if enacted into law, might conflict with, or alter, the political or administrative activities of the State Department have been the subject of consultation between State Department officers and members of specially created subcommittees.[83] So implicit has been the faith of the Committee in the correctness and thoroughness of the subcommittees' work that it has always adopted their recommendations.

It must be apparent that the step of public examination may be, and frequently is, omitted. Resolutions of inquiry, requesting the Secretary of State to supply certain information, are correctly predicated on the assumption that the only official data are in the possession of that officer. Hence the Secretary's reply offers sufficient grounds for proceeding directly to a consideration of the resolution.[84] Joint resolutions authorizing the acceptance of invitations of foreign governments to, and providing for participation in, international expositions and conferences invariably skip the hearing stage and move from the Committee's calendar to the deliberative stage.[85] In many respects the

83 66th Cong., 3rd Sess. (1921). H. R. 15857, *Further Regulating the Granting of Visés by Diplomatic and Consular Officers*, was modified to limit the discretion of these officers. *Cf.* H. R. 15953 which was the bill offered after consultation with the State Department.

70th Cong., 1st Sess. (1928). H. R. 447, *Pan American Highway*, was referred to a subcommittee of three to confer with the State Department. Minutes, C. F. A. As a result of these consultations the subcommittee acquiesced in the Department's suggestion that the commission contemplated in the bill was premature and should wait on further diplomatic negotiations with the Latin American countries. A recommendation was therefore made to postpone consideration and confine congressional activity to a sympathetic resolution. The resolution adopted at the Havana Conference contributed to the subcommittee's decision. *Cf. Calendar*, C. F. A., p. 16.

A subcommittee of three with the assistance of individuals from the whaling industry perfected the language in S. 3413, *Whaling Treaty Act*, 74th Cong., 2nd Sess. (1936). Hearings, p. 117 ff.

84 *Cf.* 75th Cong., 3rd Sess. (1938). H. Res. 409, *Jews in Roumania*. A report was requested on January 26, 1938, and received three days later. On February 1, it was considered in the Committee and an adverse report submitted to the House. *Calendar*, C. F. A., p. 29.

85 *Cf.* 74th Cong., 1st Sess. (1935). H. J. Res. 210, *For Participation of the United States in a Universal and International Exhibition at Brussels*,

Committee's examination is a foretaste of the scrutiny to which the House will subject the measure.

This is the testing ground of a bill. Its legislative destiny is shaped and adapted to the circumstances. Behind closed doors the cross-currents of patriotism and politics move and jockey for position. Party advantage must frequently compete with national expediency. Action may be stopped, deferred, or hastened, as the Committee reacts to the sentiment of outside forces. A joint resolution expressing the thanks of Congress for the work of Secretary Hughes at the Havana Conference in 1928 was held in abeyance lest its failure to pass the House embarrass the Secretary.[86] Another phase that occupies the Committee's attention is the alteration of measures in the light of testimony taken or correspondence received. A bill establishing a commission to facilitate the construction of a Pan American highway was diluted to a sympathetic resolution when the cost was revealed and until the State Department could ascertain the interests of other governments in the project.[87] Lengthy preambles to resolutions, thereby exposing them to a point of order, have been reduced to concise statements.[88] Rather than report a bill amended in the course of its deliberations, the Committee has preferred to reintroduce it. " You do not raise so many questions," observed Mr. Linthicum.[89] The perfection of phraseology is only one part of its work. As indicated below, it weighs its role in the broad field of policy determination, and more specifically in the treaty-making power, recognition, and war powers, to suggest a few.[90]

Belgium, in 1935. Introduced on March 12, 1935, it was considered the following day and ordered favorably reported. Calendar, C. F. A., p. 16.

86 Minutes, C. F. A.

87 70th Cong., 1st Sess. (1928). H. R. 447.

88 69th Cong., 2nd Sess. (1927). H. Con. Res. 45, reintroduced as H. Con. Res. 46. Fourteen " whereas " clauses were reduced to one.

89 66th Cong., 3rd Sess. (1921). Hearings on H. R. 15857, cited, p. 52. Cf. 70th Cong., 1st Sess. (1928). H. J. Res. 1, Prohibiting the Exportation of Arms, Munitions, or Implements of War to Certain Foreign Countries, was reintroduced, first as H. J. Res. 171, finally as H. J. Res. 183.

90 See infra, especially Chap. V.

The Committee's deliberations do not necessarily end with the discussion of substantive and jurisdictional questions. It must anticipate the hurdles, mainly legislative in character, that lie ahead and integrate its work with that of the whole House, the Senate, and even the executive. To the chairman is entrusted the task of finding the most expeditious means of handling the bill.[91] Congressional debate over changes in the 1935 neutrality law resulted in a compromise bill to extend its terms for a year. Because the date of expiration, February 29, 1936, was rapidly approaching, the chairman, anticipating acquiescence in this arrangement by the Committee, arranged with the Speaker for recognition to suspend the rules in order to pass the bill. Under the rules debate was thereby limited to forty minutes on the motion to suspend the rules.[92] Only the strenuous exertions of Chairman McReynolds to secure recognition from Speaker Rainey made possible the passage of the resolution providing for membership in the International Labor Organization in the last days of the Seventy-third Congress.[93] Less urgent items usually have coupled with them the Committee's instruction to the sponsor that he " take advantage of every legislative opportunity to secure its passage on the floor." [94] In substance, it directs him to do the best he can without disrupting the routine of legislative work.

The Committee has not felt itself precluded from consultation with outside sources during this second stage. Of this conduct there can be no censure; on the contrary, it displays a de-

91 See *infra*, p. 102 f.

92 74th Cong. (1935-1937). Minutes, C. F. A. Chairman Flood, in 1914, arranged for recognition by the Speaker to suspend the rules even before the bill (to give effect to the fisheries treaty with Great Britain) had been discussed or hearings held by the Committee. 63rd Cong., 2nd Sess. Hearings on H. R. 13005, part 1, p. 6.

93 Private information.

94 Such instructions were given Mr. Garner when the Committee authorized a favorable report on H. J. Res. 278, dealing with the mutual guaranty of sovereign and territorial integrity of the governments of America. 61st Cong. (1909-1911). Minutes, C. F. A.

gree of flexibility in approach that merits praise. No records tell
the story but by inference and observation a reasonably accurate
summation may be advanced. Members, the minority included,
in their private capacity have access to more than one door of
the various executive offices. Documents and details, too confidential to be circulated, are placed at the disposal of those who
care to ask.[95] While the warmth of the reception may not always
be greatest in the offices of department heads, there is a tendency on the part of the permanent functionaries, in the absence
of express orders to the contrary, to provide adequate " background " material. To the legislative freshman with no long-
range experience or perspective in diplomatic affairs it is an
instructive practice. Barring decided personal prejudices or
strong party attitudes which may command his allegiance, a
member must give serious thought to the observations of those
in daily touch with the multiple angles of our foreign affairs.
Sometimes the chairman or a specially delegated subcommittee
has been instructed to engage in discussions with the State Department or appropriate agencies and report back to the full
Committee.[96] Even the Legislative Reference Division has prepared memoranda of an historical character for the Committee's guidance.

House committees, and the House itself, cannot be entirely
oblivious of the substantive and procedural actions of the Senate
and its committees. The perfection of legislation requires both
coordination and compromise between the two Houses and their
corresponding committees. So far as the Foreign Affairs Committee is concerned, the simultaneous introduction of identical
bills in both Houses, either at the request of the State Department or by mutual agreement of the chairmen of the two Committees, has occasioned no general confusion. Should the Senate

95 *Infra*, p. 67, note 105.

96 On January 12, 1932, Messrs. Linthicum and Hull were instructed to
discuss with the State Department a joint resolution pertaining to the prohibition on the exportation of arms. 72nd Cong. Minutes, C. F. A.

act first, the Committee chairman, by motion or through a special rule, calls up the Senate measure, thus obviating the necessity of sending another measure to the Senate.

The threat of interminable debate in the Senate may even force the House Committee, against its better judgment, to modify its position and even refrain from pressing its considered conclusion. Less than two months after the meeting of the second session of the Seventy-fourth Congress the neutrality resolution of 1935 was due to expire. The Committee immediately began a discussion of the administration measure introduced by the chairman. By the end of January, 1936, it reported out the resolution with slight amendments.[97] Debate in the Senate revealed the hopelessness of pushing through any legislation embracing new doctrines in the few weeks before expiration of the old act. Anticipating defeat for the resolution if it reached the Senate, the House Committe instructed its chairman to take no further action until the Senate acted. Senator Pittman's announcement, on February 12, that his Committee had approved an abridged neutrality bill (S. J. Res. 198) extending the law to May 1, 1937, was followed the same day by the introduction of an identical measure in the House by Mr. Kloeb. The following day the Committee met. "After some discussion and reading the two bills it was decided to redraft and introduce another bill in the name of Mr. Kloeb. The redraft was to contain some of the provisions of the administration neutrality bill (H. J. Res. 422), namely section 5, which was incorporated in the new draft." [98] The redraft, H. J. Res. 491, was the measure that received the President's approval on February 29, 1936.[99] Working against time, the Committee could not insist that the Senate adopt its views. To have been adamant in its attitude would have brought into the open a

97 74th Cong., 2nd Sess. H. Rep. 1928.

98 74th Cong. Minutes, C. F. A.

99 74th Cong. Pub. res. no. 74.

controversy that the administration wanted to avoid, especially in an election year.[100]

In the previous Congress, the Seventy-third, the Committee refused to accommodate itself to the Senate's amendments on a resolution prohibiting the exportation of arms.[101] As it passed the House, the executive had the power to discriminate in the application of an arms embargo; the Senate amendment eliminated this provision and made the embargo applicable against both or all belligerents.[102] Subsequently, the chairman allowed the measure to lie on the Speaker's desk and expire with the end of the Congress. " The (Foreign Affairs) Committee was absolutely the other way, and I saw no reason to go on with that contest. Mr. Fish (ranking minority member) knew about it," explained Mr. McReynolds.[103]

8. Relations with the Executive

The exigencies of practical politics have diluted the pure theory of the separation of powers. Nowhere is this more evident than in the relations between the executive departments and the committees of Congress. The " intimate but open relations " that characterize the connections between cabinet and Commons in England are relegated under our congressional system to committee rooms where, less publicized and more informally, the executive agencies make known their needs and

100 *Cf.* statement of Rep. Richards, *Cong. Rec.*, March 11, 1936, p. 3619. "...Both political parties are afraid of the subject (neutrality), as this is election year and there is no desire to offend any of those foreign racial groups now so powerful in our country..." Chairman McReynolds defended his support of the compromise measure on the ground that he did not want "to lose the neutrality legislation we have." *Ibid.*, February 17, 1936, p. 2240. Most of the opponents objected, not so much to the bill, as to the suspension of the rules to pass it, thereby granting only twenty minutes to each side, with no opportunity for amendment.

101 73rd Cong., 1st Session. (1933). H. J. Res. 93.

102 *Ibid.*, H. Rep. 2040 (2 parts) ; S. Rep. 101.

103 Chairman McReynolds' statement may be found in the hearings on the *National Munitions Act*, 74th Cong., 1st Sess. (1935), p. 17.

desires. The committee room is symbolic of a practice of bringing the two branches into more intimate relations; a telephone call, a memorandum, or a luncheon conversation may be less conventional but equally effective. Personal and political associations, too, weigh heavily in the process. Friendships formed while serving in the House have unquestionably been an asset to Secretary Hull in creating a sympathetic atmosphere for his proposals, especially among the older, and more influential, members. Conversely, the same channels keep the Secretary informed on current developments and attitudes of the House and Committee on Forign Affairs.[104] The late Mr. Moore, one time counselor of the State Department, whose congressional experience included membership on the Foreign Affairs Committee enjoyed the confidence of many of his former colleagues. These illustrations are suggestive, not exhaustive. Nothing short of a volume could convey in detail the character and multiplicity of contacts that bring together the legislative and executive branches. Perhaps one authenticated incident may sharpen the picture. A congressman, harrassed by his constituents to protest with all the vigor he could muster against the actions of a particular foreign government, knew as well as anyone that the State Department was exerting its best efforts to alleviate the situation. The Department in turn understood the pressure to which he was subjected. A conference was arranged with a ranking officer of the Department and the situation thoroughly surveyed. Nothing not already public information was imparted to the congressman. But he was able to inform the press that he had called the Department's attention to the matter and was doing all he could to secure a favorable solution. The Department retained a sympathetic friend in the House, the congressman was relieved, and the constituents appeased.

104 Since 1898, Mr. Hull has been the only Secretary of State to have served in the House with the exception of Mr. Bryan whose congressional service antedated his cabinet post by twenty years. Mr. Knox and Mr. Kellogg each served in the Senate prior to assuming the secretaryship, as did Mr. Hull.

Sketched against the background of the federal structure, the State Department stands in sharp relief. Not only is its personnel small, but in the last fifteen years it has been increasingly recruited with regard to merit. Add to this the professional training that most of the positions require and it is apparent that congressmen find it no outlet for patronage. By the nature of its activities, moreover, it can offer few personal services that bring public recognition to the representative in his district. A passport difficulty may be untangled or a missing relative abroad located—probably nothing more glamorous.[105] In times of mounting budget demands the Department has been parsimonious in its requests, a characteristic which has won it frequent commendation.[106] Presidential prerogatives in foreign affairs tend to deflect attacks on the Department and its policies toward the President although his judgment is undoubtedly shaped by consultation with its officers. Perhaps the most sustained criticism of a departmental policy in recent years has been that directed against Secretary Hull's reciprocal trade program. This is the exception, however, rather than the rule.

Lastly, the State Department stands unique among executive agencies in that it makes no annual report to Congress. Except for the annual message of the President, supplemented by special messages, Congress has no comprehensive picture of the ramifications of foreign relations. Even members of the two congressional committees charged with examining legislation on this subject, as a body have only fragments of information.

105 " Mr. Huddleston... I find I do not get a reply from the State Department inside of about two weeks.
" Mr. Flournoy. If you have any such case in the future, I would like you to call it to my attention.... Instructions have been given to the clerks to give precedence to inquiries from members of Congress." 69th Cong., 1st Sess. (1926). Hearings on H. J. Res. 205 and H. R. 9782, *Extension of Passport Control*, p. 52.

106 " I have never thought you (the State Department) complained loud enough when they (the Budget Bureau) cut your department. You should have more money." Mr. Linthicum to Assistant Secretary Olds. 70th Cong., 1st Sess. (1928). Hearings on H. R. 13179, *To Provide for the Reorganization of the State Department*. Files, C. F. A.

Yet abstruse but important facts may be acquired by an admix-
ture of personal contact and perseverance.[107] Chairman Porter,
in 1920 and 1921, took a personal interest in a joint resolution
that came over from the Senate providing for the appointment
of a commission to confer with the Canadian Government or
the provincial governments relative to the removal of restrictions on the exportation of pulpwood. The State Department
kept him informed of its efforts to settle the matter through
diplomatic channels. Disgruntled at the Department's inability
to secure favorable action, he secured the cooperation of the
Speaker and the Committee on Rules to put the resolution
through the House. Although moving contrary to the Department's desires, Mr. Porter was at all times conversant with its
efforts to reach a conciliatory agreement on this matter.[108] The

[107] Secretary Hull informed the Committee: "... I have always said that
any Member of Congress, whether in the House or in the Senate, could know
anything that I know about our foreign affairs, if he desired. Of course, that
implies some degree of cooperative effort along certain lines to the extent
that there should be no undesirable publicity in regard to those fairly numerous phases of our foreign affairs which for manifest reasons, should not be
made public." 77th Cong., 1st Sess., *Lend-Lease Bill*, cited, p. 7; also p. 23,
25, 31, 45.

Representative Newton, interested in the famine conditions prevailing in
Germany, visited the State Department to consult with officials and examine
consular reports on the situation. The data he thus gathered were presented
to the Committee in support of H. J. Res. 180, *Relief for Women and
Children in Germany*. 68th Cong., 1st Sess. (1924). P. 1 ff.

Addressing the Senate on the information possessed by the Senate Foreign
Relations Committee on conditions in Spain prior to the Spanish-American
War, Senator Sherman said: "... The Senator from Massachusetts (Mr.
Lodge) went to the State Department and was furnished by the Secretary
of State, Mr. Olney, with all those private papers, which show more than
any other the condition of affairs in Spain and the purposes of that country
as therein revealed.... The contents of those papers were never disclosed
to the public at large." 54th Cong., 1st Sess., March 12, 1896. *Cong. Rec.*,
p. 2725.

[108] 66th Cong., 2nd Sess. (1920). Hearings on S. J. Res. 152, *Authorizing
the Appointment of a Commission to Confer with the Dominion Government
or the Provincial Governments ... as to Certain Restrictive Orders in Council
Relative to the Exportation of Pulpwood therefrom to the United States*. Also,
Files, C. F. A. President Wilson gave the measure a "pocket veto." It was
passed again in the Sixty-seventh Congress and signed by President Harding.

comment of one congressman that " outsiders can make all the inquiries (of the Department) they want but are not able to get anything in printed form upon this thing or that thing " is a half-truth.[109] It depends upon the inquirer and the nature of the inquiry; nor is it regarded as the height of wisdom to put everything " in printed form."

In the performance of its administrative duties pursuant to an act of Congress the Department takes upon itself the initiative in recommending such changes in the law as it may deem necessary. The interested official or officials within the Department approach a member of the Committee, invariably the chairman, with a draft measure and request its introduction. So far as can be ascertained, this has never been denied. Under a statute of May, 1918, Congress gave the President power, for the duration of the war, to regulate entrance into and departure from the United States.[110] " In October, 1919, Congress in anticipation of this act ceasing to be operative through a formal declaration of peace passed another act, which continued the regulations respecting the entry of aliens into the United States through control by the consular or diplomatic visé." [111] This

109 70th Cong., 1st Sess. (1928). Hearings on H. R. 13179, *op. cit.* In 1912, Mr. Garner prepared a report on a joint resolution which sought to compel the State Department to press the claims of certain American citizens against Mexico through diplomatic channels instead of having their claims adjudicated by Mexican courts. " Mr. Garner stated that after preparing his report he had conferred with the Acting Secretary of State (Huntington Wilson) who told Mr. Garner that the State Department desired that its confidential letters on the question be omitted from the report, believing that it might prejudice the course now being pursued by the Department with the Mexican Government. Mr. Garner read a letter addressed to him by Mr. Wilson along the same lines. Mr. Legare moved that the Committee approve the report drawn by Mr. Garner as expressing the views of the Committee and also setting forth the position maintained by the State Department but without officially quoting the language of the Department used in any of the communications to the Committee or any of its members, after one more conference with Mr. Wilson. Motion adopted." 62nd Cong. (1912). Minutes, C. F. A. *Cf.* H. Rep. 556 of the same Congress.

110 65th Cong., Pub. no. 154. 40 *Stat.* 559.

111 66th Cong., 3rd Sess. (1921). H. Rep. 1280.

act expired on March 4, 1921.[112] Early that year a bill drafted by the Department was introduced to continue the granting of visés by diplomatic and consular officers until July 1, 1922.[113] Its phraseology made entrance into the United States contingent upon the presentation of a valid passport from the individual's government. Several members expressed themselves vigorously that this vested the Secretary of State with too much discretion and permitted him to debar entrants, not because they were inadmissible under the immigration laws but because they could not get the consent of their government to leave their native land. The difficulties of Irish immigrants with the British Government were stressed. To limit the discretion of the Secretary of State, and indirectly of consular officers, there was included, after informal conferences with the Department, a provision permitting such aliens to enter the United States upon the issuance by a consular officer of a document in lieu of a passport.[114]

Although the House plays no constitutional role in the treaty-making process, legislation giving effect to a treaty must, of course, receive its assent.[115] Bills on this subject are referred to

112 66th Cong., Pub. no. 79. This act never became operative because the act of the previous Congress did not expire until peace was made in August, 1921.

113 66th Cong., 3rd Sess. (1921). H. R. 15857.

114 *Ibid.* H. R. 15953. *Cf.* H. Rep. 1280. Bills authorizing appropriations for the settlement of international claims originate in the State Department and are forwarded to the chairman. Simultaneously the President sends a message to Congress together with a report from the Secretary of State. See, for example, 68th Cong., 1st Sess. (1924), H. R. 7558, *Authorizing a Payment to the Norwegian Government.* The message and report may be found in S. Doc. 52.

115 Secretary Olney forwarded to Chairman Hitt, April 27, 1896, a draft of an act made necessary by the conclusion of a convention between Great Britain and the United States, providing for the settlement of certain claims presented by the former. " In view of the expected speedy adjournment of Congress," he wrote, " I desire to get the legislation necessary for the execution of the convention under way with as little delay as possible.... As independent legislation, it should, I take it, originate in the House. It may be, however, that the best way of accomplishing the object is to have

the Foreign Affairs Committee. Customarily the Committee takes no action until the Department has requested that the necessary legislation be enacted. To expedite the work of the Committee and to insure the inclusion of all the details the request is usually accompanied by a draft bill for introduction by the chairman.[116] The draft measure for the protection of fur seals and sea otter was the result of conferences between representatives from the Department of State, Treasury, Justice, Commerce and Labor.[117] Likewise, the bill for the protection of migratory birds was the work of the Departments of State and Agriculture.[118] A variant of this practice is found in the measure to carry out the terms of the Lake of the Woods convention of 1925. Congressman Wefald of Minnesota drew up the original bill which was referred to the State Department for its observations. Secretary Kellogg returned it with minor amendments noted thereon and in this form it was reintroduced.[119] The Whaling Treaty Act of 1936 came to the Foreign Affairs Committee by way of the Senate. There is no evidence that it

its provsions tacked on to some appropriation bill pending in the Senate. If that be so, will you kindly advise me to that effect, in which case I will at once communicate with Mr. Sherman...." Mr. Hitt, after consulting Mr. Sherman, suggested that it should be added to "some appropriation bill." Secretary Olney then addressed his request to Mr. Sherman. State Department Archives.

116 See *infra*, chap. V.

117 62nd Cong., 2nd Sess. (1912). Hearings on H. R. 16571, *Protection of Fur Seals and Sea Otter*, p. 6.

118 64th Cong., 2nd Sess. (1917). Hearings on H. R. 20090, *Protection of Migratory Birds*, part 1, p. 3. Although it is not stated explicitly that the bill was drafted by the two departments, the testimony of the representative of the Department of Agriculture makes this clear. A similar deduction regarding the preparatory work of the State Department may be drawn from Secretary Lansing's remarks on the bill to cede the Danish West Indian Islands to the United States. *Ibid.* Hearings on H. R. 20755, part 1, p. 3 ff.

119 69th Cong., 1st Sess. (1926). Hearings on H. R. 9872, *Lake of the Woods*, p. 2. Congressman Wefald was not a member of the Foreign Affairs Committee.

had been submitted to the Committee prior to its passage by the Senate.[120]

Not all relations between the Committee and the executive can be explained as precisely as those touching on administrative and treaty matters. There are many aspects of their interdependence that are determined by the ebb and flow of the current domestic and foreign situation rather than by any routine capable of simple description. Through the expression of an opinion or a tactfully worded request the Department has been able to make its views known and thereby acts as a spur to or a brake on the Committee's action.[121] Difficult negotiations with the Mexican Government, touching, in part, on the deviation of the Rio Grande River, were facilitated by the prompt passage of an authorization to appropriate funds for the payment of claims to the Mexican Government for the killing of two Mexican citizens by sheriffs in Oklahoma. The Committee's favorable report was hastened by the knowledge that its action would expedite a satisfactory settlement of more important issues pending between the two governments.[122] On the other hand, a Senate measure to assert jurisdiction over the Bering Sea beyond the three-mile limit reached the Foreign Affairs Committee. Its passage by the House would have proven embarrassing to the Department in its negotiations with the Japanese for an amicable settlement of the fishing dispute. There is reason to believe that

120 74th Cong., 2nd Sess. (1936). Hearings on S. 3413, *Whaling Treaty Act.* Treaty Series 933; 52 *Stat.* 1460.

121 Memoranda particularly on technical subjects have been drafted in the Department and sent to the Committee for its guidance. At the request of Chairman Flood, Secretary Lansing sent him a memorandum on the controversial McLemore resolution. " I should call to your special attention that these memoranda are sent so that you may use the substance of the information contained in them, but without quoting the memoranda in any way as being the statements of the State Department, or otherwise referring to them as views of the Department." Carlton Savage, *Policy of the United States toward Maritime Commerce in War* (Washington, 1936), II, p. 463. See also, James B. Scott (ed.), *President Wilson's Foreign Policy* (New York, 1918), pp. 411-424.

122 72nd Cong., 2nd Sess. (1936). H. R. 13534. H. Rep. 1793. Files, C. F. A.

the Department was able to present so effectively its case to the Committee that the bill was pigeon-holed.[123]

Well-intentioned but ill-conceived legislative projects have been toned down and perfected through the intercession of the State Department. Reference has already been made to the Pan American highway project in 1928. The original McLeod bill to create a commission for the building of the highway was warmly received as a link in Pan American unity. One objection raised by the Committee, however, was the large sum of money to be spent by a roving commission. A second objection, pointed out by the Department, was the fact that the United States' part of the highway was nearing completion. It seemed proper, therefore, to have the initiative taken by the other countries since their problem was much greater. At the same time the Habana Conference passed a resolution recommending to the Pan American Congress of Highways, scheduled to meet in the summer of 1928, but postponed until 1929, " the consideration and adoption of agreements that will be conducive to the construction of a longitudinal communication highway to traverse the continent . . ." Although only a resolution, it was interpreted by the Committee as a step worthy of encouragement. " In order to bring the matter before Congress and to take action in conformity with " the Habana Conference resolution, and also to eliminate the expensive commission proposed, the Committee reported out a joint resolution authorizing " the several agencies of the Government " to " lend such cooperation and assistance as may be feasible and appropriate with a view to having the matter thoroughly considered by the approaching conference." [124]

123 75th Cong., 3rd Sess. (1938). S. 3744. See Philip C. Jessup, "The Pacific Coast Fisheries," *Amer. Jour. of Inter. Law*, XXXIII (1939), p. 129.

124 70th Cong., 1st Sess. (1928). H. Rep. 1124. The report contains an analysis and an historical background of the efforts to link the Americas by inter-communication. The original bill was H. R. 447. The measure approved by the President was H. J. Res. 259. 45 *Stat.* 490.

The deepening economic crisis of the early 1930's was tackled by Congress on many fronts, one of which was that of monetary stability. At the instigation of the silver interests the House Committee on Coinage, Weights and Measures held hearings in the spring of 1932 " to investigate the cause and effect of the present depressed value of silver." [125] This Committee concluded that an international monetary conference was necessary to restore " the commodity price level through the stabilization of international exchanges by restoring the equilibrium in the metallic bases of the money system." [126] The report included a draft, introduced by Chairman Somers, authorizing the President to call such a conference, and enumerated therein the points on which the conference should deliberate.[127] In his message to Congress of December 8, 1931, President Hoover had declared that " any effort to bring about our own recuperation has dictated the necessity of cooperation by us with other nations in a reasonable effort to restore world confidence and economic stability." [128] Even before the Lausanne Conference convened to handle the financial (and political) complications of reparations, the British Government was sounding out the State Department regarding a general economic conference as a sequel to Lausanne. The " general " character of the proposed conference was narrowed by the insistence of the United States that reparations, governmental debts owed the United States,

---

125 72nd Cong., 1st Sess. (1932). Hearings on H. Res. 72.

126 *Ibid.*, H. Rep. 1320. The Republican minority concurred in the advisability of having the President call such a conference. *Cf.* remarks of Representative Eaton (Colo.), May 16, 1932, *Cong. Rec.*, p. 10359. Mr. Eaton noted that a law of March 3, 1897 (29 *Stat.*, 624) that had never been repealed, gave the President authorization to appoint commissioners for an international conference on gold and silver.

127 This became H. J. Res. 385. Mr. Somers had exchanged correspondence with prominent Englishmen and Frenchmen on the desirability of an international conference. All had responded favorably. Hearings, cited, pp. 235, 323-4.

128 72nd Cong., 1st Sess., December 8, 1931. *Cong. Rec.*, p. 23.

and tariff rates be omitted from the agenda.[129] Upon these terms the Department announced its acceptance of the invitation. For the President, therefore, to sign a resolution favoring a conference touching solely on monetary matters would have defeated the purposes of the general confernce. Secretary Stimson felt justified in observing that " the end in view (world recovery) should be pursued along the road which has now opened "— a general economic conference.[130] The Committee thereupon contented itself with a simple resolution " approving and encouraging the efforts to hold an international conference," depending upon the Secretary's assurance that the objectives of the original measure would be included in the scope of the conference agenda.[131]

The hiatus that separates the Department and the Committee has been narrowed by the habit, developed more rapidly in the post-war years, of the latter forwarding legislative proposals to the Department for its observations. In recent years these requests have been confined mainly to major legislative proposals on subjects capable of stirring up congressional debate. No quantitative determination of the influence of these replies on congressional opinion is possible; but it is correct to say that they carry weight, even with the minority. Early in 1935 Mr. Knutson (Rep., Minn.) introduced a bill to prohibit the bringing into the United States of government securities of foreign countries which have defaulted in their contract obligations to the United States and also to forbid their advertisement for sale anywhere in the United States and the carrying of them through the mails. Like the original Johnson bill, it would have inflicted great hardship on American citizens by limiting them in the disposal of their securities and would have been of dubious value in stimulating debtor nations to make payments. While the Department refrained from opposing its passage, it deemed

129 *The New York Times*, June 3, 1932. The same issue also contains a chronological summary of the negotiations.

130 Department of State *Press Release*, June 4, 1932, pp. 545-546. Secretary Stimson's letter to Mr. Linthicum is included.

131 H. Res. 247. *Cf.* H. Rep. 1561.

the measure inadvisable. This was sufficient to kill it in Committee.[132]

The expiration of the Washington and London Naval Treaties at the end of 1936 and the disturbed conditions in Europe and the Far East led Representative Fish (Rep., N. Y.) to introduce two resolutions, one calling a conference of the signatories of the Kellogg Pact at Washington, the other authorizing the President to convoke a naval disarmament conference. Both were referred to the Department for its opinion. So far as can be ascertained, the Department showed no enthusiasm for conferences, apparently believing that nothing positive could be accomplished while failure would be dramatized and the situation made more critical. In any case the Committee, after receiving the Department's comments, failed to report either resolution.[133]

In an effort to restrict the President's powers in one sphere of international affairs—that concerning conferences—the 1913 Deficiency Act provided that "hereafter the Executive shall not extend or accept any invitation to participate in any international congress, conference, or like event, without first having specific authority of law to do so." [134] Apart from the question

132 75th Cong. (1937-1938), H. R. 2043. *Calendar*, C. F. A., p. 3. Despite a favorable report by the Senate Judiciary Committee on the original Johnson bill, the State Department objected to its passage and the measure was dropped. W. H. Shepardson, *The United States in World Affairs, 1934-1935* (New York, 1935), pp. 69-70.

133 75th Cong., 1st Sess. (1937). H. J. Res. 269 and 271. *Calendar* C. F. A., p. 18.

134 37 *Stat.* 913. This act, titled "a bill making appropriations to supply deficiencies in appropriations for the fiscal year 1913 and for prior years," was signed on March 4, 1913, by President Taft, one of his last presidential acts. In giving its advice and consent to the Treaty of Berlin in 1921, by which the United States and Germany resumed relations, the Senate attached reservations, one of which read: "That the United States shall not be represented or participate in any body, agency or commission, nor shall any person represent the United States as a member of any body, agency or commission in which the United States is authorized to participate by this Treaty, unless and until an act of Congress of the United States shall provide for such representation or participation..." 67th Cong., 1st Sess., October 18, 1921. *Cong. Rec.*, p. 6438.

of appropriations or authorizations for them, the President and the Secretary can make, and have made, commitments which, if unfulfilled by subsequent congressional action, would place the United States in an awkward position vis-à-vis the other nations. The unsettled and indeterminate status of international communications following the World War suggested the feasibility of an international conference on this question. The idea of a conference, according to Secretary Lansing, grew out of the discussions of the Council of Five at the Peace Conference. By an informal agreement, nowhere clearly described, Washington was chosen as the meeting place. The Secretary then presented a bill authorizing the holding of the conference already agreed upon. " It was assumed that Congress would authorize it? " asked Chairman Rogers. " No," replied Mr. Lansing, " there was no assumption, except it was understood that we would appeal to Congress for the privilege of extending the invitation." The chairman then asked : " Does the matter stand in such a light as to make it rather embarrassing in our international relations, if Congress should not pass the resolution? " To which the Secretary answered : " I think it would be rather embarrassing, and I am sure that it would be unfortunate." [135] There is no evidence to indicate that the Committee resented this *fait accompli*. The bitter controversy it engendered in the House turned on the question of Senate confirmation for the delegates, the Republican majority, with the Paris Peace Conference fresh in mind, contending for Senate approval.

135 The testimony of Secretary Lansing on this subject may be found in 66th Cong., 1st Sess. (1919). Hearings on H. J. Res. 205 and H. R. 9872, *Extension of Passport Control*, p. 20 ff. At the conclusion of his testimony on passport control the chairman, to relieve the Secretary of a later examination, questioned him on international communications. A few days later an entire meeting was devoted to this question, at which Mr. Walter Rogers, an expert on international communications, testified. *Ibid.* Hearings on H. R. 9822. The bill passed both Houses and was approved by the President. 41 *Stat.* 367. *Cf.* Henry M. Wriston, *Executive Agents in American Foreign Relations* (Baltimore, 1929), pp. 144-147.

The inability of the Committee to appropriate money has not always made its members insensitive to the right of Congress to perform that function. The State Department, in settling the claims of the government against Persia for the assassination of the American vice consul, Mr. Imbrie, and the assault upon his wife in 1924, agreed that the money paid this government —$110,000—should be used for the education of Persian students in the United States. When the Department sought authorization for the establishment of a trust fund to carry out this commitment, the Committee balked. Apart from the criticism leveled against certain American officials for their conduct in settling the matter, the Committee resented the disposition of money without prior congressional approval. On the other hand, in the interest of improved relations with Persia the Committee could hardly refuse the authorization. It solved the dilemma by awarding $25,000 to Mrs. Imbrie for injuries she herself sustained and authorizing the remainder to be put in a trust fund for Persian students. Before the House acted on this, the Senate sent over a measure giving Mrs. Imbrie $30,000, but making no provision for the disposition of the balance. There is no record, report, or debate that explains the Senate's action. It was this bill that finally became law.[136] The Committee, had it been disposed to inquire into the broad question of policy, could have studied thoroughly the events transpiring in Persia that gave rise to hostility to foreigners and indirectly led to the assassination of Mr. Imbrie. This was the period when various foreign interests were pressing the

136 44 *Stat.* 1973. The details of the Imbrie case may be found in 69th Cong., 1st Sess. (1926), H. Rep. 985. Mrs. Imbrie had previously received $60,000 as compensation for the death of her husband. The sum of $110,000 was determined as the cost of sending an American cruiser to Persia to bring back the body of Mr. Imbrie. The Committee's files contain a complete transcript of the exhaustive hearings. At the request of the Department these were not printed. Because the Persian government has not consented to the publication of the correspondence relating to this case, the State Department has not deemed it appropriate to publish anything " since such publication would detract from a proper understanding of the case." *Foreign Relations of the United States, 1924,* II, p. 539.

Persian government for oil and communications concessions. The Committee glossed over these details and devoted its efforts to impressing upon the Department the need for congressional authority whenever an outlay of money was involved.[137]

The observations made thus far have pertained to measures which, if passed by both Houses, would require the President's signature, an act tantamount to executive endorsement of their content. Under such circumstances it is understandable that the executive branch should concern itself with those measures that may conflict with the lines of foreign policy initiated independently of the legislature. Reference has already been made to the modification of bills and resolutions as a result of departmental comments. There remain to be considered the relations of the State Department and the Committee over simple and concurrent resolutions since neither requires the President's signature.[138] The Committee uses these resolutions " to go on record "; in a word, to inform the executive of the legislators' sentiment on matters that may be beyond immediate congressional control. Because the resolutions represent the deliberative judgment of the Committee—and the House—(and of the Senate in the case of the concurrent resolution)—there is a mutual reluctance on the part of the Committee to invite comments by the Department and, on the part of the latter, to volunteer advice. In 1913, when the chairman sought the opinion of the Department on the Rainey investigation of the Panama Canal he was informed that " although the Department does not desire to be understood as being opposed to any further investigation of the subject which might seem to the House of Representatives to be useful, yet the question to which the resolution refers is now the subject of negotiation with Colombia with a view to a mutually satisfactory settlement of all pending differences." [139] Although this is one of the most outspoken

137 Cf. *Foreign Relations*, cited, p. 539 f.

138 This does not cover the resolution of inquiry. See *infra*, p. 90.

139 63rd Cong. (1913-1915). Files, C. F. A.

expressions by the Department on a simple resolution, its carefully phrased disapproval typifies the attitude taken by the executive branch toward resolutions that convey, implicitly or explicitly, a lack of confidence in executive conduct of foreign
affairs or suggests any circumscription of presidential discretion.[140]

A resolution carries more weight with the executive when it
expresses the sense of the House on matters that ultimately require legislative action. As a prelude to negotiations with foreign countries the President is put on guard as to the temper of
the House or Congress.[141] Yet the Committee has been reluctant
to press this advantage when an international accord is anticipated because in doing so it restricts the President's bargaining
powers and imposes upon him a limitation of action that may
defeat an effort for international settlement. This was the reasoning that lay behind the Committee's discussion in 1933 of
resolutions requesting that the American delegates to the World
Economic Conference be instructed to work for the remonetization of silver on the basis of 16 to 1. Senator Wheeler's resolution expressing the Senate's views on a fixed ratio passed
that body without a dissenting vote on May 8, 1933. Several
representatives sponsored companion measures which were referred to the Foreign Affairs Committee because they presumed
to instruct delegates to an international conference.[142] The diver-

140 72nd Cong. (1932). H. J. Res. 317, *Authorizing the President to
Prohibit by Proclamation the Making of Loans or the Extension of Credit
to a State or States Violating the Kellogg Pact*, was not opposed by the
Department because the issuance of the proclamation was at the President's
discretion.

141 So thoroughly had the Senate rejected President Wilson's request for
power to accept a mandate over Armenia that House leaders saw no reason
to press for action in that body. The Democratic minority of the Committee
interpreted the refusal as "a direct, deliberate, gratuitous insult to the head
of the Nation." 66th Cong., 2nd Sess. (1920). H. Rep. 1101 (majority and
minority reports).

142 72nd Cong., 1st Sess. (1932). H. Res. 129 and 141.

gent views of the members may be gleaned from the following extracts of the hearings :[143]

. . . To declare in this room what should be the declaration would be presumptuous ; . . . the Committee would be taking upon itself, and, in turn, the House would be taking upon itself this very, very difficult task of determining what should be the ratio between silver and gold.

. . . It would be most unfortunate if you did not give this conference a full and free hand, but there would be no harm in expressing an abiding hope that silver will be monetized. I do not think that would embarrass them in the slightest, or make any difference in the result. But to come down to figures, and attempt here to anticipate what ratio is desirable, and instruct your conferees— because this would be practically an instruction—it seems to me would be most unwise . . .

. . . I think it is proper for Congress to express its view on anything it desires ; but the question is as to the advisability of practically instructing the conferees as to a definite ratio, a fixed ratio if that is known to the persons with whom they have to deal, because it limits their operations so that they have not a full and free chance to obtain the best they may in the conference.

They (the Europeans) will do everything they can for their own best interests, and nobody can blame them for that. That is one reason why I think we should not instruct our conferees in such a way that they will be bound so that it will be impossible for them to get the result they hope for.

We are confronted now with a question of policy, growing out of the fact that the Senate has already unanimously adopted a resolution instructing the delegates . . . to work for the remonetization of silver at a ratio of not to exceed 16 to 1. It seems to me that the action of the Senate calls for an expression on the part of the House. Otherwise, the situation would be left open to the objection, when the conferees got over there, that the Senate of the United States, while a very important law-making body, is not the Congress of the United States, and the question might well be asked, or it

143 73rd Cong. (1933-1935). Files, C. F. A.

might well be said, that if the Congress of the United States favored the remonetization, or rehabilitation of silver, it should have expressed itself.

If we could return the matter to the status quo, and the Senate had adopted an indefinite resolution, I can not say that I would have any quarrel with that. But it has not seen fit to do so. It took this resolution up by unanimous consent, and adopted it without a single objection. Now, the question is, is the House going to confuse the situation by adopting a materially different resolution . . .

Since the close of the war we have been sending delegations and observers and everybody else to Europe to take part in conferences and whatever they agreed to, Europe was never sure the thing they agreed to was satisfactory to the United States, because they would bring it back here and it would be kicked over. Now I think we must send instructed delegates there with reference to this thing, at least, and, if Europe does agree to that, she knows when they bring it back here it will be accepted by the Congress . . . that we are the last word in accepting whatever is done. And I think that will have more force, because Europe can say, then, " Here is something that, if we accept, we know the United States will stick by it, because the Congress, both Houses of the Congress, have said, in definite language, that this is what they will agree to."

By a vote of six to five that disregarded party lines the Committee reported out a resolution urging the American delegates to " strive to secure an international agreement for the coinage of gold and silver at a definite fixed ratio " but failing to specify what the ratio should be.[144] The legislative jam at the end of the first session prevented its adoption by the House.

Valuable though they may be as a gauge of public sentiment, the executive branch has evaluated resolutions of expression with an eye to the international repercussions their adoption may

144 H. Rep. 195. In the minority report Representative Martin (Colo.) presented at length the arguments of the silver bloc. Despite instructions to the American delegation, one of whom was Senator Pittman of Nevada, to work for a favorable silver plan, the conference contented itself with a resolution on silver couched in general terms. See Edwin W. Kemmerer, *Kemmerer on Money* (Philadelphia, 1934), chap. VIII.

stimulate. Secretary Hay reinforced his protest to Russia on the treatment of Jews by including a House resolution.[145] In 1906, two years later, resolutions expressing sympathy with the Jews in Russia were referred to Secretary Root for his suggestions as to the use to which they could be put. Unlike his predecessor, he did not find them of assistance in handling the situation:[146]

These resolutions do not appear to be the exercise of any legislative power conferred upon Congress by the Constitution, but to be merely an expression of opinion upon matters which, so far as they may be the concern of this Government, form a part of the foreign relations which the Constitution requires the President to conduct upon his own responsibility, or with the advice and consent of the Senate. The resolutions could not, therefore, if adopted, be regarded as responsible official action, and I cannot conceive that their adoption would accomplish any good purpose. I am rather inclined to think that they would tend, by producing irritation and antagonism, to aggravate the dangers of the unfortunate people whom they are intending to aid.

Mr. Root's attitude is perhaps not typical of the reception accorded congressional opinion, especially where that opinion coincides with the general line of policy being pursued by the executive. Secretary Olney even went so far as to encourage the passage of a concurrent resolution requesting the President to enter into negotiations for the settlement of the boundary between the United States and Canada. " With this supplementary legislation [sic], the Department is of opinion that the resolution would valuably cooperate with and strengthen its efforts to conclude a convention for this purpose." [147]

145 *United States Foreign Relations, 1904*, p. 790.

146 State Department Archives. *Cf.* Philip C. Jessup, " The Defense of Oppressed Peoples," *Amer. Journ. of Inter. Law*, XXXII (Jan., 1938), p. 119. Also Philip C. Jessup, *Elihu Root* (New York, 1938), II, p. 66.

147 *Ibid.*, Olney to Hitt, Jan. 24, 1896. To secure congressional endorsement for the convocation of an international conference dealing with the exemption of all private property at sea, not contraband of war, from capture or destruction by belligerent powers, Secretary Hay sent to Senator Cullom

When, in 1896, the Committee was snowed under with resolutions expressing a variety of opinions and calling for a wide range of action against Spain because of her Cuban policy, they were turned over to an ad hoc subcommittee to produce a draft incorporating these diverse views and also those embodied in the Senate joint resolutions which had been referred to it.[148] The result of its labor was a concurrent resolution condemning Spanish policy and threatening intervention " if necessary." Lest the resolution leave the President in doubt as to the degree of support Congress would give him, the Committee added the amendment " That Congress pledges its support to the President in carrying out the foregoing resolutions." It was then reported out, although Chairman Hitt withheld the Committee amendment from the House at the request of members of the Committee. The significant shift from joint to concurrent resolution was the subject of debate in the Senate. Senator Sherman's defense was illuminating. " If . . . we had changed them to a joint resolution, they would necessarily have to be sent to the President . . . and at a critical period of the war in Cuba, he would have been compelled to determine upon his executive action in ten days. All we desired, however, was the moral influence of the declaration of Congress. We did not wish to place the President in a dilemma.[149] The Senate finally approved the concurrent resolution. In the eyes of one commentator, " as a solemn declaration of American policy it was, perhaps, just a trifle silly. For it still left everything to the President and he, of course, paid no attention to the resolution." [150]

and Representative Hitt a draft of a resolution proclaiming "that it is the sense of the Congress of the United States that it is desirable . . . that the President endeavor to bring about an understanding among the principal maritime powers . . ." on this subject. He asked for its introduction as a joint resolution, an unusual request since it was designed strictly as a consensus of congressional sentiment. March 25, 1904, State Department Archives.

148 54th Cong. (1895-1897). Minutes, C. F. A.

149 *Ibid.*, 1st Sess., March 12, 1896. *Cong. Rec.*, p. 2724.

150 Walter Millis, *The Martial Spirit* (New York, 1931), p. 50.

The necessity for coincident action by the Senate and a judicious regard for the executive's role have kept at a minimum resolutions on foreign affairs, even when party differences divided the House from the executive. That hardy perennial, the Irish question, frequently tested the mettle of the Committee during President Wilson's administration. A joint resolution of December, 1918, " requesting the commissioners plenipotentiary of the United States of America to the International Peace Conference to present to the said conference the right of Ireland to freedom, independence, and self-determination " presumed to instruct the President's agents.[151] To ignore it would have given the President's opponents a political advantage. Under the guidance of Chairman Flood the Committee reduced it to a concurrent resolution, conveying the sentiment " that it is the earnest hope of the Congress . . . that the peace conference will favorably consider the claims of Ireland to the right of self-determination." [152] The Republican leader, Mr. Mann, sarcastically remarked that it was the intention of the Democrats " to let the President out from signing it. They (the Committee) reported a concurrent resolution which, when it passes this House, is so much waste paper, until it has passed the Senate." Mr. Mann's prophecy came true when the measure only received the approval of the House a few hours before the expiration of the Sixty-fifth Congress.[153] In the following Congress, controlled by the Republicans, Mr. Mason tried a new approach with a bill providing for a salary for a minister to Ireland, and hoped thereby to secure recognition of Ireland's independence through the appointment of a diplomatic agent.[154] This was blocked in the Committee by a coalition of both parties and Mr. Mason contented himself momentarily with a concurrent resolution that Ireland be granted a government of its own choice.[155]

151 65th Cong., 3rd Sess. (1919). H. J. Res. 357.
152 H. Con. Res. 68. Minutes, C. F. A.
153 65th Cong., 3rd Sess. (1919). *Cong. Rec.*, p. 5035.
154 66th Cong., 1st Sess. (1919). H. R. 3404.
155 66th Cong., 2nd Sess. (1920). H. Con. Res. 57. Files, C. F. A.

The last session of Congress under President Wilson had before it a joint resolution authorizing and empowering the President " at his discretion, to invite the Governments of all nations to send accredited delegates to an international convention to be held in the United States to consider ways and means of bringing about joint disarmament." Mr. Mason rose to the occasion and offered an amendment in Committee to insert after the word " nations " the following : " and also all peoples who are being governed by force, and without their consent, and who are seeking the right of self-determination." As interpreted by the author, the amendment would embrace India, South Africa, and the Philippine Islands as well as Ireland. The comment of one member received the endorsement of most of the others : " To put this amendment into that resolution, in my judgment, would kill the resolution, but if it did not kill the resolution, it would kill the effect of the conference because Great Britain would not attend, and I feel like [sic] bringing about a conference for disarmament is of more importance than to pass useless resolutions in reference to people who may be entitled to the right to select a government of their own." By a vote of nine to two the amendment was rejected.[156]

If passage of resolutions has been infrequent, at least the threat of House action has served at times to stir the executive branch. Chairman Porter's concurrent resolution requesting the President to enter into negotiations with China to draft new treaties which would take the place of the unequal treaties on jurisdictional rights and customs dues was ignored by the State Department until it had been reported out of the Committee. " That was followed in a few hours by a statement from the State Department which might never have been issued except for that," commented Representative Moore.[157] Before report-

---

156 *Ibid.*, 3rd Sess. H. J. Res. 424. Files and Minutes, C. F. A.

157 69th Cong., 2nd Sess. (1927). This remark was made during the hearings on *Conditions in Nicaragua and Mexico*, cited, p. 83.

ing it out, however, the Committee had discussed rather thoroughly two issues : first, should the Secretary of State be invited to give testimony, and second, the effect of such a resolution on negotiations. Mr. Burton whose long experience included that of a delegate to the opium conference recalled that " the resolution of Congress enabled me to speak not only for the President but for the Congress of the United States, and it added tremendously to the force of our representations." As for the first matter, the Committee divided without reference to party affiliation. Those favoring an invitation to the Secretary contended that an expression by the Committee without a full knowledge of the diplomatic circumstances might make more difficult the fulfillment of the resolution; those opposing the invitation, however, pointed out that the Department would be put in the position of " forming our opinions " and " then it cannot act independently as it should act. We have a perfect right, and it is not only our right but our duty, to express how we feel in reference to this situation."

In discussing the desirability of reporting out resolutions expressing the sentiment of the House, the Committee has pondered the effect of their passage both on Congress and on the executive. Judged by the cross-fire of questions, a confusion of thought exists on the subject.[158] The struggles of oppressed peoples elicited the attention of the members through the introduction of resolutions requesting the President to designate a " tag day " to assist them. In the Sixty-fourth Congress alone three such days were urged upon the President, one each for

158 During the hearings on a resolution, *In Behalf of the Armenians*, the Committee repeatedly asked the witnesses what they hoped to obtain by requesting the President to protest the persecution of the Armenians to the de facto Government at Angora and also to take up with Great Britain, France, and Italy the possibility of a conference to consider the establishment of an Armenian nation. Congressman Cooper summed up the hopes of the proponents and the beliefs of the Committee when he declared that "the object of this resolution would be to secure by its adoption a statement of the public opinion of the United States of America on what are indisputed and indisputable facts." 67th Cong., 2nd Sess. (1922). H. Res. 244, pp. 8-20, *passim*.

the Armenians, the Lithuanians, and the Ruthenians.[159] Only the last of these was in the form of a joint resolution, and therefore it required the President's signature. So numerous were these resolutions that representatives wondered whether Congress was not doing more than expressing its sympathy and really committing itself to give financial aid. But when it came to a vote, the Committee showed little hesitation in endorsing those that asked for nothing more than a request of the President.[160] Anxious to endorse the overthrow of the Czarist regime, the Committee took up a concurrent resolution congratulating the Russians on the establishment of a republican form of government. But there was considerable uncertainty among the members whether a republican government had been actually set up by the March revolution. After some inconclusive discussion, it was amended to congratulate the peoples of Russia on the establishment of " institutions of popular government." [161]

Mr. Husted's resolution on the Fiume situation was indicative of the distrust felt by many that President Wilson would use American troops for the settlement of disputes in which this country had no immediate interest.[162] It expressed the sense of the House that " the United States should not participate in any military or naval operations against the Italian forces under the command of Gabriel d'Annunzio, now investing the city of Fiume, and should not attempt to influence the action of said forces or of their commander by show or threat of force or otherwise." [163] The question the Committee could not resolve

159 S. Con. Res. 12, H. Res. 258, and H. J. Res. 350.

160 Cf. Hearings on Relief of Suffering Population of the World, 66th Cong., 3rd Sess. (1921). The preamble to H. Con. Res. 70 was interpreted by the Committee as implying a moral obligation on the part of Congress that the money collected would be administered and accounted for by that body. It was therefore changed to a simple statement that the needs of the suffering populations of the world could be met only by contributions from the American people. H. Con. Res. 71.

161 65th Cong. (1917-1919). Minutes, C. F. A.

162 The Siberian expedition and its corollary, the use of armed forces by the executive, were the subjects of resolutions of inquiry. See infra, pp. 96 f.

163 66th Cong., 3rd Sess. (1921). H. Res. 308. Files, C. F. A.

was whether the war power had as yet ceased and how far it (the Committee) could check the President's use of armed forces.

. . . If we ourselves have not taken it [the war power] away from the President, is it not true that if the President wants to put our men there, legally he has a right to do it, under whatever form it may ᴸ done?

That ıs former Austrian territory, and we declared war against Austria and authorized the use of our armed forces. So until peace has been signed with Austria, legally, at least, it seems to me that the President has a right to carry on the war there, if he wants to, with anybody he chooses, in that field.

We are not seeking to take away from the President any troops, or the right to make war, but we are merely expressing the sense of the House that we should mind our own business in an affair that we do not and cannot understand.

. . . In the exercise of the power that he is given, he has brought us into this situation. Now, unless we take it away from him, I do not see much good in advising him, because he would say that he knows this just as we do, and a great deal better . . .

I would like to get a resolution adopted in this House to the effect that we should not interfere there in any way whatever . . . I think it would be a good thing if the Executive knew what the attitude of the House was on that proposition.

Do you think that if this resolution is adopted by the House it would have any perceptible effect or influence upon the Executive?

I cannot answer that question. I do not know what effect it might have. I think it should have an effect, whether it would or not, I cannot say.[163a]

This indecision on its own powers as well as those of the President resulted, as so frequently happened, in a failure to take any action in preference to that which might bring into the open

163a 66th Cong. Files, C. F. A.

a clash between the two powers or subject the Committee to a rebuff for trespassing on executive prerogatives.[164]

9. THE RESOLUTION OF INQUIRY

The resolution of inquiry is one of the oldest legislative devices by which members seek information from the executive.[165] Rules and precedent have given to it a unique status.[166] It cannot be buried or ignored in a committee; provision is made that " all resolutions of inquiry . . . shall be reported to the House within one week after presentation." [167] Once referred to a committee, it is privileged for report and consideration at any time after the seven legislative days. Failure on the part of the committee to report may result in a motion to discharge the committee, a motion which in the case of the resolution of inquiry is privileged.[168] On matters of foreign affairs the qualification " if not incompatible with the public interest " is appended to the resolution.

The apparent purpose of the resolution of inquiry is to gather facts on a particular situation. But to what use will these facts be put? That is the question that the Foreign Affairs Commit-

164 To encourage the idea that it was not partisanship that led him to defend the President, Mr. Begg, an opponent of the several resolutions investigating American activities in Nicaragua and Mexico, raised the question what " the standing of a nation in the minds of the nations of the world (would be) if we were to ... pass a resolution ordering the withdrawal of troops, and it should pass both Houses of Congress? " Mr. Huddleston, a critic of the President's policy, replied with an equally altruistic answer: " It would show that the Congress of the United States was capable of a brave, just, and patriotic action. It would show that Congress was jealous of our national honor and was unwilling to be committed to the policy of the intimidation of the weak and helpless and unfortunate ... " 69th Cong., 2nd Sess. (1927). *Conditions in Nicaragua and Mexico*, cited, p. 43.

165 *Cf.* Hinds, *Precedents*, III, sec. 1856, for a history of the rule.

166 *Ibid.*, sec. 1856 ff.

167 Rule XXII, sec. 5 (1934 ed. of the Rules of the House).

168 The ordinary motion to discharge a committee is not privileged; but the practice of the House has given privilege to the motion in cases of resolution of inquiry. See Clarence Cannon, *Precedents of the House of Representatives* (Washington, 1935), VI, sec. 415.

tee ponders in preparing its report for the House. The answer is usually resolved in the light of what the Committee believes to be the motives of the sponsor. Broadly speaking, two purposes lead to the introduction of these resolutions. One of these rests upon the assumption that, with complete information before it, the members will be able to frame effective legislation or will have a solid basis in fact for formulating an opinion. In short, it is a prelude to further legislative action. The projected legislation is likely to be restrictive in scope just as the resolution expressing the sense of the House or of Congress will lean toward the critical. In 1913, the Committee had before it two resolutions, one making an inquiry of the State Department and the other, a joint resolution, censuring a foreign government; both dealt with the persecution of the Jews in Roumania.[169] Representative Moore, in pressing for prior con-

169 63rd Cong., 2nd Sess. (1914). Hearings on H. J. Res. 183 and H. Res. 138, *The Jews of Roumania.* After a lengthy preamble the first of these resolved " That it is the sense of the American Congress that the interests of civilization, the rights of humanity, the principles of eternal justice, and the dignity and sanctity of international law demand that the signatory powers of the treaty of Berlin compel Roumania to observe the stipulations of the treaty of Berlin in the matter of the treatment of the Jews," and secondly " That the Secretary of State be requested to transmit a copy of this resolution to the Governments of Great Britain, Germany, Austria, Russia, France, Italy, and Turkey."

The second " Resolved, That the Secretary of State be requested to inform the House whether any communication has been had with the Roumanian Government or the powers signatory to the treaty of Berlin in relation to the observance of said treaty, or with respect to a naturalization convention between the United States and the Roumanian Government; and if so, and no conclusions have been reached thereon, whether the United States has such interests with respect to said treaty and the operation thereof as to make further diplomatic negotiations desirable." This " resolve " clause was preceded by a preamble which, under the ruling of several Speakers, nullifies the privileged status of a resolution of inquiry. The ruling was apparently not invoked in this case. *Cf.* Hinds, *op. cit.*, sec. 1877: " The privilege of a resolution of inquiry may be destroyed by a preamble, although the matter therein recited may be germane to the subject of the inquiry."

In 1888, the Committee made a privileged report on a resolution of inquiry pertaining to the boundary dispute between Great Britain and Venezuela. In place of the original resolution it offered a substitute identical in wording

sideration of his resolution of inquiry over that which undertook to rebuke the Roumanian Government, made the point that his " would be the more diplomatic of the two resolutions and more in line with what the American Jews desire to obtain. It would be the first step toward obtaining information officially that we do not now seem to have. . . . When we get this information . . . we would be in a position to take further action. . . . The adoption of the Chandler resolution (the joint resolution) at this time . . . would be premature, in view of the fact that the committee is not officially informed . . ." [170]

The other purpose represents the endeavors of the minority or dissident members of the majority to smoke out the executive from his exclusive domain and use the data obtained to snipe at the administration's foreign policy. The task of the majority, especially the chairman, is to check the passage of those resolutions aiming to embarrass the executive, for their wording contains a strong implication of criticism of the executive. President Wilson's settlement of the Panama Canal tolls question with the aid of the Democratic majority in both Houses aroused the Republicans. Representative Knowland called upon the President for " all correspondence which has passed between the United States and Great Britain relating to the question . . ." " What is the real purpose of this resolution? " he was asked by a member of the Committee. " Simply to get more light on the subject than we have now." "And what

in the " resolve " clause but with an altered preamble. The chairman explained: "As the resolution is intended to be simply a resolution of inquiry, it seemed proper that the Committee should present it with a preamble leading to such a resolution." 50th Cong., 1st Sess., March 7, 1888. *Cong. Rec.*, p. 1827.

170 *Op. cit.*, p. 37, 39. While not opposed to the Moore resolution, Mr. Chandler felt that the facts were already known. " I have been up to the State Department, and I had a talk with Mr. Bryan. He received me very cordially, and I violate no confidence when I say he told me he was in sympathy with the purpose of my resolution and was in sympathy with any movement that would stop the oppression of the Jews. But he added that the question of precedent would have to be settled." P. 22.

are you going to do with the light after you get it?" queried another member. "Diffuse it," was the cryptic reply.[171]

During the same period the Mexican policy of the President was a subject of frequent discussion, although partisanship was more restrained. Early in 1914 the Committee had before it Representative Ainey's resolution requesting the President to transmit information "concerning treatment of American citizens and other persons in Mexico." Mr. Ainey explained:[172]

I believe that in our form of government there is a responsibility which rests upon the legislative side as well as upon the executive side for the safeguarding of American interests, American lives and American property in other countries . . . I think it becomes my duty in my official way to bring these matters to the attention of this Committee, and ultimately to the attention of the distinguished President of the United States, in order that we may have an opportunity of knowing just what are the conditions in Mexico, and if legislatively we may be able to help in bringing about a peaceful solution of the Mexican trouble. I think it is our duty both to acquire information and our duty to act in such a way as will bring about the safeguarding of American rights. . . . The purpose of my resolution is that we may be enabled to know what they (the President and the State Department) are doing and what information they are acting upon. I say that because I believe we have the right to that information as well as the President of the United States and the Secretary of State . . .

Similarly, Representative Kahn pressed for the adoption of his resolution in 1914 calling on the Secretary for "such letters or documents or instructions given or sent to Hon. John Lind," the President's representative in Mexico, on the ground that the latter's action was inconsistent with his expressed desire not to interfere in Mexico. "It puts the President in a very embarrassing position when you take into consideration his statement to

171 63rd Cong., 2nd Sess. (1914). H. Res. 452. Files, C. F. A. Charles Seymour, *The Intimate Papers of Colonel House* (Boston, 1926), I, p. 190 ff., discusses the settlement of the tolls question with Great Britain.

172 63rd Cong., 2nd Sess. (1914). H. Res. 429. Files, C. F. A.

the Congress of the United States," remarked Mr. Kahn. The publicizing of such information, observed the congressman, would allay the suspicions that Latin American nations may have regarding the United States.[173]

Within the scope of this survey the years from 1913 to 1921 were the most prolific in numbers of resolutions of inquiry referred to, and acted upon by, the Committee. They fall broadly into two categories, viz., those touching on President Wilson's relations with Latin American nations, especially Mexico, and those dealing with problems arising out of the war. So great was the general concern of congressmen on these questions that an adverse report would hardly have stopped discussion. On the other hand, for the executive to have answered the queries would have endangered the negotiations then in progress or would have drawn upon it for data not easily revealed. The Committee's problem was to appease the demands with a minimum of embarrassment to the State Department. Take, for example, Mr. Dallinger's resolution on conditions in Russia.[174] He called upon the Secretary of State for the following:

First, The present condition of business and the amount of commodities now on hand and now being produced in Russia; and the possibilities of trade relations between Russia and the United States.

Second, Whether as a matter of fact under the present de facto government in Russia there is any protection to the individual in his life, liberty, and property—

(a) If an individual accused of crime is given a fair trial, with the right of appeal to a civil judicial tribunal.

(b) If there exists in Russia today any freedom of the press or the right of free speech.

(c) If private property is subject to seizure by governmental authorities without payment of proper compensation and without the process of law.

173 *Ibid.*, H. Res. 561. *Cf.* George M. Stephenson, *John Lind of Minnesota* (Minneapolis, 1935), chap. XIV-XVII.

174 66th Cong., 3rd Sess. (1921). H. Res. 635.

Third, Whether it is a fact that the soviet government of Russia and the Third Internationale are engaged in a systematic and organized propaganda throughout the world to destroy—

(a) Nationality and love of country.

(b) The organization of society into families.

(c) All forms of religion, and particularly the Christian religion.

These questions bordered closer on a request for expressions of opinion—barred from resolutions of inquiry—than to a solicitation of factual material. Hence the Committee resorted to a hearing. It may be observed, parenthetically, that hearings or lengthy discussion on resolutions of inquiry were characteristic of this period. Although more than seven legislative days had elapsed, Mr. Dallinger preferred to have the Committee report his resolution " in some form, or else obtain the information desired directly from the Secretary of State." " I have no basis for introducing this resolution," he added, " other than that there has been a great deal of talk about the resumption of trade relations with Russia, and it has been strongly urged that we should recognize the soviet government of Russia . . ." [175] The hearings on this resolution were most thorough and even included testimony of ranking department officers. By the time the Committee had completed its hearing to determine whether the Secretary should be asked to supply these data, it had probed into all phases of Russian activity and left nothing for the Department to add!

Representative Ainey's resolution inquiring into steps taken by President Wilson to safeguard American lives and property in Mexico reflected the uneasiness felt by many members of both parties on the President's Mexican policy.[176] Although the Committee was divided in opinion on the policy being pursued, it was recognized that congressional discussion would further stimulate an already sensational press. By agreement with Mr. Ainey, the Committee decided to invite Secretary Bryan to appear in executive session. Pending the Secretary's coming, Mr.

175 *Ibid.*, p. 1.

176 63rd Cong., 2nd Sess. (1914). H. Res. 429.

Ainey did not take advantage of the expiration of the legislative week to move to discharge the Committee. When Mr. Bryan presented himself before the Committee early in March, 1914, his explanations were frank and complete. He made out a good case for not revealing all that was available, mainly because the press, through distortion, aggravated the situation. Mr. Ainey who joined in the questioning, although not a member of the Committee, was apparently satisfied with the Secretary's comments for he refrained from pressing for passage of his resolution.[177]

Two resolutions making inquiry into the President's control of the armed forces were the occasion for extended scrutiny and examination into foreign relations.[178] Constituents were alarmed by the dispatch of American troops to Siberia and the reports of the conditions under which they were living. In some districts organizations of relatives of the troops were formed and descended upon Washington to press for their immediate return to this country. Representative Rhodes called upon the Department for data on the situation. Before this was forthcoming the Committee gave over a session to a discussion of the President's authority for sending soldiers into a country against which no war had been declared.[179] The prevailing view was that the declaration of war against Germany and Austria-Hungary gave him permission to fight only those countries and to carry on operations elsewhere incidental to that primary object. The question which the Committee found itself unable to answer was whether the Siberian expedition was part of the attack against the Central Powers. On this point it sought enlightenment from ranking officers of the War and State Departments.

177 Files, C. F. A. In connection with the Committee's consideration of H. Res. 504, 74th Cong., 2nd Sess. (1936), touching on the Italian-Ethiopian conflict, a member of the State Department appeared before the Committee and explored the broad implications of the resolution.

178 66th Cong., 1st Sess. (1919). H. Res. 250 (re Siberia). Minutes and Files, C. F. A. 66th Cong., 3rd Sess. (1921). H. Res. 646 (re Cuba). Minutes and Files, C. F. A.

179 Cf. supra, pp. 85 f.

The War Department's representative explained the military function of the American forces in Siberia—to aid our Russian ally and, secondly, to keep open the avenue of access to the Czechoslovak troops fighting the German and Austrian prisoners. Beyond this the Committee probed into sales of munitions and supplies to Russian leaders. The State Department official refuted the statement that the President had exceeded his constitutional authority by moving troops into Siberia without specific congressional authorization and justified this incident on the ground that it was necessary to prevent aid from reaching the " general enemy." But constitutional issues paled into the background as it was disclosed that behind the intervention by one of the great Powers in Siberia lay ulterior motives that forced joint intervention upon the American Government as a counterpoise. In the absence of more complete records one may only infer that this revelation proved decisive in leading the Committee to look favorably upon the President's action.

General Crowder's mission to Cuba, in 1921, led to a further examination of the President's use of armed forces abroad and its repercussions on foreign relations. Representative Mason asked the President not only to state why the officer was sent to Cuba but upon what authority he (the President) acted. More than two weeks elapsed from the date of introduction before the Committee discussed its disposal. Aside from the author of the resolution, other members were reluctant to press the President on this point, one prominent Republican contending that " the President is doing the proper thing in this matter." By one vote short of unanimity the Committee tabled the resolution and Mr. Mason admitted defeat.

The swift flow of international affairs in the first two administrations of President Franklin D. Roosevelt has not resulted in a greater use of resolutions of inquiry. Measured by numbers, by content, by the attention given them in the Committee, the House, and the State Department, they have played no part in keeping Congress abreast of the executive's reaction to foreign affairs. All eighteen resolutions of inquiry that came to the Foreign Affairs Committee in the years from 1933 to 1940 were reported adversely with the recommendation that they be not passed.[180] The reasons for the scant consideration given them lie partly in the resolutions themselves and partly in the answers given.

The rules rigidly exclude an inquiry into motives, objectives, or opinions; only a request for strictly factual material is permitted. Stress is placed on the " what," not on the " how " and " why " which are of more interest to the House. Questions, therefore, must be pointed rather than exploratory. There is no bar to a series of related questions within one resolution or a number of resolutions on the same subject. Precise questions invite precise answers that give only an episodical treatment of foreign affairs. Unlike the question hour in the House of Commons, the resolution of inquiry lacks the benefit of publicity. A minister who rises to answer in the most ambiguous language at least has the attention of the House and probably of the press. In contrast, the resolution of inquiry moves in an atmosphere of semi-privacy. So far as its introduction and reference are concerned, these are merely noted at the end of the day's proceedings in the House. The Committee no longer follows the custom of the Wilsonian period of discussing whether the resolution should be sent to the State Department. Instead, the Committee sends it along to the Department for its reply.

The rules would appear to assure the author of a resolution of inquiry either a report " if not incompatible with the public interest," or the privilege of publicizing his query through the use of a discharge motion. This last is a cumbersome procedure to which no member has resorted on resolutions before the Foreign Affairs Committee. Only once in the last eight years has the Secretary fallen back upon the " escape clause," perhaps

180 The resolutions of inquiry referred to the Committee on Foreign Affairs for each of the four Congresses were: 73rd Cong. (1933-1934), none; 74th Cong. (1935-1936), three; 75th Cong. (1937-1938), five; 76th Cong. (1939-1940), ten. Fourteen of the eighteen resolutions came from minority members. Ten of them were introduced by two members of the Foreign Affairs Committee, Mr. Fish and Mrs. Rogers, who were active critics of the President's foreign policy.

because the President finds in his constitutional prerogative sufficient means to stem congressional attacks upon his policy.[181] No matter what the Secretary's reply, resolutions of inquiry have invariably been buried in adverse reports to the House with nothing more than a small obituary in the *Record*. Some adverse reports contain the information supplied by the Department. Mrs. Rogers' resolution requesting information relating to the protection of the American legation in Addis Ababa was answered at length by Secretary Hull. His letter and accompanying dispatches from the American Minister were incorporated in the adverse report.[182] On the other hand, two resolutions calling for information on American investments in Mexico elicited replies from the State Department too confidential to be printed in a public report.[183] The adverse reports on them added the statement that " such information available to the Department of State as is consistent with the public interest has been furnished your committee and is on file," thus affording any interested representative an opportunity to examine the Department's replies for his own guidance. Confident that discretion would restrain the publication of his replies, the Secretary was able to answer the resolution with reasonable completeness and thereby fend off further inquiries.[184]

181 At the conclusion of his testimony on the Ainey resolution, Secretary Bryan was asked whether he did not think it would be better for the Committee not to report this resolution. " I think so," replied the Secretary, "although I have no objection to the Committee doing what it wants to do, because the President can protect himself and the interests that are intrusted to him under the constitution and under the authority of your resolution." 63rd Cong. (1914). Files, C. F. A.

182 74th Cong., 2nd Sess. (1936). H. Res. 504, H. Rep. 2661. For similar reports, *cf.* 75th Cong. (1937-1938). H. Rep. 1651, 1751, 1809, 1831, and 2231.

183 76th Cong., 1st Sess. (1939). H. Rep. 24 on H. Res. 18 and H. Rep. 162 on H. Res. 107. Representative Kennedy's resolution (no. 78) requested a reply from the Secretary within fifteen days.

184 *Cf. The New York Times*, February 8, 1939.
Secretary Root responded to Mr. Hitt's request for information and correspondence relating to the arrest, detention, fine, and imprisonment of an immigrant by the Hungarian Government by giving the details as recorded by the Department. He noted, however, that no claim by or on his behalf

Another device for curtailing insistence upon a knowledge of executive policy without the attendant publicity of a report is the quiet endeavor of the chairman to obtain the necessary details and pass them on to the author of the resolution. A resolution of inquiry into religious conditions in Mexico in 1935 was answered by the Department, but the Committee deemed desirable an adverse report with no accompanying explanation in the light of the Department's reply. By agreement, however, the

had been presented. "Under these circumstances the expediency of adopting the Resolution is questionable, and I am not disposed to advise doing so. All the correspondence for which it is proposed to call has, however, been collected and is open to examination by any member of the Committee or of the House if desired." State Department Archives, Jan. 5, 1906.

A month later Mr. Root wrote Representative Adams about a resolution calling for information relating to the conduct and transactions of Mr. Sorsby, formerly Minister to Ecuador. His reply read, in part:

2. The second paragraph of the resolution, which relates to the promotion of Sorsby and the reduction of Bridgeman, should be stricken out. That is purely a question of appointment of a foreign minister and a foreign consul which is committed by the Constitution to the President with the advice and consent of the Senate, and the President cannot hold himself answerable to the House of Representatives for reasons which actuate him in the exercise of that Constitutional power.

There is no earthly reason why you should not know what the facts are, and I am perfectly ready to inform any member of the Committee or of the House personally of the facts; but I cannot advise the President to answer such a question officially. State Department Archives, February 7, 1906.

In 1930, the Senate by resolution of inquiry called upon President Hoover for "letters, minutes, memoranda, instructions, and dispatches" relating to the negotiations of the London Naval Conference "to the end that the Senate may be able to do and perform its constitutional obligations with respect to advising and consenting to and ratifying such treaty or rejecting same." 72nd Cong., 1st Sess., S. Res. 320. President Hoover replied: "This treaty, like all other international negotiations, has involved statements, reports, tentative and informal proposals as to subjects, persons, and governments given to me in confidence. The Executive, under the duty of guarding the interests of the United States, in the protection of future negotiations, and in maintaining relations of amity with other nations, must not allow himself to become guilty of a breach of trust by betrayal of these confidences. He must not affront representatives of other nations, and thus make future dealings with those nations more difficult and less frank. To make public in debate or in the press such confidences would violate the invariable practice of nations.... I have no desire to withhold from the Senate any information having even the remotest bearing upon the negotiation of the

information was divulged to the sponsor and the report was withdrawn.[185] An earlier resolution on the same subject was similarly handled in order to forestall discussion on the floor of the House.[186] Such a settlement was predicated on the twofold assumption that even an adverse report would give unwarranted and disproportionate attention to a situation that was occupying the Department and that the author of the resolution would be placated by the material put at his disposal.

The Department's policy in recent years of answering resolutions of inquiry has been responsible for their declining importance. A response, no matter how abbreviated or perfunctory, is a sound procedure; it disarms the inquirer without necessarily informing the House. To hide behind the cloak of incompatibility with public interest only heightens congressional criticism and increases suspicion of executive policy. Moreover, a personal visit to the Department provides a quicker and more extensive reply than can be had by means of the resolution of inquiry. There is a further reason for congressional apathy toward resolutions of inquiry, a factor that can be stated more readily than it can be evaluated. That is the increased publicity facilities of the White House and the State Department. The press release is only the most obvious product of the publicity

treaty. No Senator has been refused an opportunity to see the confidential material referred to, provided only he will agree to receive and hold the same in the confidence in which it has been received and held by the Executive ... " He believed it to be incompatible with the public interest to comply with the resolution. S. Doc. 216. The Senate thereupon adopted the Norris reservation which stipulated " that in ratifying said treaty the Senate does so with the distinct and explicit understanding that there are no secret files, documents, letters, understandings or agreements which in any way, directly or indirectly, modify, change, add to or take away from any of the stipulations, agreements, or statements in said treaty..." July 21, 1930. *Cong. Rec.* p. 390.

185 74th Cong., 1st Sess. (1935). H. Res. 277. *Calendar*, C. F. A. Only by consent of the House may a chairman of a committee withdraw a report. *Cannon's Precedents in the House of Representatives* (Washington, 1939), p. 90.

186 69th Cong., 1st Sess. (1926). H. Res. 137. Minutes, C. F. A. *Ibid.*, 2nd Sess. (1927). H. Res. 371 and 388. Files, C. F. A.

machinery. More valuable to the correspondents is the interpretative background material they are able to obtain. While it can rarely be quoted directly, it serves to enlarge their perspective and sharpen their stories.[187] It is an interesting reflection on the democratic process in foreign affairs that the press is often given a closer view than are members of Congress. That, I believe, accounts for the greater number of reprints of editorials, columns, and news accounts in the *Congressional Record*.

10. THE CHAIRMAN

The chairman of a House committee has a variety of duties and privileges as well as a degree of prestige by virtue of his office. Within the committee he is the ranking majority member and presides at its meetings. Since the rules of the House are also the rules of the committee " so far as applicable," he is in many respects a miniature speaker, the head of a " little legislature." He has the power of recognition and the right to appoint subcommittees. The conduct of hearings is entrusted to him, including arrangements for the appearance of witnesses. Seniority in committee service accords him a deference among the younger and less experienced members, especially of his own party. His advice, even when unsolicited, can hardly go unheeded.

The chairman of the Committee on Foreign Affairs, more than the chairmen of most legislative committees, seldom has any independent views to urge upon the Committee or the House. Whatever legislative program is presented to the Committee is essentially executive in origin. That is to say, at least the broad outlines are. The President's strategic position in foreign policy has had the effect of producing a succession of chairmen who have accommodated their legislative actions to his wishes. One unique exception to this generalization was the opposition of Chairman Belmont, in the 1880's, to the demands

---

187 For an enlightening account of the relations between the press and the State Department, see Bertram D. Hulen, *Inside the State Department* (New York, 1939), chap. VIII, The Press Conference System. Mr. Hulen has been covering the Department for almost twenty years.

for legislation for an interoceanic canal—a resistance more noteworthy because of the demands within and outside of Congress for such a project. For a variety of reasons but chiefly because of "the confusion and uncertainty which existed in the treaty relations between the United States and other governments respecting the guarantee of the neutrality and free use of the proposed canal" he refused to support the recommendations of the majority of his Committee.

This matter continued through four Congresses. As chairman of the Committee on Foreign Affairs (for two Congresses), it was my duty to present for consideration the subjects which had been referred to the committee, to appoint the necessary subcommittees to consider them, and also to formulate the general procedure and the order in which the various subjects were to be taken up. I was, therefore, able to create the delay I considered so necessary. For this purpose, I found the Consular Reform Bill very useful.

The endorsement of an interoceanic canal by both major parties in the 1888 election led him to withdraw his opposition in a most unusual way. He asked the Speaker to transfer the canal question from his committee to the Committee on Commerce. This was done and the House speedily adopted the Committee's report favoring a canal.[188]

In the intervals between legislative activities the chairman of the Foreign Affairs Committee performs an essentially negative function, that is, he blocks action by the Committee. Not accustomed to the niceties of diplomacy, the Committee (and the House, too) does not always appreciate the value of inaction. The President and the Secretary of State have had to turn to him—sometimes to the House leaders—to hold in check the restive urge of Congress to "do something," action that would only complicate the administration's task. Perhaps the most notable example in recent years was the struggle over the McLemore resolution. President Wilson laid down the strategy

188 Perry Belmont, *An American Democrat* (New York, 1939), chap. XI.

of forcing a vote on the resolution in order to defeat it. Although the resolution, warning American citizens not to travel on armed ships, had the approval of an overwhelming majority of the House, its cumbersome preamble cost it much support. " Under Presidential pressure both the Rules Committee and the Committee on Foreign Affairs refused to permit a simple resolution of warning to be substituted for the unpopular McLemore resolution." The administration feared that a failure to have a record vote on this resolution would be followed by the introduction of one more aceptable to the House and, therefore, more embarrassing to the President. A grumbling House voted to table it, 276 to 142, and gave the President a technical victory.[189]

The disposition of the McLemore resolution was due to the combined efforts of the House leaders, of whom the chairman of the Foreign Affairs Committee was only one. On other issues that have not yet generated heat beyond the Committee walls the chairman is a self-constituted diplomat moving between the Committee and the executive. Immediately after the signing of the Treaty of Versailles in June, 1919, inquiries came to the Committee regarding the return of the soldier dead from France in fulfillment of promises made to the families of the deceased. A ranking officer of the Department informed Chairman Porter that the promise was " awkward but for the time being we can refuse to fulfil it on the perfectly adequate ground that the French will not permit us to move the bodies." This explanation not only failed to satisfy the Committee but aroused its ire because of the anxiety of many constituents. Several measures having been introduced on the subject, the Committee threatened to report one of them and debate the whole issue on the floor of the House. Fearing the effects of a protracted and sharp debate on Franco-American relations, the chairman forestalled Committee action by carrying the issue to Secretary Lansing.

189 The details of the struggle on the McLemore resolution are given in Charles C. Tansill, *America Goes to War* (Boston, 1938), chap. XVII. See, also, 64th Cong., 1st Sess., *Cong. Rec.*, March 7, 1916. *Cf. supra*, p. 13, ft. 8.

The Secretary, in turn, called upon Ambassador Wallace for vigorous action in Paris until the latter was able to secure a favorable reply from the French Government. Satisfied with the explanations given by the latter, the chairman quietly passed the information to interested members and the matter never became the subject of a public debate.[190]

During the 1920's the chairman was called upon frequently to block measures before the Committee that would have aggravated our relations with Mexico, had they passed. Unfortunately neither the minutes nor the files of the Committee throw much light on the nature of the discussions or the line of argument pursued. The curt minute: " The chairman made a statement to the committee bearing on the Mexican situation. No further consideration was given the matter " describes the extent of action on a concurrent resolution requesting the President to " adjust " relations with Mexico in 1922.[191] Two years later the Committee looked with favor upon Mr. Fairchild's resolution to prohibit the shipment of arms to any foreign powers. Its passage would have denied military aid to the Obregon government in Mexico in its effort to put down the de la Huerta revolt. Mr. Porter read to the Committee a specially prepared statement by Secretary Hughes and supplemented it with his own reasons for believing that action should be delayed. These proved sufficient to induce the Committee to postpone action indefinitely.[192]

190 66th Cong. (1919-1921). Files, C. F. A. During the hearings, in 1914, on the Panama Canal Tolls, Chairman Flood stated to the Committee: " I am authorized to say by the President there has been absolutely no correspondence between this Government and Great Britain during this administration on this subject." 63rd Cong. Files, C. F. A.

191 67th Cong. Minutes, C. F. A. In the same Congress Chairman Porter opposed a joint resolution favoring the establishment in Palestine of a national home for the Jewish people. When the Committee voted to report it favorably, he asked that another member present it on the floor. This was done by Mr. Fish, the author of the resolution. Minutes, C. F. A.

192 68th Cong. Files, C. F. A.

Chairman Porter, in 1926, tried to satisfy Representative Boylan's request for data from the State Department on the expulsion of American citizens from Mexico. He presented a digest of his conversations with Departmental officials and secured for Mr. Boylan a copy of a departmental report on the situation, hoping thereby to appease the Congressman. When the latter pressed a concurrent resolution favoring the withdrawal of " diplomatic recognition " until the Mexican Government had changed its religious policies, the Committee deemed it politically expedient to hold hearings. Again the Department communicated with Mr. Porter who presented the information in an open session of the Committee. At the conclusion of the hearings the Committee found the Department's policy, as explained by the chairman, to be sufficiently satisfactory and thereupon dropped the question.[193]

More recently, the Committee, acting upon the suggestion of Secretary Hull, agreed to report adversely a resolution inquiring into our relations with Mexico. When Mr. Bloom, then the acting chairman, made the report, he moved that it be tabled, the effect of which was to prevent debate. The House supported him. The author of the resolution, Martin J. Kennedy of New York, called this an " unstatesmanlike device." His protest, it would appear, was directed more against the Committee's unwillingness to disclose the Secretary's report than against the procedure followed, a procedure which is not unusual in the case of adverse reports.[194]

Until the executive decides that his powers in foreign policy must be implemented by legislation, the legislative career of the chairman of the Foreign Affairs Committee is hardly more distinguished than that of the average congressman. Once the need for legislation is apparent, the chairman takes his cue from the President. The more far-reaching the proposals, the more prominent is the role cut out for the chairman. Calls at the White House, interviews, hearings, confidential memoranda,

193 69th Cong. Minutes and Files, C. F. A.
194 76th Cong., 1st Sess. (1939). *The New York Times*, February 8, 1939.

and conferences brighten his routine and enhance his legislative —and public—stature. It may be argued that he can refuse to present the President's request for legislation. That is possible. But in foreign affairs the judgment of the chairman is no match for that of the President or the Secretary of State. The President's request implies that he has need of the legislation for the successful prosecution of his policy. To refuse to press the legislation opens the chairman to charges of obstructing the foreign policy of the country—not the President—an accusation too serious for him to combat singlehandedly. In recent years the executive has often communicated his wishes to the chairmen of the House and the Senate committees in order that the legislative processes might be hastened. The psychological effect has been to stimulate the activity of the House committee in order that it may compete on more favorable terms with the better known and more powerful Senate Committee on Foreign Relations.

When President Cleveland wanted to settle the vexatious matter of the Canadian fisheries, he turned to the chairman of the Foreign Affairs Committee, Perry Belmont, and, together with Secretary of State Bayard, acquainted Mr. Belmont with the background as well as the policy he (Cleveland) planned to pursue. " The conferences with Bayard," wrote Mr. Belmont, " ended in my being entrusted with the presentation to Congress of the measure defining the policy of the administration." Not only did Mr. Belmont draft the bill—a severe measure providing for reprisals if the British did not end their discrimination against American fishermen in Canadian waters—but he also arranged for the whole Committee to meet with President Cleveland in order to obtain the President's viewpoint. We have Mr. Belmont's word that the meeting was a success. " We gave him our full confidence, having been convinced by personal contact that we could safely entrust to him the far reaching powers of the proposed measure." So successfully did the chairman and his committee present the President's views to the House that only one negative vote was cast against the bill. The Republicans in the Senate were not willing to entrust the President with the broad powers given him in the House bill. They were able to put through a much weaker measure which the House finally accepted and the President reluctantly signed.[195]

The support of the majority of the Committee does not necessarily mean that the chairman will be able to carry the House with him. Against his views are those of the Senate and possibly the President, either or both of which may not accord with his. Such was the case when Congress undertook to request President Harding to call a limitation of arms conference. The short session between his election in 1920 and his inauguration in 1921 had failed to resolve the question, Republican House and Senate leaders maintaining that the President-elect would tackle the problem after his inauguration. Only the insistence of Senator Borah that a provision be included in the naval appropriations bill on this matter stood in the way of a harmonious view among congressional leaders; but it was sufficient to prevent the passage of the bill. The special session, meeting a month after President Harding took office, again tackled the naval appropriations bill. Not until he had expressed himself as favorable to congressional expression on the subject of arms limitation was the Borah amendment added to the bill after it reached the Senate. Briefly, this amendment authorized and requested the President to call a conference of the United States, Great Britain, and Japan to agree upon substantial reductions in naval expenditures for the next five years. But the President took the position that the Senate amendment was too specific, permitting him no discretion to enlarge the agenda or to include other nations. Chairman Porter, after a visit to the White House, prepared a joint resolution " concurring " in the declared purpose and intention of the President to call a conference. Mr. Porter's move was predicated upon two assumptions: first, that the President was capable of acting upon this matter without the authorization of Congress, and secondly,

195 Belmont, cited, chap. XII. See also, Allan Nevins, *Grover Cleveland* (New York, 1932), p. 410 f.

that President Harding was willing to take the initiative. His joint resolution was submitted to, and approved by, the Republican members of the House Committee on Foreign Affairs. A favorable report to the House was made the same day that the resolution was introduced. It was hoped that it would serve as a guide—something in the way of unofficial instructions to the House conferees on the naval bill who would incorporate its content into the bill in place of the " narrow, restricted and unsatisfactory " language of the Borah amendment. Yet the House conferees—Republicans and Democrats—preferred the Borah amendment. Under these conditions the Republican leader, Mr. Mondell, sought an opportunity to drop the Porter resolution as gracefully as possible without the embarrassment of a vote. The opportunity came, first, when the President wrote him a letter expressing indifference to the form which congressional expression took and, secondly, when the Senate receded from the increased appropriations it had previously asked for the navy. Since the Senate had yielded on so many points, argued Mr. Mondell, it was unreasonable to ask it to surrender its views on the arms conference. Actually, Senator Borah was prepared to fight for his amendment, if it were challenged by the House, thereby precipitating a debate which both Houses sought to avoid as the end of the fiscal year approached. The House receded from its position and acquiesced in the Senate amendment which was put in the naval appropriations bill.[196]

While the immediate issue here—naval appropriations— presents no evidence of a fundamental cleavage between the House and the Senate, the subordinate point of congressional expression is of importance for this study. The capitulation of the House was, first, a recognition of the power of the Senate rules. Fearful that one Senator—an influential one, it must be admitted—could delay legislation, the House surrendered the studied judgment of its own leaders to that of the Senate. Per-

---

196 66th and 67th Cong. (1919-1921; 1921-1923). Files and Minutes, C. F. A. Also 67th Cong., 1st Sess., *Cong. Rec.*, June 29, 1921.

haps the spirit of compromise warrants commendation for the House, especially since the President, in whose behalf the Foreign Affairs Committee adopted its chairman's proposals, gave up the struggle to impress his views on Congress. It would appear from the *Record* that the House's retreat on opposition to the Borah amendment was in the nature of a *quid pro quo,* the Senate having receded from most of its amendments increasing appropriations. Balancing one against the other, the House leaders expressed the feeling that theirs was the better of the bargain. Victory on the question of appropriations outweighed defeat on a less immediate problem. The final House vote on the Borah amendment, 332 for, 4 opposed, would support the thesis that the House was " money-minded." Fresh from its victory over President Wilson in foreign affairs, the Senate enjoyed a psychological advantage over the House. While the acquiescence by the House on such an issue may be of no immediate consequence, if repeated over a period of years, it has the danger of creating within the House a sense of its own impotence in foreign affairs.

An indication of the chairman's influence, both within the Committee and the House, may be gathered from a study of measures which he has sponsored as compared with those introduced by other members of the Committee and with those introduced by non-members of the Committee. The Seventieth Congress, during which Mr. Porter, a Republican, was chairman, and the Seventy-fifth, when Mr. McReynolds, a Democrat, was chairman, have been used as illustrations.[197]

	70	75
Measures introduced by the chairman	50	50
Action taken by the Committee on these measures [198]	38	48
Enacted into law	20	36

197 These statistics have been gathered from the *Calendar* of the Foreign Affairs Committee.

198 The phrase, "Action taken by Committee," refers to any consideration given to the measure by the Committee, whether in the form of general discussion or hearings, without reference as to whether or not it was reported out.

Measures introduced by other members of the Committee 30	20
Action taken by the Committee on these measures 15	9
Enacted into law 3	3
Measures introduced by non-members of the Committee 77	82
Action taken by the Committee on these measures 30	30
Enacted into law 5	12

It is apparent, therefore, that the blessing of the chairman is a prerequisite, at least for Committee action. And without a Committee report, the House has virtually no opportunity to pass upon a measure. Unless the issue is of great public moment, and few before the Foreign Affairs Committee can thus be classified, the chairman may use the power of his office to follow his own bias on the subject. To deluge him with petitions and expressions of opinion borders on the futile. Unless constituents in his own district take action, he has little to fear from public opinion. Nor is it likely that, midst the welter of congressional issues, the press will single him out for condemnation. Even if he were so honored, the attack would probably be ephemeral rather than prolonged. Those who assail his power must remember that he is but one of forty-seven chairmen, all part of an entrenched machine designed to separate the wheat from the chaff in the legislative mill.

Finally, party ties and personal friendships have given the chairman an influence far beyond the legislative halls.[199] In thirty-four of the forty years herein considered the political

It should be remembered that a large percentage of the measures introduced by the chairman represent Department requests.

199 George H. Haynes, in his study of *The Senate of the United States* (New York, 1939), makes this statement: In 1835 Speaker Bell set aside the claims of J. Q. Adams to the chairmanship of the House Committee on Foreign Affairs in order to place at its head a friend of the administration. He later declared that he made that appointment " without the slightest interposition of the Executive " and justified his act thus: " The Committee on Foreign Affairs has charge of the branch of the public interest and business of the country placed by the Constitution more exclusively within the control of the Executive than any other. I consider the appointment of a political friend of the Executive as the chairman of that committee not to be an act of mere liberality but of patriotic duty." Vol. I, p. 302.

faith of the House has been identical with that of the executive. Those, therefore, who have controlled the House have been confreres of the President and of many whom he has chosen for associates in the executive branch. More than likely, it has not been a friendship springing out of an identity of immediate partisan objectives but one that has developed over years in party conclaves and conventions. The unorthodox composition of President Franklin D. Roosevelt's cabinet stands as an exception. This personal relationship does not easily lend itself to examination although a failure to identify it would ignore one of the most important elements that link the legislative with the executive branch. When the House heard of the death of Chairman McReynolds, obituary remarks made by his colleagues threw some light on this personal equation. Mr. Fish, ranking minority member, observed: " Due to his long friendship with the Secretary of State, Mr. Hull, of the State of Tennessee, he was able to bring to that Committee (Foreign Affairs) additional information which was helpful in all our deliberations . . ." Congressman Shanley commented that " he acted as a liaison between an equally great State Department and its beloved head, Cordell Hull, and this body of legislators . . ." [200]

[200] 76th Cong., 1st Sess., *Cong. Rec.*, July 11, 1939.

The problem of the relations between committee chairmen and executive officers is inherent in the doctrine of separation of powers and must always be reckoned with in any realistic study of the committee system. Chairman Ingersoll of the Foreign Affairs Committee made this observation almost a century ago: " My constant official intercourse with him (Calhoun) was so free that I found him as Secretary of State, with a president with whom I had neither personal nor party intimacy, both more familiar, imparting and satisfactory than their successors, President Polk and his Secretary of State, Mr. Buchanan, both of my party and my friends, but shy, secret if not timid, and reserved. As head of the committee supposed to be in daily confidential communication with them concerning foreign affairs, and fortified confidentially with Executive plans, measures, motives, and expectations, I was debited in Congress with much more than they ever let me, or even perhaps let each other know and expected and constrained by my Executive superiors to maintain, perform and explain what I knew no more of than almost everybody else." W. M. Meigs, *Life of Charles Jared Ingersoll*, pp. 272-273.

CHAPTER III

THE FOREIGN SERVICE AND THE STATE DEPARTMENT

DURING a congressional debate, in 1855, on a bill reforming the diplomatic and consular services, Mr. Perkins paused to comment on the casual interest which Congress had shown in the development of these services from the beginning of the government.

The great interest felt at the formation of our Government in adjusting internal affairs, and the establishment of the Constitution, as a kind of international law between the states themselves, diverted attention from the importance of a well regulated system of intercourse with foreign nations; while the general confidence reposed in the moderation of General Washington . . . checked all disposition to question the amount of power left to be exercised at his discretion. . . . Our early legislation conferred upon the President a degree of discretion over foreign intercourse more in accord with the spirit of the English than of our own Government.[1]

Had Mr. Perkins been disposed to examine further into the congressional attitude toward our foreign service, or had he served in Congress during the post-Civil War years, he would have been able to add another significant observation on this matter—the hostility shown by many members of Congress, especially toward the diplomatic branch. In 1798, "Mr. Nicholas gave it as his opinion on our foreign intercourse that the United States would be benefited by having no ministers at all." [2] Mr. Goodrich held "that we ought to have no political foreign relations. That gentleman prided himself on being of peculiar sentiments, but on this occasion he was not so. It had long been the sentiment of this country. It was a sentiment

1 32nd Cong., 2nd Sess. *Cong. Globe.* January 11, 1855, App., p. 356. Mr. Perkins was chairman of the Foreign Affairs Committee.

2 5th Cong., 2nd Sess. *Annals of Congress.* January 18, 1798, p. 851.

introduced into all our treaties but one (the treaty of alliance with France in 1778), and it would be found in the ' Farewell Address ' of the late President of the United States." [3] Eighty years later Mr. Hewitt, although not committed to the abolition of the diplomatic service, favored its reduction. " Whenever the diplomatic relations can be made to subserve the interests of commerce, I would preserve and strengthen them, but where they connect themselves with political questions in which we have but little direct or collateral interest, I would reduce the expenses and enlarge the efficiency by consolidating them under not more than two general heads, as I have proposed for Europe . . ." [4] Indeed, the recurring theme, whenever Congress discussed legislation pertinent to the diplomatic and consular services, whether in appropriation or general legislative bills, was the relative uselessness of the former and the commercial gains that flowed from the latter.[5]

For more than half a century after the founding of the government both services received the scantiest attention from congressional committees and Congress itself. An act of 1790 gave the President a lump sum of $40,000 annually to be used " for the support of such persons as he shall commission to serve the United States in foreign ports " with the proviso that the total salary and outfit for any one minister was not to exceed $9,000.[6] Not until 1818 did Congress vote an appropriation for specific posts in the diplomatic service.[7]

3 *Ibid.* January 26, 1798, p. 934. Mr. Gallatin was reported: " Gentlemen might, if they pleased, call it a paltry saving, but having first established the fact that these officers were not only unnecessary but dangerous, though the saving was not large, it ought to be made." *Ibid.* January 19, 1798, p. 887.

4 45th Cong., 2nd Sess. *Cong. Rec.* March 11, 1878, p. 1650.

5 Mr. Burrows, reporting the diplomatic and consular appropriation bill, March 2, 1882, said: " In distributing this sum, while the committee (on Appropriations) have not lost sight of the diplomatic service, we have sought especially to sustain, encourage and foster the consular service, that channel through which we hope to build up our trade with the nations of the earth ..." 47th Cong., 1st Sess. *Cong. Rec.*, p. 1552.

6 1 *Stat.* 198.

7 3 *Stat.* 422.

The origins and growth of the consular service were equally inconspicuous. Apart from the act of 1792, specifying the functions of consuls and the fees they might collect, no further legislation on this subject was forthcoming until 1856. Nevertheless, the subject was one of frequent comment in and out of Congress, especially the abuses and inequalities of the fee system and the incompetent personnel. Secretary Livingston, in 1833, and Secretary Buchanan, in 1846, reported to Congress on the need for reform.[8] A special committee of the House studied the matter in 1845. By 1855 the newspapers and various Chambers of Commerce had publicized the inadequacies of the service. Under these stimuli the Committee on Foreign Affairs bestirred itself and reported out a bill which, when enacted into law, was the first comprehensive legislation on the foreign services.[9] The salaries for diplomatic representatives at the several posts were stipulated, with proportionate amounts for lesser officials. Similarly, a consular schedule with a specified compensation was attached, including a prohibition upon business ventures where the salary was over $1,500. No doubt aware of the slow response by Congress to improve the machinery of international intercourse, the bill empowered the President to issue such diplomatic and consular regulations and instructions pertaining to their functions as he might deem necessary so long as they were not contrary to the law.

Another half century passed before Congress altered the legislation of 1856. Such fundamental improvements as came during this period were usually the result of executive orders rather than legislation. Only during the annual debate on the appropriations for the diplomatic and consular services did Congress show interest in their operation. But it was not an interest calculated to improve their deficiencies. The usual gesture for economy was tempered by political spite and spoils. A former diplomat, Eugene Schuyler, wrote of the system:

8 29th Cong., 2nd Sess. (1846). H. Doc. 12.
9 33rd Cong., 1st Sess. (1854). H. Rep. 348. 11 *Stat.* 52.

It would . . . be an almost impossible thing that the Committee on Appropriations should be composed wholly of good men; and unless the chairman were a man particularly interested in foreign affairs, in nine cases out of ten the Subcommittee on Appropriations for the Consular and Diplomatic Service would be composed of persons possessing no previous acquaintance with the subject. The subcommittee of the House then took up the estimates presented by the Secretary of State and prepared a bill. It was not content with the present establishment, and refused to be governed by the General Law or the Revised Statutes. It raised a grade here, established a consul there, pared down a salary in one place, abolished a mission in another, made an important change in a third, and so on. Some of these changes were often excellent and even necessary, but the principle of new legislation in an appropriation bill was, according to the rules, wrong, unless it were " in the interest of economy." The main idea of the subcommittee seemed to be to reduce the appropriation to the lowest limit, from motives of economy, they said; not that the nation at large cared for, or even knew of, this saving of ten or twenty thousand dollars to the detriment of its interests, but because the reputaton of being economical, and " watchdogs of the Treasury," would possibly help them in their district, and their constituents might believe them worthy of a new election. The bill was then reported to the House; the party strength was drilled to support the committee. Every amendment was voted down, for the men whose salaries were sometimes retroactively abolished were too far away to be heard; no changes were made save of one kind; some objector invoked the rules of the House against every slight increase of pay or grade as " new legislation," but any diminution was passed without notice, because although it had evidently the same character, it was " in the interest of economy." From the House the bill went to the Senate. The general theory of the Senate committee is to reject every change made by the House, and to return pretty closely to the Law of the last Congress, restoring what had been omitted, and adding a few largish appropriations for unforeseen expenses, secret service money, or as it is technically expressed, for " expenses in carrying out the Neutrality Act," and the like. These are necessary to bargain with. The Senate passes the amended bill with slight debate, except in unusual cases. We have now reached the last days of the session, when there is no time for the detailed consideration of any measure. The House, on motion of the member in charge of the bill, rejects, without debate, all the Senate amendments, and suggests a Committee of Conference; the Senate in like way refuses to recede, and accepts the conference. The two committees, or as many as choose to attend, then meet in secret conference, bargain with each other, give and take, each yield in part, and report the result back to their respective houses in such a technical form that it is impossible to understand it without a careful examination of all the papers; it is read hastily by the clerk, and it is passed without debate. It may, and frequently does, contain new matters never before proposed in the open House. And thus six men have secretly decided upon an important law and have forced it through Congress.[10]

How this operated in specific instances may be seen, for example, in 1866, when the House refused an appropriation for the minister to Portugal because he indulged in a " most foul and vulgar abuse of Congress " in a personal letter to Secretary Seward.[11] The following year it eliminated from the appropriation bill funds necessary for the maintenance of the legation at the Holy See, thereby forcing a termination of American relations with the Vatican.[12]

Between 1885 and 1920, the Committee on Foreign Affairs displaced the Appropriations Committee in the handling of diplomatic and consular appropriation bills. There is nothing to indicate that this change in jurisdiction stimulated congressional

10 Eugene Schuyler, *American Diplomacy* (New York, 1886), pp. 26-28.

11 39th Cong., 1st Sess. *Cong. Globe*, pp. 2619-2620, 3943, 3952, 3959. *Ibid.*, 2nd Sess., pp. 845-850, 1501-1504, 1505-1508, 1548, 1844-1854. 40th Cong., 2nd Sess. *Cong. Globe*, pp. 1201, 1725-1729, 1746-1847, 1887, 1944, 1960.
The Deficiency Appropriation Act of March 3, 1869, included this item: " For a sufficient amount to pay the regular salary of the present minister-resident at Portugal, and the exchange thereon, from the first day of July, 1866, so long as the same was withheld from him." 15 *Stat.* 315.

12 This item was stricken out by an amendment offered by Mr. Stevens, chairman of the Appropriations Committee, because, among other reasons, it (the Holy See) " prohibits free worship by American citizens within its jurisdiction of the Christian religion." 39th Cong., 2nd Sess. *Cong. Globe*, pp. 850-851, 883-885. The following year, 1868, an attempt to put the item back in the appropriation bill was defeated, 59-48. 40th Cong., 2nd Sess. *Cong. Globe*, pp. 1219, 1223.

attention toward the improvement of the two services. Even as late as the end of the nineteenth century the minute books suggest that the Foreign Affairs Committee, as a Committee, evinced little interest in their efficient functioning. Under date of March 18, 1892, this laconic item appeared: " Mr. Blount (the chairman) reported a bill for the diplomatic and consular appropriations for the year ending June, 1893. Same was adopted." [13] On January 12, 1898, " Mr. Hitt reported the diplomatic and consular appropriation bill. After discussion, he was directed to report it favorably." [14]

Secretary Root had carried over to the State Department the same penchant for reorganization that he had displayed in the War Department. The statute of April 5, 1906, reorganizing the consular service, while an act of Congress, was pushed through only by the diligent efforts of the Secretary, aided by groups and individuals outside of Congress who were anxious to improve the service.[15] Essentially, however, the reforms of this period—and this applies to the diplomatic branch, too—were the work of the executive branch.

In its self-appointed capacity as " watchdog of the Treasury " the House, acting through its committees, gave far more attention to the consular than to the diplomatic service.[16] The

---

13 52nd Cong. Minutes, C. F. A.

14 55th Cong. Minutes, C. F. A.

15 *Cf.* Jessup, *Elihu Root,* II, chap. XXXI.

16 The following excerpt from a House debate is illustrative of the way the House approached the appropriations for the diplomatic service.

Mr. Holman: I have before me one of these state-papers, dispatches of Government—one of these mysterious documents that seem to overawe our sense of economy. Let us read what valuable facts come to us from this little monarchy (Greece) at a cost of $7,500 a year and contingent expenses. See what a voice comes from that land of scholars and nurse of arms:

Mr. Read to Mr. Fish

Legation of the United States,
Athens, April 25, 1875 (Rec. May 27)

This dispatch is so important that the time of its being received is mentioned!

Sir: The king and the queen attended the imposing ceremonies at the cathedral last evening, the Greek Easter eve. They arrived in a state

reports of the Appropriations Committee, and later the Foreign Affairs Committee, were weighted with studies of the gains—actual or potential—derived from the enlargement of the various consular posts. Because they served as patronage outlets for congressmen, personnel reform was dealt with most cautiously. The emphasis fell upon the fact that the posts were virtually self-supporting through the collection of fees for consular services. The Senate, on the other hand, paid more heed to the diplomatic posts, possibly because it recognized more clearly than the House the utility of those officers in the conduct of foreign relations. Although the Constitution confers upon the President the right to appoint ambassadors, subject to Senate confirmation, no appointments to that rank were made

carriage, preceded by outriders and followed by a strong escort of cavalry.

The scene was a most impressive one as they ascended the steps of the broad platform before the cathedral accompanied by the various members of their court in brilliant dress, and were received with appropriate solemnities by the Metropolitan and his clergy. The king——"

How important to be minute and careful in speaking of kings, when a gentleman employed at a salary of $7,500 a year, to note the movements of a king and report them to our Department of State——

The king was in the uniform of a general officer——

That is valuable information. The State Department must have been greatly edified by this valuable intelligence!

The king was in the uniform of a general officer, with the ribbon of his royal order on his breast. The white satin robes of the queen seemed to steal the color from her cheek.

(Laughter)

My friend from New York (Mr. Cox) suggests that this was very gay. He must not indulge in such levity. This is a solemn state paper—a costly and valuable one. This is a specimen of the special dispatches sent by our high-salaried ministers at the expense of the industrious people of this country. . . . You can see that this famous diplomat was inspired by the old poets of that country. Anacreon could scarcely have expressed a handsomer simile. We can see the effect of Grecian literature in this ambitious diplomat.

*   *   *   *   *

In the vicinity of the cathedral, from an early hour, every available space was packed with a living mass——

Now, I call the attention of my friend from Ohio, and want him to observe how far this is republican Greece that we all revere and love——

Yet not a murmur arose.

Either the people of that little monarchy were so completely subjugated that "not a murmur arose," or else they were beholding with contempt this

until the act of 1893 specifically provided for them whenever any foreign government expressed a willingness to appoint a man of equal rank.[17] This clause was inserted by the Senate as an amendment to the appropriation bill and accepted by the House. Under this provision ten ambassadorships were created. In 1909, however, this act was repealed, again on the initiative of the Senate, and a new clause was inserted, prohibiting the President from creating ambassadorships " unless the same shall be provided for by an act of Congress." [18] Pursuant to this bill several ministries were raised to embassies, for example, Spain, Argentina, Chile, and Belgium; in the case of Peru, an appropriation bill, in 1919, provided for an ambassador to that country.[19] China, however, presented a different case, the Pres-

pageantry to which we contributed by sending a representative there at $7,500 a year.

* * * * *

At the close of the rites, their majesties returned to the palace. Everything must be detailed.

At the close of the rites their majesties returned to the palace, while their subjects retired to their homes to celebrate with feasting and joyous songs the arrival of Easter, after many weeks of rigid fasting.

John Meredith Read.

There are five or six other equally valuable state-papers in that volume from the same source. Does my friend from Ohio think that the overtaxed people of this country can afford to pay a gentleman $7500 a year to get up these puerile descriptions of the fetes of a petty monarchy? 44th Cong., 1st Sess. February 7, 1876. *Cong. Rec.*, p. 923.

17 *27 Stat.* 497. In 1875, the act of 1856 was amended to read: "Ambassadors and Envoys Extraordinary and Ministers Plenipotentiary shall be entitled to compensation at the rates following, per annum, namely ... " Then followed the specific salaries named in the act of 1856. " Those to all other countries unless where a different compensation is prescribed by law, each $10,000." 18 *Stat.* 483.

18 *35 Stat.* 672. This change was made on the floor of the Senate as an amendment of the Committee on Appropriations. 60th Cong., 2nd Sess. February 23, 1909. *Cong. Rec.*, p. 2926. The House, oddly enough, disagreed with the amendment, but in the Conference Committee it receded from its position. *Ibid.* February 26, 1909. *Cong. Rec.*, p. 3330.

19 *38 Stat.* 110; 40 *Stat.* 1325; 41 *Stat.* 291. No statute was enacted authorizing the appointment of an ambassador to Peru and fixing his salary. In

ident announcing the elevation in grade without prior congressional authorization.[20]

The Foreign Affairs Committee has shown some confusion of thought on the right of Congress to legislate on the matter of appointment of ambassadors. In 1921, during a discussion on a joint resolution " authorizing the appointment of an ambassador to China," the Committee pondered the question whether it could *authorize* the President, since, as some contended, his authority flowed from the Constitution.[21] Other

1923, Congress made provision, in the Second Deficiency Act for 1923, for an ambassador to Cuba. In this instance Congress seems to have departed from its usual practice and kept its action strictly within its constitutional power by the use of the following language: " The compensation of an Ambassador to Cuba, when hereafter appointed, shall be the sum of $17,500 per annum, and the salary appropriated for the fiscal year 1923-1924 for an Envoy Extraordinary and Minister Plenipotentiary to Cuba is hereby made available for the salary of an Ambassador, and there is hereby appropriated for that purpose for the fiscal year 1924 the additional sum of $5,500." 42 *Stat.* 1160.

20 Department of State *Press Release*, May 18, 1935, pp. 335-336.

21 66th Cong. Minutes, C. F. A. This question of the powers of the President and of Congress with respect to the appointment of ambassadors and ministers came under discussion in the House of Representatives on January 28, 1921. The President had appointed ministers to Finland and to the Kingdom of the Serbs, Croats, and Slovenes, and the appointments had been confirmed by the Senate. The appropriation bill under consideration in the Committee of the Whole contained appropriations for the salaries of those ministers. A point of order was made against those two items because there was no legislative enactment by Congress authorizing the appointment of the ministers, and fixing their salaries and authorizing appropriations therefor. The chair held that the President had ample constitutional authority for the appointment of the ministers and that, inasmuch as the appointments had been made in conformity with the provisions of the Constitution, there was ample authority in law for Congress, if it desired to do so, to appropriate for the payment of their salaries, and therefore that the point of order would not lie. In the course of his statement the chair referred to the act of 1909 and observed that that act had no effect upon the constitutional power of the President except the practical effect of serving notice upon him that thereafter he must not make ambassadorial appointments except upon the authority of the Congress of the United States in the sense that he should know that Congress would sanction his action in the appointment by appropriating for its support before it could be made effective. 66th Cong., 3rd Sess. *Cong. Rec.*, pp. 2164-2173. On May 19, 1939, a similar point was made against the

members advanced the idea that Congress was limited to a simple designation of the rank to be held by our representative. The Committee, in preparing its report, fell back upon the language contained in its report in 1919, wherein the President was authorized to appoint an ambassador to Belgium.[22] This measure, which had received the assent of President Wilson, had been drafted in the State Department, thus creating the presumption that the executive did not regard the language as an encroachment on his prerogative.

In an endeavor to put into law what had been achieved by executive order in the way of a career system, Representative Flood sponsored a " State Department bill " in 1915, the chief feature of which was the appointment of an officer to a grade rather than a post. Equally important, considering the personnel shortage that confronted the Department at home, was the provision permitting officers, both diplomatic and consular, to be transferred to Washington for a tour of duty in the Department.[23]

The test of the structure developed by the legislature and the executive over more than a century came during the World War. Before American entry the limited facilities of the foreign services were taxed by the obligations assumed in looking after the interests of the belligerents in those countries where their diplomatic and consular services had ceased to function. Economic dislocation caused by the War, although immediately favoring the United States, increased the burden on the services. Secretary Lansing, testifying before the Committee in 1920, stated:

Since 1913 our ships engaged in foreign trade have increased 357 per cent. Our passport correspondence has increased 991 per

appropriations for ambassadors to Colombia, Panama, Union of Soviet Socialist Republics, and Venezuela. Following the 1921 ruling of the chair, the point of order was overruled. 76th Cong., 1st Sess. *Cong. Rec.*, p. 5864.

22 66th Cong. H. Rep. 268 (Belgium) ; H. Rep. 1323 (China).

23 This was the Flood-Stone bill, 38 *Stat.* 805. For the debate on this bill, see 63rd Cong., 3rd Sess. January 18, 1915. *Cong. Rec.*, p. 1777 f.

cent, and the foreign trade has increased over 100 per cent. . . . We still have war going on in Russia and Siberia, Turkey is in a state of ferment, and the relations between this country and Germany and Austria and Hungary have not yet been restored. We are being constantly urged to give assistance to the various countries in Europe that are suffering, and economic assistance is required. That means renewal of trade relations. The result is that we have very heavy responsibilities imposed upon us, and we have to discharge our legal and moral duty in safeguarding the interests of our own Government and people abroad. We have to utilize the great opportunities we have in the matter of commercial and industrial interests, and, in addition, we must furnish economic aid to these countries. . . .[24]

Moreover, increased living costs, accentuated by unstable economic conditions and relatively slight increases in appropriations, impaired the morale of the personnel.[25]

The very paucity of legislation, however, left to the Secretary a wide degree of discretion in the disposition of personnel, thereby permitting the Department to operate more efficiently than it might have, had it been bound by legislative restrictions. Mr. Carr testified:

It was only the fact that Congress left an enormous amount of latitude in the hands of the Secretary of State that enabled us to go through the war with both branches of the service as successfully as we did. Where it was necessary we could increase the number of men in a class; that was particularly true in the case of the Consular Service because occasionally we would need a consular officer somewhere and could not have sent him without much delay if we had not had so much latitude.[26]

The need for reform, dramatized by the War and urged on by industrial and exporting groups, was stimulated by the loss of the power to report appropriations by the Foreign Affairs

24 66th Cong., 2nd Sess. *Hearings on Diplomatic and Consular Appropriation Bill*, pp. 5-6.
25 *Ibid.*, pp. 159-160.
26 *Ibid.*, pp. 90-91.

Committee. The first gesture by the Committee in this direction came in a bill reported by the Republican majority and characterized by its sponsor, Mr. Rogers, as " an attempt to modernize the basic laws relating to our foreign intercourse." Its aims were expressed thus in his report on the bill:

> It is believed that such an enactment as that now proposed will be useful and desirable in making instantly available the current legislative will as to the subject matter; furthermore, it will grant the authority to the Committee on Appropriations, which is now lacking (though necessarily often exercised), to make foreign service appropriations in character and amount in accordance with the needs of the country; and, finally, it will, when the Committee on Appropriations goes beyond the four corners of existing law, prevent the making in the House of points of order against items the retention of which is essential to the national welfare.[27]

It is significant that this bill was referred to as one " relative to the *foreign intercourse* of the United States " rather than, as were subsequent measures, " relative to the *foreign service* of the United States." It embraced a potpourri of subjects, most of them having little or no connection with the personnel problems of the services. Ministers were to be commissioned to a class, not a post; an increased sum was set as the maximum for the acquisition of the embassy in Paris; an appropriation of $5,000 was authorized for the family of a Japanese subject accidentally killed in Hawaii by an American soldier; the United States Court for China was placed under the supervision of the Secretary of State; small salary increases were granted foreign service officers serving as interpreters. The report of several minority members attacked the commissioning of ministers to a class as an invasion upon the right of Senate confirmation.[28] A second criticism, more trenchant and pertinent, was directed against those provisions that would prevent points of order being raised in the House on appropriations for the for-

27 67th Cong., 2nd Sess. (1923). H. Rep. 646.
28 *Ibid.*, part 2.

eign service. The House Rules state that "no appropriation shall be reported in any general appropriation bill, or be in order as an amendment thereto, for any expenditure not previously authorized by law . . ."[29] The majority proposal permitted the Committee on Appropriations to report out bills pertaining to the foreign service with no other justification in law than "the needs of the country." Further, a member would be denied the right to raise a point of order against such proposed appropriations. Thus, the Senate and the President, it was argued, would be parties to a law enabling the House to nullify its own rules. Mr. Stedman wrote:[30]

The spectacle of a representative body proposing enactment of a law to secure exemption from the operation of rules established by itself for the government of its own procedure is without parallel in the whole range of parliamentary experience in this or any other country inhabited by civilized beings.

Before this measure came to a vote, the Committee had before it another bill which, after being reported by the Committee and passed by the House, was lost in the legislative congestion in the Senate at the end of the Sixty-seventh Congress.[31] Reintroduced in the following Congress with slight modifications, it passed both Houses and received the President's approval on May 24, 1924. Mr. Rogers, assisted by the State Department, worked out a more coherent measure pertaining to the personnel problems of the foreign services. In the words of Mr. Carr "the novel feature of this bill is the combination which it contains of those things which have been adopted by Congress in the past in one form and another and its application of them to the foreign service."[32] The principal objects of

29 Rule XXI.

30 *Supra*, H. Rep. 646, part 2.

31 68th Cong., 1st Sess. (1924). Hearings on the *Foreign Service of the United States*. Appended to these hearings are those held in the Sixty-seventh Congress, fourth session, on the bill that did not come to a vote. *Cf.* 68th Cong., 1st Sess. H. Rep. 157.

32 Quoted from the reprint of the hearings, 68th Cong., 1st Sess., p. 151.

the bill may be grouped under four heads: first, the amalgamation of the diplomatic and consular services; second, the adoption of a single revised salary scale applicable equally to officers in the foreign service; third, the authorization, when necessary, of representation allowances to representatives at foreign capitals; fourth, the extension of the civil service retirement act to members of the foreign service.[33] To delineate the relative parts played by the House, the Senate, and the State Department is not possible on the basis of extant materials. The absence of debate in, and the unanimous approval by, the Senate eliminates that body as a factor in shaping this legislation. The technical content points rather conclusively to an active role by the State Department. That Mr. Rogers should have devoted himself to pushing this legislation over a period of five years is a tribute to his patience even if his motives cannot be clearly discerned. Apart from his alertness in recognizing the defects of the old system, he was especially critical of the appointments made by President Wilson and expressed himself at length on this point before Congress.[34] It should be noted, however, that in building up the evidence in behalf of his measures, he called upon members of both parties for support. Once the earlier measure, designed to harmonize practice and rules, was dropped, the Committee responded to his arguments. This spirit was carried into the House and in the final vote on the Rogers bill only twenty-seven voted in the negative. Several years later, the Department, following separate investigations by the House and the Senate into alleged discriminations by the Foreign Service Personnel Board, recommended remedial legislation and also sought to overhaul the office of clerks in the foreign service. The bill embodying these proposals, popularly called the Moses-Linthicum Act of 1931, came as a result of congressional criticism

33 67th Cong., 4th Sess. H. Rep. 1479.

34 *Cf.* 65th Cong., 3rd Sess. January 21, 1919, *Cong. Rec.*, p. 1826. "When we look over the appointments to the Latin American Republics, mostly under the regime of Secretary Bryan, we can not fail to be startled at the complete lack of consideration given to merit, ability, or useful experience."

of the operation of the Rogers Act as well as from a desire to extend the merit system to non-career men.[35]

If the attention of Congress and the Foreign Affairs Committee to the foreign service has been sporadic and indifferent, the part they have played in shaping the Department itself—the home office—has been even less distinguished. Two months after its first meeting the House devoted itself to the establishment of executive departments, chief among which was a Department of Foreign Affairs. The lengthy debate which ensued centered not around the functions to be performed by that Department but on the President's right to remove its head.[36] On July 27, 1789, the President signed the bill formally creating the Department. Within two months it assumed functions not pertinent to foreign affairs—keeping the records of the country and publishing acts of Congress—and its name was accordingly changed to the Department of State. Congress continued to pile on the Department a miscellany of duties which interfered with the effective operation of its primary function—foreign affairs —particularly since no adequate provision was made for increased personnel. In a report to the House in 1846, Secretary Buchanan lamented that he " had no time even for a careful or regular perusal of the leading foreign journals," so much of his time being devoted to minutiae that should be delegated to subordinates.[37] Particularly time-consuming was the requirement that the Secretary alone could sign a paper, no matter how unimportant. The only relief Congress offered, apart from a moderate enlargement of the personnel from time to time, was to transfer these additional duties to new agencies as they were created.

It is not too sweeping a statement to say that the fundamental changes within the Department's organization came through

35 46 *Stat.* 1207.

36 1st Cong. *Annals of Congress*, pp. 368 f., 473-608. Also Hunt, chap. IV, for summary of debates on removal from office.

37 29th Cong., 1st Sess. H. Rep. 552.

the action of several secretaries rather than Congress or its committees. Secretary McLane, in 1833, specified the duties of the various members and laid out functional divisions within the Department. Geographical bureaus made their appearance on orders from Secretary Fish, while it remained for Secretary Knox to establish the regional divisions into which the Department is now arranged.

Congress approached the problem of the "home service" most seriously in 1928. Following a four months' investigation by a special Senate Committee—the Moses Committee—into the shortcomings of the Rogers Act, the Foreign Affairs Committee started a "friendly survey" of the home office. A speech delivered by Representative Davenport in January, 1928, during a debate on the State Department appropriations bill was apparently the starting point for serious thinking on the subject.[38] In the middle of April, 1928, Chairman Porter introduced a bill—H. R. 13179—providing for the reorganization of the State Department. Although the bill never left the Committee, hearings were held on it, together with kindred measures, during May. It was designed to break down the salary inequalities existing between the foreign and home services, but more important from the policy-making side, to keep the career men in the field and restrict their influence in shaping policy. Two under-secretaries and six assistant secretaries were specified, not more than three of the eight at any one time to have been foreign service officers within seven years preceding their appointment. Moreover, the administration both of the foreign service and of the home service was vested in an Assistant Secretary of State "who has not been a Foreign Service officer . . . within seven years next preceding his appointment." Some of the comments made by witnesses indicated that the Department itself was aware of its deficiencies. The fault, however, was put upon the Bureau of the Budget for inadequate appropriations to correct them. On the basis of statements made

38 70th Cong., 1st Sess. January 6, 1928, *Cong. Rec.*, p. 1097 f.

by Senator Moses before the Committee, it was evident that a reorganization would then have hard sledding before the Senate; indeed, the reforms he proposed for the foreign service were not enacted into law until 1931. The Committee, therefore, confined its activities to the hearings, making it plain, however, that reorganization could and should be initiated by the Department itself.[39]

* * * * * * * * *

During the House debates in 1940 on the annual appropriation bill for the State Department an amendment was offered by Mr. McCormack to strike out the appropriation for the salary of the ambassador to the Union of Soviet Socialist Republics.[40] The justification for this amendment, explained Mr. McCormack, was the " breaching " of the promise made by the Soviet Government, when diplomatic relations were renewed in 1933, not to engage in subversive activities within the United States. The disclosures of several congressional committees, of which the Dies Committee was the latest, indicated to Mr. McCormack and others that the Soviet Government had not fulfilled its promise. The conflict between Russia and Finland added to the unpopularity of the former.

Amidst all the emotional outbursts comparatively little attention was given to the point whether the action of the House in striking out the appropriation would affect our diplomatic representation in Moscow. It was the contention of Mr. McCormack that " the question of diplomatic relationship in itself rests with the executive branch of the Government, but under the Constitution we have the power of expressing our own views as a body when appropriation bills are under consideration. In rare cases, such as in the case of the Soviet Union, we are justified in exercising our constitutional power." While

39 70th Cong. Files, C. F. A. *Cf.* August C. Miller, Jr., " The New State Department," *Amer. Jour. of Inter. Law*, XXXIII (July, 1939), p. 500, for an analysis of administrative changes in the Department.

40 76th Cong., 3rd Sess. February 7, 1940. *Cong. Rec.*, p. 1173.

several proponents of the amendment admitted that it was not the proper procedure to alter diplomatic relations in an appropriation bill, they pointed out that this was the only course left to them. Bills designed to accomplish this had been shelved in the Foreign Affairs Committee allegedly because of the State Department's influence.[41] On a vote by division the amendment carried, 88 to 86; but a subsequent vote by tellers resulted in its defeat, 105 to 108.[42]

Had the appropriation been eliminated, would it have accomplished its object of severing diplomatic relations with Russia? An examination of pertinent statutes suggests the possibility of developing a line of argument that would answer this query in the negative. The law clearly prohibits the continued use of the ambassador's services on a voluntary basis.[43]

. . . Nor shall any department or any officer of the Government accept voluntary service for the Government or employ personal service in excess of that authorized by law . . .

Some compensation, no matter how small, must be forthcoming from the Government if the ambassador is to retain his post. The State Department bill includes, among other items, the following:[44]

Emergencies arising in the Diplomatic and Consular Service: To enable the President to meet unforeseen emergencies arising in the Diplomatic and Consular Service, and to extend the commercial and other interests of the United States and to meet the necessary expenses attendant upon the execution of the Neutrality Act, to be expended pursuant to the requirement of section 291 of the Revised Statutes (31 U. S. C. 107) . . . $225,000 . . .

Could the President draw upon this emergency fund for an

41 See, e. g., the colloquy between Mr. Fish and Mr. Allen of Pennsylvania. *Ibid.*, pp. 1180-1181.

42 *Ibid.*, p. 1180.

43 31 *U. S. C.* 665.

44 76th Cong., 3rd Sess. H. R. 8319.

amount as small as one dollar in order to meet the requirement of compensation? That portion of the Code referred to in the bill reads:[45]

Whenever any sum of money has been or shall be issued, from the Treasury, for the purposes of intercourse or treaty with foreign nations, in pursuance of law, the President is authorized to cause the same to be duly settled annually with the General Accounting Office, by causing the same to be accounted for specifically, if the expenditure may, in his judgment, be made public; and by making or causing the Secretary of State to make a certificate of the amount of such expenditure, as he may think it advisable not to specify; and every such certificate shall be deemed a sufficient voucher for the sum therein expressed to have been expended.

The phrase, "in pursuance of law," is the key phrase. In 1893, Congress provided that whenever any foreign government expressed a willingness to raise a legation to an embassy, the President could reciprocate by appointing a man of equal rank. Accordingly, an ambassador was appointed at St. Petersburg. Except for the period when diplomatic relations were severed, the salary for the ambassador to Russia has been based upon the 1893 statute. The office, therefore, was created in pursuance of law and the President could give the ambassador compensation from the emergency fund.

However cogently one may argue this question from the legal viewpoint, there are certain ethical implications that must be examined. The continued appropriation by Congress for the Department's emergency fund rests upon the assumption that such money will not be used for purposes for which Congress has definitely declined to make regular appropriations. The President's signature to an appropriation bill which denies funds for a particular post implies that he agrees to this deletion. If the wishes of Congress were not respected by the executive, the necessary comity that must pervade the relations of these two branches of the Government would be impaired and Congress,

45 31 *U. S. C.* 107.

understandably, would feel justified in omitting or seriously curtailing appropriations for the emergency fund.

Later in the day, Mr. McCormack offered another amendment, providing that no appropriation contained under the title " Foreign Intercourse " shall be used for the maintenance of an embassy in the U. S. S. R. or for salaries of officers at that post. This amendment, defeated 38 to 95, followed the precedent of 1867 when Congress withheld funds for the maintenance of the officers and of the physical property occupied by them at Rome. In view of the adverse vote on the first amendment, this amendment lost much of its force and simply carried out Mr. McCormack's announced intention to amend the bill at those points where provision was made for any appropriations pertaining to the embassy at Moscow. Had the first amendment passed, this subsequent one would have been a logical sequel. It would have forestalled any circumvention through the appointment of a foreign service officer as chargé d'affaires, thereby providing the United States with a degree of representation, even though of lesser dignity than that accorded by the presence of an ambassador.

Should the President deem it imperative that a special ambassador be present in Moscow to carry out a particular mission, it is believed that he would not be acting contrary to the spirit of the emergency fund if compensation for this individual came from that source. Presumably the representative would not be designated the ambassador from the United States. Rather, he would be the President's personal representative with the rank of ambassador, such as the recently appointed envoy of President Roosevelt to the Vatican who presented a private letter from the President instead of the usual letter of credence. By and large he would be entitled to the courtesies and amenities accorded regularly accredited ambassadors.[46]

46 I am indebted to certain members of the Department of State who have given me the benefit of their thought on this subject.

CHAPTER IV
APPROPRIATIONS

SOME remarks may well be made at this point on the power of appropriations as exercised by the Committee on Foreign Affairs. In common with several other committees, its right, under the House rules, to report appropriations was nullified by a change in the rules in 1920, coincident with the establishment of the Bureau of the Budget. Since that date it has had only the right to *authorize* appropriations, the final step of reporting appropriations resting with the Committee of that name.

The examination of bills appropriating money or authorizing its appropriation has continued to be close since the turn of the century. The measures which have come before the Committee involving monetary matters have been confined to a few subjects—diplomatic and consular offices, the fulfillment of treaty obligations, claims of foreign governments and their subjects, and international congresses and conferences. The successive reorganizations of the diplomatic and consular services by executive order and legislation, coupled with the Committee's loss of power to report appropriations, have diminished the Committee's control—and that of Congress too—to which these services were subjected in the nineteenth century.

Of the remaining subjects involving appropriations, only those appropriations pursuant to treaty commitments, discussed below, can be said to have had some direct bearing on the foreign relations of the country. Both claims settlements and participation in international conferences have been approached by the Committee less from the legal angle than from the viewpoint of the goodwill engendered. In the case of claims settlements the Committee has used as a point of departure the detailed reports submitted by the various government departments —State, Navy, and War principally. In 1936, an omnibus claims bill was introduced, by request, by Chairman McReynolds.[1] Included in this bill was a payment of $240,000 to Great Britain and Japan as the share of the American Government " incident to an undertaking to deport enemy aliens from China to Australia during the World War." Although a subcommittee, after discussions with the State Department, recommended the payment of all claims, the full Committee struck out the payments to Great Britain and Japan because of the former's default on the war debts and the latter's treatment of American citizens in China.[2] This attitude, however, has been the exception in the disposition of claims cases.

Prior to the World War, when international conferences were less numerous, the Committee was disposed to discuss the value to be derived from American participation. In the post-war period it has looked upon them as a necessary function in the life of a responsible state. In anticipation of the scrutiny given appropriation bills on the House floor, the Committee wisely examines them with care before they leave the Committee. A joint resolution inviting the nations to a World's Dairy Congress carried no amount, merely authorizing and requesting the President to issue invitations. Chairman Porter stated the thought in the minds of other members when he pointed out that " a reasonable construction of this resolution carries with it the implication that the United States is going to pay the expenses of this Congress and thereby you give the President blanket authority to go on and spend all the money he might see fit, and I do not understand how Congress upon receipt of those bills could refuse to appropriate the necessary amount of money if we passed the resolution in its present form." [3] To push the measure as it stood carried " an implication of an appropriation " which would jeopardize its passage in the last days of Congress. As a safeguard, therefore, the Committee adopted an amendment providing " that nothing herein con-

1 74th Cong., 1st Sess. H. R. 6612. H. Rep. 2872.

2 Ibid. Files, C. F. A.

3 63rd Cong., 3rd Sess. (1921). H. J. Res. 459. Hearings, pp. 13-15.

tained shall be construed to create any pecuniary obligation on the part of the Government of the United States." [4]

A joint resolution " to provide an appropriation " for expenses of participation in a general disarmament conference also specified no sum, but included the language " that so much as may be necessary is hereby authorized to be appropriated . . ." [5] After examining Mr. Carr on the tentative budget he had drafted, it was agreed to insert the sum of $450,000 in lieu of the general language of the original resolution.[6] It is worth noting, however, that the failure of Congress to authorize or to appropriate the necessary funds would not preclude participation by the United States. During the hearings in 1928 on the reorganization of the State Department that point was raised by a member of the Committee. The gentleman testifying for the Department replied that " if we have any money in our State Department emergency fund, it comes out of that. That is the only way . . . there is no law against it." [7] To the executive disregard of the act of 1913, prohibiting American participation in international conferences " without first having specific authority of law to do so," may be added the ability of the State Department to circumvent reliance upon Congress for funds through the use of the contingent funds, placed at the disposal of the executive since 1793.[8] Thus, one of the few financial checks which the Foreign Affairs Committee, and Congress, might use over the executive is capable of evasion in spite of a " self-imposed limitation by Congress of its (i. e. Congress') right to appropriate for specific objects and to scrutinize and investigate expenditures." [9]

4 *Ibid.* H. Rep. 1273.

5 72nd Cong., 1st Sess. (1932). H. J. Res. 163. Hearings.

6 *Ibid.* H. Rep. 30.

7 70th Cong., 1st Sess. H. R. 13179. Files, C. F. A.

8 1 *Stat.* 299. See also, Henry M. Wriston, *Executive Agents in American Foreign Relations* (Baltimore, 1929), pp. 129-152.

9 Wriston, p. 123.

While it is commonly held that the House may use the appropriation power as a check on the executive in his conduct of international affairs, it must not be forgotten that the House may use that same power to assist him in foreign affairs against the dilatory tactics of the Senate. The best example is found in the endeavor of the Foreign Affairs Committee to secure favorable House action on a joint resolution authorizing an appropriation for the United States' share of expenses in the maintenance of the World Court. The resolution is treated in the section on treaties below.[10] It is sufficient at this point to note that the late Professor Garner was of the opinion that " if such an appropriation were made and continued permanently, the effect would be to make the United States for all practical purposes a member of the Court, since that appears to be the only legal obligation which membership in the Court involves, and as for the right of the United States to make use of the Court, it already has that right." [11] There are historical precedents for this argument. Congress has appropriated money for the support of international organizations in the absence of treaty obligations. An example of this is the annual appropriation for the Interparliamentary Union for the Promotion of International Arbitration, for which, said Mr. Carr, " there is no [authorization] statute or treaty." [12]

10 *Infra*, p. 173 f.

11 James W. Garner, "Acts and Joint Resolutions of Congress as Substitutes for Treaties," *Amer. Jour. Inter. Law*, XXIX (July, 1935), p. 483.

12 72nd Cong., 2nd Sess. Committee on Appropriations. Hearings on *Department of State Appropriation Bill for 1934*, p. 215.

CHAPTER V
THE COMMITTEE AND TREATIES

1. NEGOTIATIONS

WHILE the House as early as 1796 disclaimed " any agency in making treaties," it did maintain the right " to deliberate on the expediency or inexpediency of carrying . . . into effect a treaty " stipulating " regulations on any of the subjects submitted by the Constitution to the power of Congress." [1] This qualifying phrase has been susceptible of broad interpretations, especially when appropriations and tariff duties have been involved. On the assumption that this thesis is correct, the House and its committees have justified their participation in the treaty-making process at any one of several points.

The tariff question became a more lively topic of discussion in committees when the United States embarked on an extensive policy of reciprocity in the 1880's and 1890's. Most of the pronouncements on the role of the House in tariff conventions have emanated from the Committee on Ways and Means, although Foreign Affairs, Judiciary, and Rules as well as the House have expressed themselves.[2] In 1880, the House, under

1 4th Cong., 1st Sess., April 1, 1796. *House Journal*, p. 492.

2 The House has followed no sharp line of practice in referring to the several committees measures which affect revenue through international agreements. As a general rule, those measures looking to the negotiation of agreements have gone to the Foreign Affairs Committee, while those designed to carry out treaty agreements have been referred to the Ways and Means Committee. For references to the Foreign Affairs Committee, see 48th Cong., 1st Sess., H. Rep. 2149; 49th Cong., 1st Sess., H. Rep. 1648; 50th Cong., 1st Sess., H. Rep. 369, 1183; 51st Cong. 1st Sess., H. Rep. 1827, 1870; 52nd Cong., 1st Sess., H. Rep. 1957; 1145; 53rd Cong., 2nd Sess., H. Rep. 878. Cited in Hinds' *Precedents*, sec. 4174. For references to the Committee on Ways and Means, see Hinds, sec. 1526, 1527, 1531.

The Judiciary Committee reported on treaties affecting revenue both in the Forty-eighth and Forty-ninth Congresses. The chairman, Mr. Tucker (Va.), made both reports, upholding the contention that " the President, by and with the advice and consent of the Senate, cannot negotiate a treaty ... whereby duties on imports are to be regulated." The second report further

Democratic control, adopted an extreme view, claiming not only the right of Congress to *execute* commercial treaties, but holding that the *negotiation* of such a treaty would " be an infraction of the Constitution and an intrusion of one of the highest prerogatives of the House of Representatives." [3] The Foreign Affairs Committee did not accept this view. The following year, during the same Congress, this Committee reported adversely a joint resolution which declared that the treaty-making power " does not extend to treaties which affect the revenue, or require the appropriation of money to execute them; but that in such cases the consent of the law-making power of the Government is required, which includes, as one of its branches, the House of Representatives." The Committee sought to reconcile the treaty-making power with Article I, section 7, wherein it is provided that all bills raising revenue must originate in the House, and section 8, declaring the right of Congress " to lay and collect taxes, duties, imposts, and excises." It denied that these constitutional clauses prevented the President from exercising his powers in regard to treaties. ". . . A treaty cannot be construed so as to destroy other powers given in the Constitution . . ." A refusal by Congress to carry out a treaty " within constitutional limits . . . might be regarded by the other party as just cause of war. But within our jurisdiction, in case of conflict between a valid treaty and a valid act of Congress, they both being the law of the land, it seems that

requested the President " to withhold final action upon the proposed convention (with Hawaii) and to condition its final ratification upon the sanction of an act of Congress..." 49th Cong., 2nd Sess. H. Rep. 4177.

In giving its consent to a convention with Mexico the Senate added the following amendment: " The present convention shall take effect as soon as it has been approved and ratified by both contracting parties according to their respective constitutions, but not until laws necessary to carry it into operation shall have been passed by both the *Congress* of the United States of America and the Government of the United Mexican States...." The Ways and Means Committee interpreted the adoption of this amendment by the Senate as " a substantial admission, in the nature of a precedent, which may be expected hereafter to govern treaties affecting the revenue." 48th Cong., 1st Sess. H. Rep. 1848. (1884).

3 46th Cong., 2nd Sess. Jan. 19, 1880. *Cong. Rec.*, p. 532.

the later law would govern. The resolution under consideration affirms a proposition which, under existing constitutional provisions, cannot be sustained." The Committee's report was tabled by the House without debate, thus upholding the views presented by the Committee.[4]

With no recorded debate on either of these propositions, it is difficult to explain the divergent views taken by the House in the same Congress on essentially the same question—the negotiation of commercial treaties. Perhaps the explanation for this inconsistency may be found in the uncertain attitude of the Democratic majority on the tariff issue.[5] Despite the insistence of a member of the Foreign Affairs Committee that the earlier resolution should be referred to that Committee which was then considering the subject, the House adopted the first of these resolutions by an overwhelming vote, 175 to 62. No record vote occurred on the Foreign Affairs Committee's report. One may challenge the contention of the House in the first case in the light of the precedents.[6] It may be noted in passing that commercial treaties have sometimes included a clause making their operation contingent upon a subsequent act of Congress.[7]

4 46th Cong., 3rd Sess. H. Rep. 225. February 14, 1881. *Cong. Rec.*, p. 1568.

5 J. L. Laughlin and H. P. Willis, *Reciprocity* (New York, 1903), chap. IV, give an adequate sketch of the political complexion that entered into the tariff question.

6 *Cf.* Moore, *Digest*, V, pp. 162-164.

7 The act to carry out the Cuban reciprocity treaty of 1902 included a proviso that "nothing herein contained shall be held or construed as an admission on the part of the House of Representatives that customs duties can be changed otherwise than by an act of Congress originating in said House." 33 *Stat.* 3.

On a resolution calling for an investigation of the convention with Hawaii in 1887—a convention which was not submitted to Congress for its approval —the Committee on Judiciary, Mr. Tucker (Va.) chairman, reported the following resolution:

> That the President, by and with the advice and consent of the Senate, can not negotiate a treaty which shall be binding on the United States whereby duties on imports are to be regulated, either by imposing or remitting, increasing or decreasing them, without the sanction of an act of Congress; and that the extension of the term for the operation of the

Again, the President has entered upon negotiations pursuant to an act of Congress, thereby securing prior assent to alterations of duties within the terms of the act.[8]

The conflict of opinion represented above on the question of negotiation of treaties has usually found the Foreign Affairs Committee taking a more modest view of the rights of the House on this subject. The Committee's view more nearly coincides with the constitutional principle that in foreign affairs the President alone may negotiate, as well as with the terms of the act of 1842, wherein the payment of agents without a specific appropriation is prohibited except that agents engaged in foreign intercourse may be paid from the contingent funds under the control of the President.[9] In a letter to President Harding in June, 1921, Chairman Porter put in terse language his thoughts on the relation of the House to treaty negotiations.

I am of the view that limitation of armament can only be brought about by a treaty and that the Constitution vests in the Chief Executive the exclusive initiative in the making of such a treaty or treaties; therefore, I am opposed to the language of the many resolutions which have been introduced in Congress on that subject, e. g., '. . . the President is hereby authorized' ; '. . . the President is hereby authorized and directed ' ; '. . . the President is herewith authorized and requested,' and other similar expressions which appear in all the resolutions and convey to the country two false impressions, namely, that you are without power to act unless author-

original treaty or convention with the Government of the Hawaiian Islands, proposed by the supplementary convention of December 6, 1884, will not be binding on the United States without like sanction, which was provided for in the original treaty and convention, and was given by act of Congress.

That the President is respectfully requested to withhold final action upon the proposed convention and to condition its final ratification upon the sanction of an act of Congress, in respect of the duties upon articles to be imported from the Hawaiian Islands.

49th Cong., 2nd Sess. (1887). The House took no action on the report.

8 See, for example, the Reciprocal Trade Agreements Act of 1934, renewed in 1937 and again in 1940. The legal aspects of the agreements are treated in William S. Culbertson, *Reciprocity* (New York, 1937), chap. V. See, also, *Yale Law Rev.*, XLVI (Feb., 1937), pp. 647-670.

9 5 *Stat.* 533.

ized by Congress, and that you are reluctant about doing so. . . . My thought in the resolution is to put the matter in its true light by recognizing your constitutional powers and to show our concurrence in your declared purpose and intention, and by appropriating sufficient money with which to pay the expenses thereof.[10]

That the Committee has been conscious of this check upon its own power may be gathered from the alterations it has made in resolutions coming before it which " authorize " the President to conduct negotiations with a particular country. These have been modified to read " request." [11] Where, however, the cost of negotiation promises to be considerable and Congress provides a specific sum in lieu of reliance on the contingent fund, the Committee has authorized the President to negotiate.[12]

Negotiations leading to treaty arrangements which ultimately require congressional action, as distinct from Senate approval, for their fulfillment have sometimes been previously approved by Congress as a precaution against later congressional opposition. In 1888, the Committee reported out a measure requesting the President to negotiate with Mexico for the creation of an international commission to determine all questions touching the boundary line between the United States and Mexico. In support of this the chairman reported Secretary of State Bayard as follows: "As such an arrangement (an international river commission) would not be effective without legislative provisions for expenses, I would prefer to have some indication of the feeling of Congress in the premises before entering on any formal negotiations." [13] The resolution recommended was

10 67th Cong. (1921-1923). Files, C. F. A.

11 60th Cong., 2nd Sess. (1909). H. Rep. 2212.

12 E. g., 67th Cong., 1st Sess. (1921). S. J. Res. 36, *Authorizing the Appointment of a Commission to Confer with the Dominion Government . . . Relative to the Exportation of Pulp Wood therefrom to the United States.*

13 50th Cong., 1st Sess. (1888). H. Rep. 1008. In 1879, the Secretary of State sought an appropriation for the appointment of commissioners to negotiate with Mexico. The Secretary assured a member of Congress " that it is almost impossible to conclude any treaty with the Republic of Mexico

drafted in the Department. The State Department sought similar approval in 1935 on a bill authorizing " the Secretary of State, with the approval of the President, to designate the American Commissioner on the International Boundary Commission to cooperate with representatives of the Mexican Government in making a study regarding the equitable use of the waters of the lower Rio Grande, the lower Colorado and Tia Juana Rivers to obtain information on which to base a treaty with Mexico relative to the uses of the waters of these rivers." [14] It was maintained in the Committee, in support of this measure, that it was impossible to make a treaty with Mexico on the assurance that it would be carried out, because expenses would be incurred in connection with the proposed treaty, the studies and surveys, and authority was lacking for the incurrence of these expenses.[15]

Public indignation may press so heavily upon Congress that, against its better judgment, it may push through a bill that in calmer moments would be pigeonholed. American indignation over the failure of the Russian Government to honor American passports issued to citizens of the Jewish faith resulted in a bill requesting the President " to renew negotiations " to correct this situation. Despite the positive views of his Secretary of State on such matters, Theodore Roosevelt signed the measure as one of his last acts before leaving the presidency.[16] It was a pleasant gesture and the responsibility passed to his successor.[17]

2. EXECUTION

Alexander Hamilton expressed himself unequivocally on the responsibilities of the House to carry out treaties. " The House

unless it be done by the method proposed in this resolution. . . . The appointment of this commission will have more prestige and influence with the Mexican people." 46th Cong., 1st Sess. H. J. Res. 117. June 28, 1879. *Cong. Rec.*, p. 2425.

14 74th Cong., 1st Sess. H. Rep. 422.

15 74th Cong. (1935-1937). Files, C. F. A.

16 35 *Stat.* 1170.

17 See, *infra*, Legislative Action in View of Treaty Action.

of Representatives have no moral power to refuse the execution of a treaty which is not contrary to the Constitution, because it pledges the public faith; and have no legal power to refuse its execution, because it is a law, until at least it ceases to be a law by regular act of revocation of the competent authority." [18] He would find few members of that body since then who would accept either his assumptions or his reasoning. Countless pages of the debates and numerous reports of committees would challenge him. Yet when the final count is taken, one could cite few examples where the House has failed to uphold " the public faith." The observation, so frequently advanced, that through control of the purse the House may exert an influence on foreign affairs, lacks substance when analyzed in the light of treaty obligations.[19] There is no instance of the House having failed to vote the necessary sum to carry out a treaty.[20]

The Committee on Foreign Affairs, followed by the House and Senate, discussed exhaustively the constitutional aspects of appropriations made pursuant to treaty commitments in connection with the payments due to Russia for the purchase of Alaska. Chairman Banks, after a review of the precedents and the observations of writers, stated in his report: [21]

18 Message for Washington to Congress, in reply to a call for papers relating to the Treaty with Great Britain, March 29, 1796. Hamilton's *Works* (ed. by John C. Hamilton), VII, p. 556.

19 See, *supra*, Negotiations, p. 137 f.

20 During the analysis of the State Department appropriation bill Mr. Caldwell, chairman of the subcommittee in charge of the bill, made the following statement: " Under the heading ' Contributions, quotas,' and so forth, we reduced the estimate by about $19,000 directed at the expenses of our participation in quarterly meetings of the Governing Board of the International Labor Organization. Your attention is called to the fact that neither this committee nor the Congress has any discretion in the matter of these funds. So long as the Congress authorizes the participation by this country in foreign conventions, it is our duty from which we have no escape to appropriate the funds necessary for that purpose." 76th Cong., 3rd Sess. Feb. 6, 1940. *Cong. Rec.*, p. 1082. *Cf.* the address of Mr. Linthicum, chairman of the Foreign Affairs Committee, titled *The Share of the Committee on Foreign Affairs ... in the Treaty-Making Power.* 72nd Cong., 1st Sess. May 2, 1932. *Cong. Rec.*, p. 9392.

21 40th Cong., 2nd Sess. (1868). H. Rep. 37.

. . . It is now conceded that the House is entitled to consider the merits of a treaty that it may determine whether its object is within the scope of the treaty power; but, if it be not inconsistent with the spirit and purpose of the Government, Congress is bound to give it effect, by necessary legislation, as a contract between the Government and a foreign nation. If, on the contrary, it is found to be in conflict with the fundamental principles, purposes, or interests of the Government, it would be justified, not merely in withholding its aid, but in giving notice to foreign nations interested that it would not be regarded as binding upon the nation, in passing laws for its abrogation, and preparing the State for whatever consequences might attend its action.

On the House floor two amendments were offered. The first, after reference to the treaty provisions involving a payment of $7,200,000, added: [22]

. . . and whereas the subjects thus embraced in the stipulation of said treaty are among the subjects which by the Constitution of the United States are submitted to the power of Congress, and over which Congress has jurisdiction; and it being for such reason necessary that the consent of Congress should be given to said stipulation before the same can have full force and effect; having taken into consideration the said treaty, and approving of the stipulations therein, to the end that the same may be carried into effect: Therefore, section 1, Be it enacted, that the assent of Congress is hereby given to the stipulations of said treaty.

22 40th Cong., 2nd Sess. *Cong. Globe*, June 30, 1868. Mr. Loughridge who introduced the amendment spoke as follows: "An attempt is being made through the means of the treaty-making power, to concentrate almost all of the power of this government in the hands of the President, subject only to the advice and consent of the Senate.... I hesitate not to say, sir, that if, without any explanation, disaffirmance, or protest, we make this appropriation, we shall, so far as this House can do it, have surrendered practically all the power of the government into the hands of the treaty-making department, and reduced this House to the position of an involuntary agent of that power with no discretion but to carry out its expressed will. ... By substituting a foreign government or an Indian tribe in place of this House, on the principle claimed by the Executive, there is nothing within the whole scope of the legislative powers of the government that cannot be done without the consent or intervention of this House..." *Ibid.*, p. 3621.

This amendment was adopted by a vote of two to one. A second amendment, declaring " that the powers vested by the Constitution in the President and Senate to enter into treaties with foreign governments do not include the power to complete the purchase of foreign territory before the necessary appropriation shall be made therefor by act of Congress " failed of adoption by only two votes. The Senate refused to accept the pronouncements put in by zealous partisans of the House. When the bill emerged from the Conference Committee, the phraseology of the House amendment was modified to read: " and whereas said stipulations can not be carried into full force and effect except by legislation to which the consent of both Houses of Congress is necessary." The clause " that the assent of Congress is hereby given to the stipulations of said treaty " was stricken out.[23] With these alterations the bill passed both Houses and was signed by President Johnson.[24] Of the results of these changes Wharton comments that " there was no action which might be regarded as taking the position that the House has the prerogative of affirming or rejecting, at its discretion, execution of a treaty when such execution is dependent on its action." [25] Never, since 1868, has the House or the Committee reverted to the stand taken on the question of appropriations pursuant to treaty commitments.

The House has given attention to the execution of treaties whose contents, apart from appropriations, embrace matters which fall within the jurisdiction of Congress. To carry out the terms of the Washington Arms Limitation Treaty the Committee on Naval Affairs reported out a bill, the first section of which authorized the President " to make such disposition as in his judgment may be proper of any capital ship of the Navy . . ." [26] This section had the approval of the State and

23 *Ibid.* July 23, 1868. *Cong. Globe*, p. 4392.

24 15 *Stat.* 198.

25 Wharton, *International Law Digest*, II, pp. 21-23, cited in Moore, *Digest*, V, pp. 228-229.

26 67th Cong., 2nd Sess. (1922). R. Rep. 888.

the Navy Departments. The debate on the floor turned on the necessity for inserting this provision in the bill.[27] It was argued by Mr. Tucker that the Constitution specifically granted to Congress the power " to provide and maintain a navy " (Art. I, sec. 8, c. 13) and " to dispose of and make all needful rules and regulations respecting the territory or other property belonging to the United States " (Art. IV, sec. 3, c. 2).[28] Since the treaty touched upon the maintenance of the navy—government property—the President was unable to carry out the treaty without the authorization of Congress. Mr. Burton, a former senator and a distinguished member of the Foreign Affairs Committee, disputed the contentions of Mr. Tucker. He held this section of the bill to be unnecessary. His arguments, however, lacked the convincing logic applied by Mr. Tucker. After examining the two extreme claims presented many times—that which asserted that the concurrence of the House is legally obligatory in executing treaties and that which advanced the thesis that the House may accept or reject at its will measures introduced for this purpose—he advanced a third point, a combination of law and moral obligation.[29]

While the right of the House to disapprove or nullify exists, there is, nevertheless, a necessary comity between the respective departments of the Government, a binding moral obligation, and it would be in violation of the established division of powers to withhold action; also that the observance of good faith in dealing with other countries requires that stipulations contained in any treaty

27 *Ibid.* May 16, 1922. *Cong. Rec.*, pp. 7062-7076.

28 Mr. Tucker also cited c. 14 (The Congress shall have the power to make rules for the government and regulation of the land and naval forces) and c. 18 (The Congress shall have the power to make all laws which shall be necessary and proper for carrying into execution the foregoing powers, and all other powers vested by this Constitution in the government of the United States, or in any department or officer thereof) of Article I, section 8. Mr. Tucker's contentions are treated exhaustively in his book, *Limitations on the Treaty-Making Power Under the Constitution of the United States* (Boston, 1915).

29 *Supra*, note 27. *Cong. Rec.*, p. 7069.

ratified in the manner prescribed by the Constitution be made effectual by action of the House.

The short debate that followed did not reveal conclusively the sentiments of other representatives. But several were impressed by the acquiescence of executive departments in the bill as reported.

Underlying this discussion is a broad question which the Committee and the House have never finally answered—how far delegates to international conferences may commit the Government in matters entrusted by the Constitution to Congress. An arrangement entered into by the President and approved by the Senate might conceivably be displeasing to the House. Two approaches to the problem have been attempted. The first of these has already been discussed in connection with the deliberations of the Committee to instruct delegates to the World Economic Conference.[30] While such resolutions of opinion, if adhered to, have the merit of informing the delegates of the extent to which the House is willing to go, they impose upon the delegates a degree of inflexibility in conference deliberations. Moreover, protracted negotiations may find the sentiment of the House shifting, particularly if an election changes the political composition of the House. The settlement of the war debts represents a second approach. Contrary to the request of the Treasury Department which sought full power to arrange settlements of outstanding indebtedness to the United States, Congress passed an act creating a separate body, the World War Debt Funding Commission.[31] This act specified the limits within which the commission could make funding arrangements. When it was found necessary, in order to reach an agreement with each of the debtor nations, to exceed these limits, the commission sought the approval of Congress. In a series of separate acts congressional approval was given to each of these special

30 *Supra*, pp. 81-82.

31 42 *Stat.* 363. *Cf.* 67th Cong., 1st Sess. (1921). Hearings on H. R. 7359, *Refunding Foreign Obligations* before the Committee on Ways and Means.

accords. The bilateral character of the negotiations in each case made for a more expeditious settlement than in the case of a multilateral conference. Moreover, preceding each of the final agreements, the subject had been explored with each of the debtor nations through diplomatic channels.[32]

The action of the Committee, as a Committee rather than as individuals, has leaned toward the views expressed by Mr. Burton. It has sought to reconcile the international responsibilities assumed in treaty form by the President and approved by the Senate with the constitutional powers entrusted to the House. Its approach has been sober and reasonable rather than perfunctory. The hearings on measures to carry out treaties have been searching. While the burden of proof has rested with those seeking the requisite legislation, the Committee has not seriously challenged either the President's right to negotiate a treaty or the necessity for the treaty. The queries directed to witnesses have kept the Committee abreast of international problems to which the House has directed its attention. The amendments it has offered have aimed at clarification and perfection.[33]

3. TERMINATION [34]

In the absence of constitutional provisions for the termination of treaties, one must turn to precedents for guidance. Three

32 See *Foreign Relations of the United States, 1924*, two volumes, for United States negotiations on behalf of World War Foreign Debt Commission for settlement or refunding of debts owed to the United States by foreign governments.

During the hearings, in 1927, on treaty relations with China Mr. Burton told the Foreign Affairs Committee that at the Opium Conference, to which he was a delegate, "the resolution of Congress enabled me to speak not only for the President but for the Congress of the United States, and it added tremendously to the force of our representations." 69th Cong. Files, C. F. A.

33 E. g. 74th Cong., 2nd Sess. S. 3413, *An Act to Give Effect to the Convention between the United States and Certain Other Countries for the Regulation of Whaling.*

34 The discussion of termination of treaties is restricted in this section. First, attention is given only to those treaties requiring notification as a prelude to termination. Second, termination is considered solely from the domestic angle without reference to the implication of international law.

possibilities present themselves and each has been used: first, that the President alone may terminate a treaty; second, that the President in conjunction with the Senate may terminate a treaty; and third, that the President together with Congress —the Senate and the House—may terminate a treaty. The first of these has been used infrequently. Through the simple process of an instruction to the American Minister to Switzerland by Secretary Hay the convention of friendship and commerce of 1859 was ended.[35] There is no indication that this step was preceded, or followed, by the action of either or both Houses of Congress. More recently, President Roosevelt, without legislative sanction or approval, served notice upon Japan that the commercial treaty with that nation would be terminated at the end of six months.[36]

Support for the second alternative comes from several sources, notably the Senate itself. President Pierce, " in pursuance of the authority conferred by a resolution of the Senate," served notice on Denmark that the treaty of 1826 would be terminated in accordance with the provisions of that treaty.[37] The occasion was the desire to end the obnoxious dues levied on ships entering the Baltic Sea via the Sound. It is of importance to note, however, that the Senate's action followed the annual message of the President to Congress in which he deemed it " expedient that the contemplated notice should be given " to Denmark.[38] There is nothing in the message to indicate that he sought action either by the Senate or by Congress. Apparently not all senators were convinced of the sufficiency of the Senate's action. A resolution, introduced by Senator Sumner, directed the Foreign Relations Committee " to consider the expediency of some act of legislation, having the concurrence of both Houses of Congress " by which the treaty " may

35 *Foreign Relations, 1899*, pp. 754-757.

36 Department of State *Bulletin*, July 29, 1939, p. 81.

37 Third annual message to Congress, December 31, 1855. Richardson, *Messages and Papers*, V, p. 334.

38 Second annual message to Congress, December 4, 1854. *Ibid.*, p. 279.

be effectively abrogated." [39] The Committee's report vigorously sustained the Senate's earlier resolution. [40] Said the Committee: ". . . The treaty . . . was created by the will of the treaty-making power, and it contained a reservation by which that will should be revoked or its exercise cease on a stipulated notice. It is thus the will of the treaty-making power which is the subject of revocation, and it follows that the revocation is incident to the will." Again, " the committee are clear in the opinion that it is competent for the President and Senate, acting together, to terminate it in the manner prescribed . . . without the aid or intervention of legislation by Congress, and that when so terminated it is at an end to every intent, both as a contract between the Governments and as a law of the land." The Foreign Relations Committee's emphasis on the Senate's prerogative was doubtless an effort to counteract the two earlier instances of abrogation in which the House had participated. To waive these earlier episodes as precedents, the Committee found extenuating circumstances in each of them. The annulment of the French treaty in 1798 was " a hostile act, as the preamble shows, and was looked upon at the time as the precursor of war, if not an act of war itself." To the Committee this action was " a rightful use of the war power." In view of the hostilities then in progress between the two countries and their subsequent extension, there is some justification for this reference to the " use of the war power " entrusted to Congress. [41] The termination of the treaty of 1827 with Great Britain, touching upon the joint occupation of the Northwest Territory, was still

39 34th Cong., 1st Sess. February 28, 1856. *Cong. Globe*, p. 528.

40 *Ibid*. S. Rep. 97.

41 Two factors are of importance in this case: first, the treaty contained no provision for termination; and second, termination was completed by an act of Congress. Customarily the action of Congress or of the Senate, where it precedes denunciation, leaves to the President's discretion the moment for serving notice of termination. " The French government did not admit that the act of 1798 effected a valid international abrogation of `the treaties." Moore, *Digest*, V, 357.

within the memory of many of the senators. A settlement with Great Britain having failed, President Polk, in 1846, asked " that provision be made *by law* " for its termination.[42] The Committee vindicated this procedure because the aim was " to make the act more impressive upon England than if authorized by the Senate alone, and especially as it was known that on the policy of giving the notice at all the Senate was by no means united." [43] This explanation ignored President Polk's reference to provision " by law " which obviously envisaged participation by the House.[44]

Philander C. Knox, President Taft's Secretary of State, wrote Mr. Taft along these lines when the latter was preparing his book on the presidency. " Personally, I have no doubt but that treaties may be terminated at any time by the same power that makes them, namely, the President and the Senate and that, as the precedents show, it is immaterial whether the action of the Senate comes before or after the Executive formally notifies the other government of the termination." [45] So careful a student as Crandall also supports this view.[46]

Against these contentions of the Senate may be cited instances where the House has weighed the matter of termination. Two illustrations were given above. President Grant, in communicating to Congress difficulties with Great Britain over the application of the extradition article of the Treaty of 1842,

42 First annual message to Congress, December 2, 1845. Richardson, *Messages and Papers*, IV, p. 395.

43 34th Cong., 1st Sess. S. Rep. 97.

44 In 1858, the Foreign Relations Committee reported on the termination of the eleventh article of the treaty of 1846 with Hanover. The Committee substituted a simple Senate resolution for the original joint resolution referred to it. 35th Cong., 1st Sess. See 56th Cong., 2nd Sess., S. Doc. 231, pt. 8, titled *Compilation of Reports of the Committee on Foreign Relations, United States Senate, 1789-1901*, p. 124.

45 November 21, 1914. Knox mss.

46 Samuel B. Crandall, *Treaties, Their Making and Enforcement* (Washington, D. C., 1916), p. 461.

wrote: " It is for the wisdom of *Congress* to determine whether the article of the treaty relating to extradition is to be any longer regarded as obligatory on the Government of the United States or as forming part of the supreme law of the land. Should the attitude of the British Government remain unchanged, I shall not, without an expression of the wish of *Congress* that I should do so, take any action either in making or granting requisitions for the surrender of fugitive criminals under the Treaty of 1842."[47] Three years later President Hayes incorporated the same thesis in a veto message to the House when he returned a bill restricting Chinese immigration into the United States in contravention of Articles V and VI of the Burlingame treaty of 1868. " The authority of *Congress* to terminate a treaty with a foreign power by expressing the will of the nation no longer to adhere to it is as free from controversy under our Constitution as is the further proposition that the power of making new treaties or modifying existing treaties " (as this bill would have done) " is not lodged by the Constitution in Congress, but in the President, by and with the advice and consent of the Senate, as shown by the concurrency of two-thirds of that body." [48]

Political expediency rather than legal contention has given to the House a voice in terminating treaties. During the Senate debates on a joint resolution looking to the termination of certain articles of the Treaty of Washington (1871) with Great Britain, Senator Edmunds spoke in the following terms:[49]

. . . The Committee [on Foreign Relations] by reporting it [i. e. the joint resolution] does not mean to have the Senate understand that we think it is indispensable that the termination should be made by a joint resolution; and the question is open and under reserve. I mention this so that there shall be no implication that the President by and with the advice and consent of the Senate

47 June 20, 1876. Richardson, *Messages and Papers*, VII, p. 373.

48 March 1, 1879. *Ibid.*, p. 518.

49 47th Cong., 2nd Sess. February 9, 1883. *Cong. Rec.*, p. 2333.

alone can not terminate it. I think he can; but to save all possible question we wish to pass the joint resolution if we can, but if we cannot we shall undoubtedly . . . ask the Senate in its constitutional capacity of an adviser in respect of the foreign affairs of the Government, to advise the President to put an end to the treaty whether we have time to get the measure through both Houses or not.

The joint resolution was passed by both Houses and signed by the President. The articles of which termination was sought dealt with the fishing privileges of Americans off the Canadian coast and had agitated members of the House as well as the Senate. It would appear from Senator Edmunds' remarks that participation by the House was more by grace than by prerogative. Yet the House did not challenge this argument.

Over a period of thirty years the House—occasionally the Senate—had before it bills and resolutions, joint and simple, that expressed indignation at the discriminatory treatment accorded American citizens of Jewish faith who sought permission to enter Russia. It was contended that the action of Russia was in violation of the treaty of 1832. The failure of President Taft to adjust the issue by treaty spurred the House, and particularly the Foreign Affairs Committee, to seek a termination of the treaty of 1832.[50] Mr. Knox has given a description of the events, as he recalled them, three years later.[51]

The House, with but one dissenting vote, passed a resolution calling for the termination of the treaty in a way that would have been most displeasing, if not insulting, to the Russian Government. This resolution reached the Senate, as I recall it, on a Thursday, and it

[50] In his annual message to Congress President Taft referred to relations with Russia in the following terms: " By direction of the State Department, our ambassador to Russia has recently been having a series of conferences with the Minister of Foreign Affairs of Russia, with a view to securing a clearer understanding and construction of the Treaty of 1832 between Russia and the United States." *Foreign Relations, 1911,* xxi-xxii. For correspondence with Russia, *ibid.,* pp. 695-699.

[51] Knox to Taft, November 21, 1914. Knox mss.

became at once apparent that this body was disposed to pass the resolution immediately and without amendment, and indeed it seemed to entertain that purpose. However, upon the insistence of Senator Cullom that it would be disrespectful to the Committee on Foreign Relations to act upon the resolution without first referring it to the Committee, and upon his assurance that he would report the resolution out of the Committee on the following Monday, the resolution was so referred.

Thereupon, and while it was under consideration by the Committee, I took the matter up with several Committee members, with the result that a decision was reached that in order to avoid having to give the notice in an improper and insulting form, you, as Chief Executive, would give notice of the termination of the treaty in accordance with its provisions without waiting for the action of the Senate and this was the course followed.

Later, December 21, 1911, Congress by a joint resolution, confirmed your act by declaring that " the notice . . . is hereby ratified and adopted." [52]

In the Committee hearings which preceded passage of the first resolution by the House no mention was made of the constitutional right of the House to share in the determination whether a treaty should be abrogated.[53] Most of the questions were directed toward the hypothetical results that would follow such an act. The presumption ran throughout that the procedure was correct. Nor is there any evidence that the Senate challenged the House. The Foreign Relations Committee had an opportun-

52 Notification of termination was delivered to the Russian Government before the Senate voted. Subsequently President Taft informed the Senate of this " as a part of the treaty-making power of this Government, with a view to its ratification and approval." Mathews analyzes the President's course as follows: (1) that he had a right to notify the foreign government of the denunciation of the treaty prior to any action by the Senate or by Congress authorizing him to do so; but (2) that subsequent approval by the Senate, as a part of the treaty-making power, was desirable, if not necessary; and (3) that the concurrence of the House of Representatives was unnecessary. John M. Mathews, *American Foreign Relations* (New York, 1938), p. 591.

53 So far as can be ascertained, the Foreign Affairs Committee has never examined this broad question.

ity to modify those portions which included the House and to reaffirm the position taken in 1856. It would appear, therefore, that the Senate tacitly acknowledged the claim of the House to share in a function which previously had been regarded as beyond its competence. While it may be argued that the President was not legally obligated to serve notice of termination, political considerations pointed the course. The success of congressional pressure here, as in the more recent abrogation of the Japanese treaty, indicates that the influence of Congress, or the Senate alone, may weigh heavily in affecting our foreign relations where they rest upon treaty commitments.

What can be said, then, as to the propriety of either legislative body seeking to bring about the abrogation of a treaty? Mathews sums up the confusion of precedents this way: [54]

> Some treaties may be more appropriately terminated by the President than by Congress, and vice versa; some may be terminated with equal effectiveness by the action of the President, or of the treaty-making body, or of Congress. Sometimes more than one method may with propriety be pursued in accomplishing the same object; although usually one method is more appropriate, that is, more in accordance with law and practice, than the others.

It is apparent, too, that one must go beyond the constitutional and legal arguments and look for guidance in the domestic and international scenes. No better illustration of this may be offered than the recent termination of the commercial treaty with Japan. The unpopularity of that nation's China policy and the resultant disregard for American rights in China laid the groundwork for action. The precise nature of the action was suggested by the resolution introduced by Senator Vandenberg, a leading Republican opponent of President Roosevelt.[55] His resolution expressed the sense of the Senate that the United States Government give appropriate notice to Japan for the abrogation of the treaty of 1911. While this resolution was

54 Mathews, cited, p. 616.
55 76th Cong., 1st Sess. S. Res. 166.

still before the Foreign Relations Committee, the President informed Japan that he gave notice, as required by the treaty, that the treaty would end after six months.[56] This was the President's device for weakening the advantage gained by Senator Vandenberg. Less dramatic were the circumstances some sixty years earlier when the Foreign Affairs Committee pondered the termination of the naturalization treaty with Prussia, necessitated by the consolidation of the various German states into the German Empire. The Committee decided " that an effort might properly be made with the object of negotiating a new treaty which would of itself operate as a termination of the present one without such formal notice being now given." [57] By thus urging a new treaty upon the President, with the Senate's approval, it denied itself an expression of policy on the content of a naturalization treaty. This preference for supersession as against abrogation came before the Committee again as late as 1927, when it had under advisement a concurrent resolution suggesting that the President enter into negotiations with China with a view to adjusting the questions of extraterritoriality and of customs. One member favored a simple resolution abrogating the existing treaties; this would be the " most satisfactory and direct method." It was pointed out, however, that these two problems were in themselves most complex and their solution hinged, in part, upon the attitude of other Powers. It was thought that a resolution such as that before the Committee would give legislative approval to the President's China policy at the same time that it accorded him the widest latitude in handling the involved negotiations preceding a change in the treaty relations between the two countries.[58]

56 See *The New York Times*, July 28, 1939, article by Arthur Krock titled " In the Nation."

57 47th Cong., 2nd Sess. (1883). H. Rep. 1893.

58 69th Cong. (1925-1927). Files, C. F. A.

4. LEGISLATIVE ACTION IN LIEU OF TREATY ACTION

Customarily Americans look upon the President and the Senate as the components in the treaty process, the former to initiate and to conclude the international agreement, the latter to lend advice and to refuse its consent if its advice is not taken. But occasionally, and at widely scattered intervals, this nice arrangement of constitutional procedure has proven incapable of functioning or unwilling to operate. In that case the expedient has been reliance upon the legislative process.

The events preceding the signing of the Jay Treaty in 1794 illustrate one means by which the legislature has exerted its influence on our treaty relations. Efforts to enter into a favorable commercial accord with Great Britain were met with coolness or, at the most, procrastinating and inconclusive negotiations. Congressional irritation was heightened by these tactics and showed itself by the attempted passage of discriminatory shipping acts. Only the moderating influence of Hamilton with his Federalist friends in Congress prevented their enactment. Washington felt constrained to place before Congress the course of events " as it might at some time have influence on matters under your consideration." [59] The outbreak of war in Europe in 1793 and the consequent repercussions on American attempts to maintain a neutral position provoked fresh outbursts of congressional indignation which even the pro-British Federalist group could not stem. An embargo on American shipping for one month, subsequently extended another month, was the first positive sign of a more virile policy. Only President Washington's nomination of John Jay as an envoy to negotiate with the British stayed congressional action on pending non-intercourse and sequestration bills.[60] While the negotiations and the treaty itself embraced many points apart from commerce, it was the threat of Congress—partially fulfilled—

59 Richardson, *Messages and Papers*, I, p. 96.

60 Samuel F. Bemis, *Jay's Treaty: A Study in Commerce and Diplomacy* (New York, 1924), chap. IX.

to use its powers over commerce that brought the negotiations to a successful end. Here, then, was a case where the President found an act of Congress more effective in securing results than the exercise of his treaty powers. His desire for a treaty was exceeded only by that of the legislature whose cooperation he enlisted. The legislative weapon was used to create a situation so unfavorable to the interests of a foreign power that a treaty was entered into to offset domestic reprisals.

The familiar details behind the joint resolutions leading to the annexation of Texas, in 1845, and of Hawaii, in 1898, need no restatement. In each case domestic issues and partisan politics were powerful enough to prevent a favorable vote in the Senate. When the Senate failed to give its consent to the ratification of the treaty with Texas by which the latter would have been annexed, President Tyler sent a special message to the House of Representatives, pointing out that " the power of Congress is . . . fully competent in some other form of proceeding to accomplish everything that a formal ratification of the treaty could have accomplished . . ." [61] But Congress was too preoccupied with the details of adjournment and the approaching presidential campaign to risk a full-dress debate.[62] In his last annual message to Congress, in December, 1844, the President recommended an alternative method that had been

61 Richardson, *Messages and Papers*, IV, p. 323. June 10, 1844. As early as May 6, Secretary Calhoun and Mr. Ingersoll, chairman of the Committee on Foreign Affairs, had agreed that in the event the Senate rejected the treaty, the latter would embody the terms "in a bill in the House." The following day President Tyler agreed to this proposal. On June 3, the President told the Texan chargé d'affaires that he planned " to send a full open message to the House to serve as an appeal to the people on that subject, when Congress adjourned (*sic*)." Meigs, *Ingersoll*, cited, pp. 265-268.

62 In a comforting instruction to T. A. Howard, American chargé in Texas, Calhoun pointed hopefully to the prospects of securing by joint resolution what had not been obtained by treaty. Senator McDuffie's resolution had been tabled, 27 to 19, but Calhoun's analysis of the vote, as well as the position of those who were absent when the vote was taken, gave a slight majority to those favoring such a resolution. The indications in the other House were still more favorable, he stated. June 18, 1844. Moore, *Digest*, I, p. 454.

brought before the Senate in the closing days of its last session.[63] He spoke of the adoption of the terms of annexation " by Congress in the form of a joint resolution or act to be perfected and made binding on the two countries when adopted in like manner by the Government of Texas." The debate which followed upon the report of a joint resolution by the Foreign Affairs Committee was discursive, to say the least. Proponents and opponents alike cloaked their ignorance of the most elementary facts in a mantle of polemics. The economic worth of Texas, of slavery, of debts, of public lands, of the navy, of foreign repercussions, to name only the more outstanding controverted points, obscured the broad constitutional issue to which few gave attention. Justin Smith has given us a neat summary of the arguments that developed around that point.[64]

To admit a foreign nation as a State would be to admit a new partner into the Union; this would require a new compact; and a new compact could be drawn by the people alone, it was argued. The power given Congress to admit new States had sole reference, the speakers often urged, to the territory already belonging to the United States,—particularly to Colonies that might not at once accept the Constitution; the territory of Texas must therefore first be acquired; it can be acquired only by agreement; any agreement with a foreign state is a treaty; the business of making treaties belongs to the President and Senate; and so those who favor the annexation of Texas by an act of Congress would destroy the constitution by too broad a construction of it. In reply it was maintained that the old time Federalists were making themselves ridiculous by insisting now upon an absurdly narrow view of the organic law; that in fact the language of the constitution was perfectly clear and precise; " New States may be admitted by the Congress into this Union." Jefferson thought otherwise, it was retorted; but even this did not check the march of the annexationists. Not all agreements with foreign nations are treaties, it was pointed out. The name of Marshall was cited in behalf of this view; and the power to admit new

63 Richardson, cited, IV, p. 345.

64 Justin Smith, *The Annexation of Texas* (New York, 1911), pp. 330-331.

States, expressly given to Congress, was pointed to as full and adequate authority to accept a new partner. Vermont and North Carolina were foreign nations when admitted to the Union, it was even insisted; but attention was called in reply to the fact that both had fought in our Revolutionary war, and both were included in the territory over which the treaty of 1783 gave the United States jurisdiction. The proceedings of the convention of 1787, one side maintained, provided that it was the intention to admit States arising from foreign territory, and one aim of the constitution was said to have been the prevention of adjacent confederacies; but these assertions were denied. On one point the opponents of the measure were rather neatly caught. Texas, it was reasonably argued, can certainly be acquired somehow by the American government; the enemies of the treaty said last winter that such an acquisition could not be effected by the treaty-making power; hence Congress must possess the necessary authority. In reply, some admitted that they had been in error; some took the ground that the power belonged solely to the people; and some retorted that the great number of annexation plans proved that the friends of that scheme understood very well the constitution would have to be circumvented in one way or another. The purpose of the constitution, others argued, was to defend the weak parts of the Union; the South, endangered by English designs, was now the weak part; therefore, the intent of the constitution would be fulfilled by protecting her. One speaker took still bolder ground, declaring that since it was the will of the people to acquire certain territory, the method of doing so was a point of no great importance; but it was easy to meet him by emphasizing the duty of Congress to obey the organic law.

Because the proposal of a joint resolution challenged the Senate's part in the treaty process, the constitutional issues were more thoroughly and maturely discussed in that body. The substance of conflicting claims has been summed up thus: [65]

On the one hand it was urged: It has been clearly settled that the authority of Congress is exclusively domestic; it would be absurd to hold that while the concurrence of the President and two-thirds of the Senate is necessary merely to purchase a bit of foreign terri-

65 *Ibid.*, pp. 340-341.

tory, a simple majority of Congress can admit a foreign nation to the Union as one of our equal States; such a doctrine is dangerous, for a margin of one member in each branch could introduce any number of alien countries and thus totally change the character of the Union; it is an unwarrantable stretch of the constitution to attribute such a power to Congress, for it evidently belongs to the people alone. The other side, however, was maintained with no less vigor, particularly by Woodbury. The power of Congress is not exclusively domestic, it was urged, since it has authority to deal with foreign nations by declaring war, taking action with reference to loans, and regulating commerce; the treaty-making power was given to the President and Senate merely for convenience in doing that work; a two-thirds majority of the Senate meant originally only a margin of four votes, and certainly that was no safer than a clear majority of both Houses; foreign nations would not be admitted to the Union, for an acceptance of the United States constitution would be necessary and only a similar people, like the Texans, would consent to that; no stretch of the constitution is contemplated, for its language is perfectly clear, precise and unlimited. Both sides appealed with more or less effect to the proceedings of the constitutional convention and the opinions of the Fathers; and in reality each side could make an argument that appeared unanswerable.

The passage of this resolution did not annex Texas; it enumerated the conditions upon which it could be admitted as a state —not a territory—into the Union. A second resolution of December 29, 1845, declared that the conditions of the earlier resolution had been accepted and consummated the annexation. A study of contemporary political events and of the final vote on the March resolution leaves one with the conviction that the debates were exercises in rhetoric. Constitutional arguments probably determined no more votes than any other argument. It was party loyalty that carried the day, with Democrats supporting the President, and the Whigs voting in opposition.[66]

66 In the House the vote was 132 to 76. One Whig voted with the majority and two Democrats with the minority. In the Senate, where it passed by a vote of 27 to 25, three Whigs joined with the Democrats to make possible its passage. Smith, cited, pp. 345-347.

No more unfavorable setting could be found for a debate on the precise constitutional issue here discussed than that which surrounded the debate on the annexation of Hawaii. The treaty by which annexation was to be effected never came to a vote in the Senate; the known opposition of a sufficient number of senators made futile an attempt to bring it to a vote. As the nation moved toward war with Spain, the advocates of annexation resorted to the alternative scheme of a joint resolution.[67] A resolution reported favorably by the Senate Foreign Relations Committee in March, 1898—between the sinking of the *Maine* and the declaration of war—was still on the Senate calendar when Dewey's victory at Manila electrified the country. The Hawaiian Islands assumed a larger stature in the eyes of the nation and a closer relationship with them was demanded in order that they might serve as a way-station for the navy in Far Eastern waters.[68] On May 4, three days after Dewey's victory, the House had before it a resolution to annex the Islands. After the Foreign Affairs Committee had heard the testimony of Major General Schofield and of Rear Admiral Walker, Representative Williams (D., Miss.) moved a substitute resolution.

> Resolved . . . That the United States will view as an act of hostility any attempt upon the part of any Government of Europe or Asia to take possession of the Hawaiian Islands, or to exercise, upon any pretext or under any conditions, sovereign authority therein.
>
> 2. That the United States hereby announces to the people of those Islands and to the world their guarantee of the independence

67 In his *Diplomatic Memoirs* (Boston and New York, 1909), John W. Foster regretted the use of a joint resolution "because of its evasion of the constitutional provision and the creation of a bad precedent," II, p. 174. In an address before the National Geographic Society, delivered in Washington on March 26, 1897, he seemed less concerned with the procedural question. "...In a matter which involves the interests and destiny of a great nation of seventy millions of people, no mere technical questions of procedure should be allowed to embarrass our action..."

68 Julius W. Pratt, *Expansionists of 1898* (Baltimore, 1936), p. 319.

of the people of the Hawaiian Islands, and their firm determination to maintain the same.

Nine members—seven Republicans and two Democrats—voted against this proposition while four Democrats supported it. By the same vote the Committee agreed to report favorably the original resolution.[69] On the House floor constitutional issues yielded to those of strategy and economics, national honor and Japanese encroachments. Chairman Hitt did not even touch on the constitutional question.[70] The ranking minority member, Mr. Dinsmore (D., Ark.), sandwiched into his speech of opposition the thought that the Islands could be admitted only as a state, not as a territory. Once the opposition of Speaker Reed had been overcome, the final vote was never in doubt.[71]

Even the Senate debate lacked vigor. Two opposition senators, Bacon and Turley, stressed the surrender of the treaty power by the Senate which was implied in the use of a joint resolution. The former also dwelt upon the distinction between the admission of Hawaii as a territory and of Texas as a state, an act which could be performed constitutionally only by Congress. " The power to acquire foreign territory not for the purpose of making it a State . . . is essentially and necessarily the subject-matter of treaty between two governments." [72] His

69 55th Cong. Minutes, C. F. A. In his report to the House, Chairman Hitt alluded to the acquisition of territory as distinct from the acquisition of a state. After citing the Louisiana Purchase, he referred to the act of August 18, 1856, authorizing American citizens to take possession of unoccupied guano islands. " They are United States territory, subject to our laws. So Midway Island in the Pacific... was occupied, and Congress appropriated $50,000, which was expended trying to create a naval station there. The manifest principle is that the power to acquire territory is an incident of national sovereignty." 55th Cong., 2nd Sess. (1898). H. Rep. 1355. The hearings are also included in this report.

70 Ibid. June 11, 1898. Cong. Rec., pp. 5770-5776.

71 William A. Robinson, Thomas B. Reed, cited, pp. 366-367. The vote in the House was 209 to 91.

72 55th Cong. S. Rep. 681. The majority of the Senate Foreign Relations Committee agreed that " it is the constitutional power of Congress that operates to annex foreign territory."

arguments were lost upon the Senate, where the Republican majority relied upon the strength of its numbers and the fervent nationalism engendered by the war to squelch the minority. As in the House, the political supporters of the President carried through the resolution.

Through the use of a joint resolution in the above instances the President courted the assistance of the House to overcome senatorial opposition sufficient in strength to block the normal treaty-making procedure. In 1919, however, it was the Senate that looked to the House to support it against the President. Unlike the two previous cases, the President was of a political faith different from both the Senate and the House. This, in itself, foreshadowed difficulties. The curtailment of normal party conflicts during the war only intensified them once hostilities ended. The Treaty of Versailles embraced issues, notably the League of Nations, which were the cause for intra-party dispute, especially within the Republican party. Thus, the irreconcilable leaders of that party had to manoeuvre to close the gap in their own ranks at the same time that they carried on their struggle against President Wilson. The acrimony and asperity that characterized the principals in this episode afforded little hope that the plane of debate would be either high or enlightening.[73]

The normal process for terminating a war by a treaty failed when, in November, 1919, the Senate rejected the Treaty of Versailles. When Congress reconvened in December, the Treaty was again discussed, compromises attempted, and finally rejected for the second time in March, 1920. During these months of senatorial palaver the House remained inactive—if not entirely passive—since the Treaty was not before it. With the second rejection, however, it showed concern, not on the question of the Treaty or of the League of Nations, upon which it

73 The most detailed treatment of the debates and issues may be found in D. F. Fleming, *The United States and the League of Nations, 1918-1920* (New York, 1932). A shorter but equally lucid account is W. Stull Holt, *Treaties Defeated by the Senate* (Baltimore, 1933), chap. X.

could not pass judgment, but on the status of the United States vis-à-vis Germany.

" The war thus comes to an end," President Wilson informed Congress on November 11, 1918, by which he meant, of course, that hostilities had ceased, not that a legal termination had been affected. Had the Treaty been accepted by the Senate, the President's simple assertion would have gained no notoriety. But after the March vote, the Republicans sharpened it into a wedge which their members in the House used to cut into the President's powers. The exigencies of the war had concentrated in the President's hands powers that could only be justified by the existence of war. The acts conferring these powers on the President contained a clause specifying the time that their operation should cease. For example, the phrase, " end of the war," used in The Trading with the Enemy Act was deemed to mean " the date of the proclamation of exchange of ratifications of a treaty of peace, unless the President shall, by proclamation, declare a prior date, in which case the date so proclaimed shall be deemed to be the end of the war." [74] The inability of the President and the Senate to resolve their differences excluded the possibility of a treaty settlement. Despite his statement that the war was over, the President showed no disposition to issue a proclamation. The only course left, argued his opponents, was a declaration by Congress. Since Congress by joint resolution " recognized the fact that war had been thrust upon us, so now it becomes the duty of Congress to give official recognition to the fact that the war is ended." [75] The resolution presented to the House specified, therefore, that the date when that resolution became effective shall be " treated as the date of the termination of the war or of the present or existing emergency . . ." Another section, looking to a restoration of reciprocal trade with Germany, stipulated that within forty-five days after the resolution became effective, the German Government must notify the

74 40 *Stat.* 412.
75 66th Cong., 2nd Sess. H. Rep. 801.

President that it has declared a termination of the war and on behalf of itself and its nationals waive any claims it would not have had the right to assert had the United States ratified the Treaty of Versailles. Unless these provisions were met, all commercial and humanitarian transactions were prohibited and a penalty clause was inserted for those who violated them.[76] In brief, the House resolution sought to accomplish two ends: first, within the domestic sphere, to declare the termination of the state of war; and second, within the international sphere, to secure from the German Government a similar declaration on its part under the threat to use congressional regulation of commerce in a discriminatory manner.

There are no extant records of what took place in the Foreign Affairs Committee; the sessions were executive. But on the House floor the Committee members played the leading roles in attacking and defending the President. For that, after all, was what the debates comprised. Constitutional arguments were the means to an end and must, accordingly, be discounted. The opposition, almost solidly Republican, placed the breakdown of the treaty process upon the President. " The President still retains all these (extraordinary) powers and refuses to surrender them unless the Senate yields to his arbitrary view as to the terms and the conditions of the treaty of peace," said Mr. Porter.[77] Since the powers conferred upon him by virtue of a state of war " remain in some mysterious way in the hands of the President until a treaty of peace has been made and proclaimed, and there is no other way to end such a state of war except by a treaty of peace, the President could maintain a

76 *Ibid.* H. J. Res. 327, Sec. 3 and 4. Section 5 read: " That nothing herein contained shall be construed as a waiver by the United States of any rights, privileges, indemnities, reparations, or advantages to which the United States has become entitled under the terms of the armistice signed November 11, 1918, or which were acquired by or are in the possession of the United States by reason of its participation in the war, or otherwise; and all fines, forfeitures, penalties, and seizures imposed or made by the United States are hereby ratified, confirmed, and maintained."

77 66th Cong., 2nd Sess. April 8, 1920. *Cong. Rec.*, p. 3346.

dictatorship just so long as he is able to hold the President's office . . ." The duty of Congress, therefore, was to terminate the state of war.[78] After an examination of the methods of terminating war, the Committee found that in this case " the usual method " (of treaty settlement) had failed; " it becomes the plain duty of Congress to declare the admitted fact that the war is ended." [79] Germany had capitulated and signed the Treaty of Versailles, with no intention or ability to resume hostilities; military hostilities had ceased. The resolution, therefore, recognized an existing situation. While assuming that a treaty between the two nations would ultimately follow, in the making of which the President would be the negotiator for the United States, it sought to work into the legislative framework the terms—admittedly broad—upon which peace could be made.

The minority, almost entirely Democratic, contested this reasoning. Conceding the right of Congress to repeal the special legislation by which the President had increased his powers, it denied the right of Congress " to declare peace, and so far as it seeks to direct the President to issue a proclamation to the German Government, it trenches upon the treaty-making powers, and is not within the power of Congress." [80] It drew its arguments from the discussions of the Constitutional Convention and the decisions of the Supreme Court.[81] Mr. Flood, spokesman for the minority, challenged the sincerity of the proponents by offering a motion to recommit the measure to the Foreign Affairs Committee with instructions to report out an amended version of the resolution. The amended resolution

78 But the resolution failed to name any belligerent but Germany.

79 *Supra*, H. Rep. 801, p. 2. In a note of July 22, 1868, to the Spanish Minister, Secretary Seward observed: " It is certain that a condition of war can be raised without an authoritative declaration of war, and, on the other hand, the situation of peace may be restored by the long suspension of hostilities without a treaty of peace being made." Moore, *Digest*, VII, p. 336.

80 *Ibid.* Part 2 of the report contains the minority views.

81 J. Ribas y Hijo *v.* U. S. "A state of war did not in law cease until the ratification in April, 1899, of the treaty of peace." 194 *U. S.* 315, 323.

would have repealed all the war legislation—as the Republicans desired—but would have omitted all reference to the termination of a state of war. After this was voted down, 171 to 222, the original resolution passed the House.

The amendments added by the Senate were in the nature of perfecting amendments. In addition to terminating the state of war with Germany, provision was made for the *repeal* of the resolution of April 6, 1917, and similarly, the repeal of the resolution of December 7, 1917, declaring war against Austria-Hungary. The sections dealing with trade relations with Germany under certain conditions and the penalties incurred for their violation were stricken out and the President was requested to open negotiations with the former belligerents. A new section was inserted, prohibiting the disposition of the property of the German Government or its nationals then in the possession of the United States until a peace treaty had been ratified and full reparation made to all persons owing allegiance to the United States for loss, damage, or injury to their persons or property caused by the German Government or its nationals.[82] Under ordinary circumstances, Mr. Porter admitted, the two Houses would send the measure to a conference committee to iron out the differences. "But such action would delay the passage of the resolution and probably subject it to a filibuster in the Senate on the conference report." The alternative, therefore, was to have the House accept the Senate's amended resolution, which it did by a vote of 228 to 130.[83] The hopelessness of the Democratic cause may be gathered from the fact that that party failed to use its allotted time in the debate preceding acceptance of the Senate's amended resolution.

President Wilson vetoed the resolution on May 27, 1920.[84] The message he sent to Congress was most disappointing to those who hoped for a resounding challenge to congressional

82 66th Cong., 2nd Sess. S. Rep. 568. The resolution, as amended, passed the Senate, 43 to 38, on May 15, 1920.

83 *Ibid.* May 21, 1920. *Cong. Rec.*, p. 7424.

84 *Ibid.* May 27, 1920, p. 7747.

usurpation of executive functions. No mention was made of this point. Instead, he dwelt upon the moral issue which had brought the United States into the conflict and lamented that " the resolution seeks to establish peace with the German Empire without exacting from the German Government any action by way of setting right the infinite wrongs which it did to the peoples whom it attacked and whom we professed it our purpose to assist when we entered the war . . ." To his supporters it must have come as a mournful message from a weary man rather than a vigorous defense by a student of constitutional government. But they stood by him and when the House attempted to override his veto, 152 opposed the move as against 220 in support, 28 short of the requisite two-thirds.[85] Had the resolution passed both Houses over the veto, would it have hampered the President in his conduct of foreign policy? Defeated politically, there was nothing Congress could do in the nature of domestic reprisals that would alter his position on this phase of foreign policy. The trade embargo inserted by the House had been stricken out by the Senate. Even had that provision remained in the resolution, the absence of trade relations between Germany and the United States would have made it fatuous. The initiative rested with the President. But the irreconcilable differences between him and Congress made futile any move that would require the consent of one or both branches of Congress.[86]

President Harding, a tractable personality with no clear convictions on foreign policy, called Congress into special session shortly after his inauguration. He invited Congress " to establish a state of technical peace without further delay " and

85 *Ibid.* May 28, 1920, pp. 7805-7809.

86 Early in 1921, President Wilson signed a joint resolution declaring " that certain acts of Congress, joint resolutions and proclamations shall be construed as if the war had ended and the present or existing emergency expired." This was the object of Mr. Flood's earlier motion to recommit H. J. Res. 327 to the Committee on Foreign Affairs. 41 *Stat.* 1359. By supporting this measure the Republicans eliminated one of their chief grievances against the President.

promised his approval of " a declaratory resolution of Congress to that effect with the qualifications essential to protect all our rights . . . Such a resolution should do no more than thus declare the state of peace which all America craves . . ." [87] The Senate acted first, Mr. Knox introducing a joint resolution similar to the amended one which had failed to pass over the President's veto in the previous Congress.[88] When it reached the House, Mr. Porter, now a strong believer in presidential prerogatives in foreign affairs, brought out of the Foreign Affairs Committee a substitute resolution.[89] This omitted all reference to a repeal of the original resolutions of 1917 and followed the President's request for a simple declaratory resolution announcing that the state of war " is hereby at an end." The justification for this change in terminology lay in the fact that the 1917 resolution recognized the existence of a state of war which " Germany had thrust upon us." Said Mr. Porter: " The ' finding of fact ' that a state of war existed is now a matter of history. It is an eternal record of fact beyond the power of Congress to repeal, modify or limit." [90] The Senate resolution was also objectionable because it sought to specify the terms of the treaty to be concluded with the enemy states, an invasion of the executive's function. The Committee's amendment therefore struck out these terms and substituted a paragraph in accord with the President's request for a statement " essential to protect all our rights." [91] After a conference between the two Houses, the Senate yielded its position and the House version, with slight alterations, received the President's assent.[92]

87 67th Cong., 1st Sess. April 12, 1921. *Cong. Rec.*, p. 175.

88 *Ibid.* S. Rep. 2.

89 H. Rep. 148.

90 *Ibid.* June 11, 1921. *Cong. Rec.*, p. 2450.

91 *Ibid.* H. Rep. 237. Neither Senator Hitchcock nor Representative Flood, the Democratic members of the Conference Committee, signed the report.

92 July 2, 1921. 42 *Stat.* 105.

So much of the debate was of a vapid character that one must look less to the arguments and more to the political complexion that pervaded the domestic scene. After the Versailles Treaty was rejected by the Senate, President Wilson's leadership in foreign policy lapsed. Constitutionally incapable of assuming direction, Congress tried to use the legislative process to circumvent the President. Whatever the basis for differences between the Democratic President and the Republican Congress —constitutional, partisan, or personal—the cleavage was sharp. Such was not the case when President Harding took office. When he invited Congress to pass a resolution which would include " the qualifications essential to protect all our rights," he sought political endorsement for the exercise of a constitutional function. Mr. Porter's argument that the Senate resolution invaded the executive's domain while that of the House did not, has little merit. The real difference between the two resolutions lay in the nature of the rights each sought to protect. The House, resolution, adopted with Senate additions, specified those rights. A study of the published correspondence leading up to the treaty with Germany shows that this resolution loomed large in the negotiations.[93] Secretary Hughes wrote to Commissioner Dresel at Berlin, August 19, 1921 : [94]

If Germany desires speedily to resume diplomatic relations and to avoid delays which can in no possible way be profitable to her, no question should be raised respecting the reference in the proposed treaty to the peace resolution. Congress made that resolution the subject of extended consideration, and there could be no agreement that is inconsistent therewith . . . The important consideration is now that Germany would stand to gain nothing by an opposition to the provision of the proposed treaty which refers to the peace resolution; on the other hand, disagreement with the resolution of Congress would give rise to misunderstanding and to protracted controversy.

93 *Foreign Relations of the United States, 1921*, II, pp. 1-35, esp. pp. 6, 18, 19, 20.

94 *Ibid.*, pp. 18-19.

The preamble to the treaty itself contains the terms of the resolution. Nor can it be said that the full implications of any congressional expression were not known to President Harding. While he was still a senator from Ohio, he voted for the original resolution which President Wilson vetoed.

When one recalls the stand taken by many House Republicans, especially those on the Foreign Affairs Committee, on the issue of naval disarmament, explanations become more tenuous. The fact that both the peace resolution and the question of naval disarmament were discussed at the same time accentuates the contrast. As previously stated on this latter subject, it was the feeling of Mr. Porter and his Republican colleagues that the President needed no direction; a resolution of concurrence was sufficient.[95] The Borah amendment which was ultimately adopted was opposed because it was an encroachment upon the executive's functions. The President himself opposed it on this ground. Although the President yielded in the face of Senate opposition and subsequently expressed indifference to the form which congressional expression took on naval disarmament, one searches with difficulty for an element of consistency in the action both of the President and his Republican supporters. Perhaps an explanation may be found in the multiple problems that faced the nation and the public reaction to them. The readjustment of the wartime economy to the conditions of peace was the first task to which the administration had to address itself. One step in this direction was the curtailment of naval expenditures. Public opinion seized on the Borah amendment as the answer to the threatened Anglo-American naval rivalry and, under pressure from their constituents, both Houses readily adopted it.[96] Such public expressions were not mani-

95 *Supra*, pp. 108-109.

96 Senator Pomerene (D., Ohio) alleged that in the Senate cloakrooms the Borah amendment was considered an attempt to tie the President's hands. "For a long time we were of the opinion that the Borah resolution was going to be overwhelmingly defeated in the Senate; but after an exchange of thought, and perhaps after hearing from home, it was decided that there

fested in the technical question of the proper procedure for the termination of the war. Once the Treaty of Versailles was removed from the political scene, the precise terms of peace were not the subject of popular discussion. Hence Congress was able to stamp its design into the peace negotiations without fear of political repercussions. The President's complacency on this subject made the solution easier. The interpretation to be placed upon the role of Congress is not easy; it is not even clear how Congress itself regarded the outcome. In the Committee files there is evidence that Mr. Porter interpreted the passage of the peace resolution as a triumph for the constitutional right of Congress to terminate war. Whether this view was shared by his colleagues cannot be ascertained.[97]

Sandwiched among the more engrossing questions of disarmament and Latin American relations in the 1920's, the legalistic debates on American adherence to the World Court were handicapped in seeking to win popular attention. Lacking dramatic possibilities and devoid of partisanship, they received little publicity. Senate discussions were sporadic and slow, frequently involved and generally uninspiring. In so far as one can detect any cleavage it was between the President and the House on the one hand and the Senate on the other. Actually the Senate itself contained many members favorable to the Court. But these were overshadowed by a small but influential group who exhibited toward the Court the attitude they had shown toward the League of Nations. It was not unusual to link the two together in an effort to demonstrate the subservience of the Court to the League. Unable to stifle debate entirely, the opponents of membership gave the protocols the senatorial equivalent of the kiss of death by adding qualifying reservations. This necessi-

would be no opposition whatsoever to it, and there was not a single Senator who had the courage to record his vote against it." 67th Cong., 1st Sess. June 30, 1921. *Cong. Rec.*, p. 3284.

97 67th Cong. Files, C. F. A.

tated international conferences to secure agreement; but the proposed agreement only evoked additional reservations.[98]

Through all these manoeuvres the House had assumed that the Senate ultimately would act favorably. Fresh from an election the House, in 1925, saw no harm in endorsing the Court and expressing an earnest desire that the United States give early adherence to the protocol. This was passed by a vote of 303 to 28.[99] Nothing further was done by the House until after the London Naval Conference when public opinion was moved by the need for more affirmative steps to secure peace. Various members of the Foreign Affairs Committee were in touch with distinguished persons in private life who were anxious to see the United States a member of the Court. As the refractory attitude of the Senate became more evident, they looked to the House to initiate a measure that would achieve the purpose. Instead of a resolution providing for membership in the Court —which would have raised the constitutional question of intrusion in the treaty-making process—Mr. Linthicum, chairman of the Foreign Affairs Committee, sponsored a joint resolution authorizing the appropriation of a specific sum as the United States' share of the Court's expenses for the year 1932.[100]

The most troublesome phase of this simple proposition centered, not around the appropriation itself, but around the implications attendant upon the appropriation. In short, would the enactment of this measure achieve the same result as the Senate's favorable vote on the protocols of adherence to the Court? The thesis developed during the testimony of distinguished witnesses was that the Linthicum resolution would not

98 The details of the World Court struggle within the United States may be found in Charles P. Howland, *Survey of American Foreign Relations, 1929* (New Haven, 1929), pp. 333-386, or Quincy Wright, *The United States and the Permanent Court of International Justice,* International Conciliation, no. 232, September, 1927.

99 68th Cong., 2nd Sess. H. Rep. 1569.

100 72nd Cong., 1st Sess. (1932). H. Rep. 1628. The Committee amended the original resolution providing for an appropriation to have it read " authorizing an appropriation." See *supra,* p. 136.

in itself put the United States in the World Court. But it would put " the United States back of, that is, in support of the court, by action of legislation." [101] A careful reading of the hearings leaves little room for doubt that proponents of the Court looked upon this resolution as a means of easing the United States into the Court through the House's coordinate power over appropriations, leaving to the Senate the task of setting up whatever safeguards it desired. Running through the testimony is a moral note, based upon the erroneous notion that the American judge on the Court was a representative of the United States. " It is absolutely unfair, it is un-American, for us to allow *our* judge to be a part of this great tribunal and to let other nations pay those expenses and not bear our proportion," said Mr. Linthicum.[102] The discussions on the Court, however, suffered nothing in comparison with those on Texas, Hawaii, or the peace resolution; on the contrary, there was an absence of pettifogging and a presence of judicious inquiry, attributable, at least in part, to the transcendence of party lines. The resolution was reported too late for consideration by the House in the spring of 1932. Before the next session met in December, the country had passed through a strenuous presidential campaign in which domestic issues obliterated foreign affairs. Hence the House never had the opportunity to pass judgment on this resolution.

The novelty of the step proposed commands attention. It was not the purpose of the resolution to impair the plenary power entrusted by the Constitution to the President and the Senate in the conclusion of treaties. While the successful precedents of Texas and Hawaii suggested the incorporation in a joint resolution of the terms embraced in the proposed treaty, the Committee preferred to rest its case upon a more impregnable position. The role of Congress in appropriations admitted of no debate. Congress had frequently appropriated money

101 Charles K. Burdick of Cornell Law School. 72nd Cong., 1st Sess. Hearings on H. J. Res. 378, *Permanent Court of International Justice*, Part I, p. 18.

102 *Ibid.* Part 3, p. 14.

pursuant to treaty obligations. Could it reverse the process and appropriate money in anticipation of the conclusion of a treaty? To answer this in the negative would imply a limitation of the appropriation power. The constitutionality of this legislation cannot be successfully challenged. From the viewpoint of policy, as distinct from law, a further examination is necessary. Secretary Stimson, in a letter of May 25, 1932, to Chairman Linthicum, wrote in part: [103]

If the early approval of these protocols [by the Senate] in some satisfactory form does not eventuate and the appropriation contemplated by your resolution is approved by both Houses of Congress, I should feel free to consider with the Senate the question of whether this Government might not with the consent of the court be able to submit to the court some types of international litigation which we are now forced to submit to special arbitrations . . .

The Secretary pointed out the saving in expense and the increased efficiency that would come from the submission to the Court of claims of American citizens against foreign governments. " Under the court's charter we have the right, although not a member of the court, to submit with the consent of the Senate, such cases to its jurisdiction." Mr. Stimson's language was misleading since " the court's charter " made no reference to senatorial consent as a requisite for submission of cases to the Court. Apart from this, several loopholes remain by which the President has effected settlements with foreign governments without reference to the Senate. In the case of claims of American citizens against a foreign government he alone may choose the time and method of seeking settlement. An executive agreement may accomplish this purpose.[104] The Senate comes into

103 *Ibid.* Part IV, p. 33.

104 The executive agreement with Egypt, providing for the arbitration of the claim of George J. Salem, is an example. State Department, *Executive Agreement Series, no. 33*, 1932. Publication no. 297. Also, Arbitration of Claim of Charles J. Harrah, based upon an executive agreement with Cuba. State Department, *Arbitration Series, no. 1*, 1929. Publication no. 75.

the picture only when a treaty is entered into to decide the method of settlement. The converse of this proposition—where a foreign government is the claimant against the United States —may be handled in a similar manner except that an award requiring the payment of money by the United States would require an appropriation. Congressional power over appropriations would be a deterrent to the use of this method. A compromis embodied in a treaty and requiring the submission of disputes to the Court would have to have the Senate's approval. If the Senate was unable to muster a two-thirds vote for approval of the protocols by which the United States would secure membership in the Court, it would appear reasonable to suppose that a similar vote would not be forthcoming for a particular treaty calling for submission of a case to the Court. In the light of the Senate's previous attitude, this supposition would not necessarily be correct. The Senate has been reluctant to approve treaties providing for settlement by judicial means which embrace all future disputes. This hesitancy arises from the fear that questions of a domestic nature, e. g. the Monroe Doctrine, immigration, and the debts of Southern states, would be brought before an international body without the Senate's prior consent.[105] This attitude has not been evident, however, in treaties dealing with a particular issue. Considered from these angles, it would have seemed desirable, in 1932, to revert to the technique used in the cases of Texas, Hawaii, and the peace resolution of 1921. A direct vote on the joint resolution for American membership in the Court would have been clear and precise, leaving no room for an accusation of equivocation.

105 See 62nd Cong., 1st Sess. (1911). S. Doc. 98, Report of the Committee on Foreign Relations, *General Arbitration Treaties with Great Britain and France*, signed on August 3, 1911. Mr. Lodge, author of the majority report, wrote, in part: " To take from the Senate, in any degree or by any measure, the power of saying whether a given question is one for arbitration or not is to destroy the power of the Senate on the most important point to be decided in connection with differences arising with any other nation."

CHAPTER VI

ARMS EMBARGO

ALTHOUGH the United States Government, in 1919, refused to approve the Saint-Germain Convention for the Control of the Trade in Arms and Ammunition, it did not relinquish its interest in the control of the arms traffic. At the request of the State Department, Congress, in 1922, extended the arms embargo resolution of 1912 to prevent the shipment of arms to nations engaged in civil war not only in Latin America but also in China.[1] The problem, however, was too far-reaching to be dealt with successfully by domestic legislation. As American relations with the League of Nations became more cordial, the administration was not averse to participation " in the proceedings of a committee established by the League to consider the subject and finally in the Conference which was called to consider the draft treaty elaborated by the experts in the commission." [2] Among the more active delegates was the chairman of the American delegation, Mr. Burton of Ohio, a member of the Foreign Affairs Committee. The details and results of the Conference need not divert us except in so far as they helped shape domestic measures. The first of five categories into which arms, ammunition, and implements of war were divided embraced those " exclusively designed and intended for land, sea or aerial warfare." Permission by the

1 Both the 1912 and 1922 resolutions were considered in the House by the Committee on Interstate and Foreign Commerce. The 1922 resolution reads: " That whenever the President finds that in any American country, or in any country in which the United States exercises extraterritorial jurisdiction, conditions of domestic violence exist, which are or may be promoted by the use of arms, or munitions of war procured from the United States, and makes proclamation thereof, it shall be unlawful to export, except under such limitations and exceptions as the President prescribes, any arms or munitions of war from any place in the United States to such country until otherwise ordered by the President or by Congress." 42 *Stat.* 361.

2 Joseph P. Chamberlain, " The Embargo Resolutions and Neutrality," *International Conciliation*, June, 1929, no. 251, p. 21.

signatory governments to export these articles was to be granted only where they were intended " for a direct supply to the government of the importing State " or to its political subdivisions. Supervision of arms shipments was entrusted to each of the signatories. Article 33 provided, however, for the suspension of supervision and publicity " in time of war." Delegates from arms-importing states noted that the burden of publicity fell upon those states while non-importing states were not required to give publicity to the manufacture of arms. To this observation Mr. Burton responded that the United States favored a convention providing for complete publicity of manufacture as well as traffic in arms.[3]

Meanwhile, two other pertinent approaches to the problem of peaceful adjustment of international disputes were in the offing. The first, the League of Nations Preparatory Commission to consider questions of reduction and limitation of armaments, started its deliberations in 1926. The other, looking to the renunciation of war as an instrument of national policy, was initiated with an exchange of views between France and the United States in the spring of 1927 and culminated in the Kellogg-Briand Pact of August 27, 1928.

Acting apparently on the assumption that legislative expression would hasten to a favorable conclusion these latter negotiations, Mr. Burton introduced, on December 5, 1927, a declaration of policy to prohibit the exportation of arms, munitions, or implements of war " to any country which engages in aggressive warfare against any other country in violation of a treaty, convention, or other agreement to resort to arbitration or other peaceful means for the settlement of international controversies." [4] Determination of the aggressor was left to the Pres-

3 *Proceedings of Conference for Supervision of International Trade in Arms and Ammunition and in Implements of War*, League of Nations Document: A.13.1925.IX, 192. The Convention was submitted to the Senate on January 12, 1926. That body gave its advice and consent on February 21, 1935, and the President ratified it, with reservations, June 21, 1935.

4 70th Cong., 1st Sess. H. J. Res. 1.

ident and all exports to an aggressor were unlawful " until otherwise proclaimed by the President, or provided by Act of Congress." The Foreign Affairs Committee, while sympathetic to legislation to control the arms traffic, did not favor the current concept of selecting an aggressor. As a result of executive discussions within the Committee, Mr. Burton reintroduced his joint resolution early in 1928. In this version the export prohibition applied not to an aggressor but " to any nation which is engaged in war with another." Once the President had proclaimed that certain nations were at war, exports of arms to them were unlawful " except by the consent of Congress," a phrase that would permit Congress to extend aid to one belligerent, possibly to both, should public sentiment so desire.[5] The Burton resolution, therefore, complemented both the 1925 Geneva agreement, signed by the United States, and the earlier domestic legislation. By making provision for export prohibition during wartime it made up the deficiency of the Geneva Convention whose terms ceased to apply when war was in progress.[6] It extended the 1922 embargo to all nations engaged in international conflict.

After perfecting the phraseology, the Committee unanimously accorded to Mr. Burton the honor of reporting the measure to the House. It was the apparent assumption of the Committee that, in view of the anti-war spirit of the country, there would be no protracted debate. But as the contents of the report and the resolution were studied, representatives outside the Committee began to have misgivings as to its purpose. The American Legion started a campaign against it and on several occasions members denounced it before the House.[7] This was one of those rare moments when a committee, acting unanimously, found itself attacked with increasing bitterness

5 *Ibid.* H. J. Res. 183. Hearings on *Exportation of Arms, Munitions or Implements of War to Belligerent Nations*, p. 134.

6 Chamberlain, p. 127.

7 70th Cong., 1st Sess. Remarks of Mr. Fish, *Cong. Rec.*, March 12, 1928, p. 4560.

by members of both parties for failing to ascertain the opinion of the executive departments. As previously noted, members of both the Military Affairs and the Naval Affairs Committees expressed an interest in the resolution and requested that hearings be held—even though the bill had already been reported.[8] Realizing the increased opposition to the resolution, the Foreign Affairs Committee acquiesced. Unlike other hearings which sought to elicit improvement in measures, the Committee adopted a defensive attitude since it had already committed itself to the resolution.

A careful reading of the hearings leaves the impression that the proponents and opponents did not find much common ground on which to argue the resolution. Secretary of the Navy Wilbur and Secretary of War Davis weighed the internal effects of its passage, contending in brief, that the measure would hamper private manufacture of arms in this country. Foreign nations, finding their munitions supply cut off when they most needed weapons, would purchase from those countries that could supply them during war as well as peace. The only representative of a " pressure group " to appear, Mr. Herty of the Chemical Foundation, also felt that " the American [chemical] industry would suffer at the expense of the foreign industry " if the resolution were enacted into law.[9] Committee members, on the other hand, reverted to the theme that profits from traffic in arms were somehow immoral and out of step with the efforts being taken to circumscribe war. Moreover, these self-imposed regulations would serve as a model for adoption by other nations so that " war would become practically impossible." [10]

The discussion on Mr. Burton's resolution did not pose sharply the question of presidential discretion. The President's issuance of a neutrality proclamation upon the outbreak of a

8 *Supra*, p. 41.

9 Hearings, cited, p. 39.

10 *Ibid.*, p. 134, remarks of Mr. Burton.

war would *ipso facto* bring into operation the terms of the resolution; upon that point there was no discretion. Nor could the President discriminate as between an aggressor and defender nation. In the lifting of the embargo against one or all belligerents, Congress retained jurisdiction.[11] Although Secretary Kellogg gave it as his opinion that the embargo could be lifted during a war, " provided such action by Congress applied equally to all the parties to a war," it was the outspoken contention of several members that the embargo could be lifted against one adversary " to protect the weaker nations." [12] Thus, instead of selecting the aggressor from the moment war started, the embargo would be applicable to all belligerents and be modified in favor of some at the discretion of Congress. In short, Congress instead of the President would decide the aggressor, a solution pleasing to Mr. Porter because it seemed to put control in the hands of Congress instead of the munitions makers.[13]

After the termination of the hearings, it was apparent that congressional opinion was sharply divided on the contents of the Burton resolution. To endeavor to push it through in the few remaining weeks of the session would only have meant its defeat. When Congress reassembled in December of that year, the Burton resolution was dropped in favor of Mr. Porter's resolu-

11 70th Cong., 1st Sess. H. Rep. 492 on H. J. Res. 183. " While Congress undoubtedly would have the right to suspend or repeal the prohibitions enumerated in the resolution, it is thought best to make specific mention of the fact that 'by the consent of Congress' the inhibition of the resolution may be removed. This would mean that, as to any or all the belligerents, Congress could remove the prohibition."

12 Hearings, cited, pp. 78-79; 33. In addressing the House on this resolution Mr. Moore (D., Va.), a member of the Committee, remarked that if Congress should lift the embargo against some belligerent, " our Government might be charged with practically waging war against the adversary belligerent; the reply is that we are strong enough to risk any such possibility, and that we must not forever take counsel of our apprehension and fears if we are to exert ourselves effectively for the promotion of peace." 70th Cong., 1st Sess. February 20, 1928. *Cong. Rec.*, p. 3268.

13 Hearings, p. 34.

tion, a reversion in part to Mr. Burton's original resolution of choosing the aggressor.[14] The resolution provided:

That whenever the President finds that in any country conditions of domestic violence or of international conflict exist or are threatened, which are or may be promoted by the use of arms or munitions of war procured from the United States, and makes proclamation thereof, it shall be unlawful to export, except under such limitations and exceptions as the President prescribes, any arms or munitions of war from any place in the United States to such country until otherwise ordered by the President or by Congress.[15]

The scope of the resolution was greater than that contemplated in Mr. Burton's resolution since its application did not depend upon a declaration of war but could be invoked when, in the judgment of the President, international wars or domestic violence threatened. It was within the President's power to decide the nations against whom its terms were applicable. In the words of Mr. Porter, " this resolution is intended to put the control of the munitions traffic in the hands of the President, who is fully informed as to conditions in foreign countries and can exercise this power with all the facts before him, as there are no two cases alike." [16] In his view the controversy between Bolivia and Paraguay, then nearing a critical stage, would require the President's action while Congress was not in session.

Although Secretary Kellogg saw no objection to the resolution, his reserved comments and pointed references to the unneutral conduct that might be engendered by its application against a particular country engaged in an international conflict, tempered the enthusiasm of the Committee to push the resolution in the two remaining weeks of the short session.[17]

14 In the interim between the first and second sessions of Congress the Kellogg Pact had been concluded.

15 70th Cong. (1929). H. J. Res. 416.

16 70th Cong. Files, C. F. A.

17 70th Cong., 2nd Sess. Hearings on H. J. Res. 416, *Prohibiting the Exportation of Arms or Munitions of War from the United States to Certain Countries.*

It was agreed that further hearings were desirable to which " some outstanding or prominent witnesses " should be invited. Public sentiment, it was felt, had not yet crystallized and until it had become more articulate, Congress would show little interest in passing the resolution.[18]

From the confusion of thought centering around the two resolutions, some observations may be advanced. First, the Committee was more interested in curbing the traffic in arms— the genesis of both resolutions—than in maintaining a position of neutrality as understood by the accepted principles of international law. Second, the views of the Committee were not the views of the House. From the fragmentary remarks made on the floor, sentiment within the House was skeptical of, if not hostile to, the resolutions, especially the Burton resolution. Except for the endorsement by several small pressure groups, as the League of Nations Non-Partisan Association, public sentiment was inarticulate and did not influence the individual members. [19] Third, the Committee displayed no partisanship on the matter of presidential discretion, a hotly debated point less than a decade later. But there is no evidence to show that President

18 *Ibid.* Minutes, C. F. A. Senator Capper introduced a joint resolution on February 11, 1929, making it unlawful to export arms to a nation which the President declares to have violated the terms of the Kellogg Pact. 70th Cong., 2nd Sess. S. J. Res. 215. It was introduced, he stated, " mainly for the purpose of starting a general discussion and study of the important questions involved, so as to form a background for intelligent handling of the question by Congress next winter." *Ibid.* February 27, 1929. *Cong. Rec.,* p. 4581.

19 H. Res. 264, introduced by Mr. Fish, expressed the House's approval of the Kellogg Pact and the willingness of that body " to participate in the formulation and enactment of legislation to effect the purpose of said general pact." 70th Cong., 2nd Sess. December 14, 1928. Mr. Fish explained that one of the reasons for introducing the resolution was to correct the current impression that the Pact impaired or limited the constitutional power of the House to declare war as a part of the Congress of the United States. Chairman Porter preferred " not . . . to do anything that is going to impinge on the prerogative of the Senate . . . Any action we might take is of no force or effect that I can see." Files, C. F. A. A motion to report out the resolution resulted in a tie vote and was therefore lost. Minutes, C. F. A.

Coolidge sought a legislative increase in his powers. The opposition of several of his cabinet would indicate, in fact, that he did not look with favor upon the Burton resolution.[20] Finally, having determined to take control of the munitions traffic out of the hands of the manufacturers, the Committee vacillated between what it termed " congressional control " and presidential control. In either case, in sharp contrast to the debates of a later period, the implications of its decision on this fundamental point caused hardly a ripple of discussion.

The Seventy-first Congress—1929 to 1931—was preoccupied with checking the domestic economic crisis. Abroad the downward trend was even more apparent for it brought in its train political alterations that disturbed the post-war structure. Foreign affairs were pushed aside in favor of domestic matters. For the Committee on Foreign Affairs this was the most inactive Congress since the World War; no major legislation came before it for its consideration.[21] When, however, the Seventy-second Congress met late in 1931, the Sino-Japanese " incident " was menacing the peace of the Far East. In a memorandum to the Japanese Foreign Minister, Baron Shidehara, Secretary Stimson voiced the concern of the United States over the situation created by the Japanese invasion of Manchuria. " It brings into question at once the meaning of certain provisions of agreements, such as the nine powers treaty of February 6, 1922, and the Kellogg-Briand pact." [22] Mr. Stimson did more than remind Japan of the commitments embodied in these two documents.[23] He sought to harmonize American policy in the

20 Senator Capper's resolution of February, 1929, S. J. Res. 215, gave the President the right to impose an embargo upon any nation violating the Kellogg Pact, the President determining the aggressor. American nationals would " not be protected by their Government in giving aid and comfort to a nation which has committed a breach of the said treaty."

21 Only three resolutions touching on the arms export question came before the Committee in the Seventy-first Congress.

22 72nd Cong., 1st Sess. (1932). S. Doc. 55, *Conditions in Manchuria*, p. 5.

23 When the League failed to take vigorous action, Secretary Stimson dispatched identic notes to Japan and China on January 7, 1932, in which

Far East with that of the League of Nations and thus to implement the Pact by means of collective security.

Such efforts were consonant with prevailing sentiment in this country and found some support in congressional circles, even among members of the Democratic majority in the House. Without much preliminary thought to the consequences or to the application in areas other than the Far East, several measures were introduced with a view to influencing the administration's Far Eastern policy. One of these, introduced by Mr. Morton Hull, a Committee member, prohibited the export and import of " any articles of merchandise whatsoever " and the making of loans or the granting of credit to any nation declared by the President to have violated the Kellogg Pact.[24] Another approach was that found in the resolution offered by Mr. Fish, also a member of the Committee and an opponent of presidential discretion in the application of legislative acts pertaining to foreign affairs.[25] His resolution, previously introduced in the Seventy-first Congress, prohibited the export of arms, munitions, or implements of war " to any nation which is engaged in war with another." The President's issuance of a neutrality proclamation would bring the act into operation.[26] Aware of the

he declared that the United States " does not intend to recognize any situation, treaty, or agreement which may be brought about by means contrary to the covenants and obligations of the Pact of Paris . . ." Ibid., pp. 53-54. See, Henry L. Stimson, The Far Eastern Crisis (New York, 1936) ; cf. A. Whitney Griswold, The Far Eastern Policy of the United States (New York, 1938), p. 410 f.

24 72nd Cong., 1st Sess. H. J. Res. 53.

25 Ibid. H. J. Res. 137.

26 Section two stipulated that upon the issuance of a neutrality proclamation by the President " it shall be unlawful, except by the consent of the Congress, to export or attempt to export any arms, munitions, or implements of war from any place in the United States or any possession thereof, to the territory of either belligerent or to any place if the ultimate destination of such arms, munitions, or implements of war is within the territory of either belligerent or any military or naval force of either belligerent." To clarify the phrase on arms, Mr. Fish not only included twelve specific categories of arms, ammunition, and munitions of war, but

far-reaching effects that either of these resolutions, if adopted, would have on foreign policy, but uncertain how either of them would fit in with the administration's policy, the Committee voted that a subcommittee of two visit the State Department to ascertain its views.[27] Of these conversations there is no record. But on February 2, 1932, a departmental communication was forwarded to the Committee, suggesting that passage of the Hull resolution was inadvisable.[28] Conditions in the Far East were so fluid that the inevitable debate preceding final passage would complicate an already delicate situation. Nor did the Fish resolution win the Department's approval. As interpreted by the latter, the resolution sought merely to extend the 1922 resolution beyond the conditions of " domestic violence " and beyond its application to particular countries. These objections could best be accomplished by a resolution analogous to that of the 1922 act. Since Mr. Fish's resolution was aimed to curtail presidential discretion, an extension of the 1922 resolution with its broad grant of power to the President would not have met his objective. Mr. Fish immediately countered with a resolution amending that of 1922, with the important modification that the finding of conditions of domestic violence or of international conflict could be made not only by the President but by Congress as well.

While this resolution was pending before the Committee, the Conference for the Reduction and Limitation of Armaments had convened in Geneva (February, 1932). Stimulated by the many proposals advanced by the delegates to handle this complex subject, several members of the Committee thought it appropriate that the Conference consider prohibitions on the sale of arms. Mr. Fish incorporated this idea in a resolution " requesting " the American delegates to the Geneva Conference

specifically excluded " foodstuffs, oil, coal, cotton, wool, leather, copper, lead, zinc, iron, lumber, automobiles or other manufactured articles not commonly or commercially known as arms munitions, or implements of war."

27 72nd Cong. Minutes. C. F. A.

28 Ibid. Files, C. F. A.

to "propose a multilateral agreement renouncing the sale or export of arms . . . to any foreign nations in accordance with the intent and purpose of the Kellogg-Briand pact . . ."[29] Mindful that the Conference had before it enough conflicting viewpoints, some members doubted the wisdom of adding to its agenda a proposal that might only stimulate arms production in some nations. One member remarked:

> I am a little inclined to think that if we instruct our delegates to make a proposal of that sort and they make other proposals for which there might be some hope, they would be received in the light of this one, they will say the Americans are proposing things they know there is no hope of getting and it would diminish the weight of other proposals they might make.[30]

The State Department, while not endorsing it, had no objection to its adoption, knowing that it did not bind the President. Moreover, it was an expression of opinion by Congress upon which the Department could not comment with propriety. Nowhere was there a careful analysis of the resolution and the relation it bore to the questions being discussed at Geneva. It was assumed that the American delegation would advance the proposal and win support for it by pointing to the resolution of Congress. The report, recommending its passage by the House, stressed that point.[31] "It is natural . . . for foreign statesmen to be suspicious of the attitude of the Congress of the United States which is not always in accord with the suggestions made by American delegates. The passage of this joint resolution would obviate that difficulty." There is no way to determine the sense of the House on this resolution since it was never reached on the House Calendar. In view of the

29 72nd Cong., 1st Sess. H. J. Res. 282.

30 *Ibid*. Minutes, C. F. A. The resolution received the support of various peace organizations, and during the brief hearings, Miss Dorothy Detzer of the Women's International League endorsed it. The hearings were not published.

31 *Ibid*. H. Rep. 941.

difficulties of the Conference in deciding categories of aggressive weapons and the confusion attendant upon President Hoover's proposal for a one-third reduction in armaments, it is extremely doubtful whether the Conference would have given attention to another complicating problem.[32]

Not until January, 1933, did President Hoover call upon Congress for legislation that would support Secretary Stimson's concept of collective security. The League was then engaged in discussing the Lytton Report, while in South America the Chaco war was entering a serious phase. " Recent events have emphasized the urgent need of more authority to the Executive in control of the shipment of arms from the United States for military purposes," declared the President. Should the Senate fail to " ratify " the 1925 Geneva Convention, he urged that " legislation should be passed conferring upon the President authority in his discretion to limit or forbid shipment of arms for military purposes in cases where special undertakings of cooperation can be secured with the principal arms manufacturing nations." [33] Both Chairman Borah of the Senate Foreign

[32] For the background of the disarmament question see Denys P. Myers, *World Disarmament: Its Problems and Prospects* (Boston, 1932). The best history of the Disarmament Conference is J. W. Wheeler-Bennett, *Pipe Dreams of Peace* (New York, 1935).

While the Committee was formulating its views on Mr. Fish's resolution, Mr. Morton Hull, still thinking in terms of the Far Eastern conflict, drafted a resolution to penalize Japan. In place of the broad trade prohibitions of his earlier resolution, his new measure was confined to prohibiting "the granting of any loan or the extension of credit " to a state (and its nationals) declared by the President to be engaged in an international conflict in violation of the Kellogg Pact. The witnesses he produced in support of his resolution analyzed the economic weakness of Japan as well as the political situation of that country. Since discretion in its application was granted the President, the executive branch saw no objection to its passage although no examination had been made of the banking and credit problems that would thereby be involved. Despite the overwhelming pro-Chinese sentiment of the Committee, most of the members showed little interest in the resolution.

[33] Secretary Stimson, in urging President Hoover to recommend to Congress legislation conferring " upon the President authority in his discretion to limit or forbid, in cooperation with other producing nations, the shipment

Relations Committee and Chairman McReynolds of the House Foreign Affairs Committee introduced identical measures in their respective bodies.[34] The Senate, without a record vote, passed the resolution nine days after its introduction.[35] The Foreign Affairs Committee demanded hearings on a measure that fundamentally altered the 1922 resolution. After hearing Secretary Stimson and Under Secretary Castle in executive session, the Committee held open hearings.[36] Two points were stressed by members of the Department: that the resolution merely extends power already conferred upon the President, but with a " very definite reservation as to when he may exercise that power," and that " other nations have the power " that this resolution confers upon the President. To meet the criticism of certain members that this extension of presidential powers was fraught with danger, Assistant Secretary Rogers prepared a memorandum titled "Arms Embargo Resolution and Neutrality " which was circulated among the Committee members.[37] Not convinced by the Department's arguments, the Committee adopted, by a vote of eleven to six, Mr. Fish's amendment limiting the application of the resolution, not to " any part of

of arms and munitions of war to any foreign State when in his judgment such shipments may promote or encourage the employment of force in the course of a dispute or conflict between nations," remarked that "there are times when the hands of the Executive in negotiations for the orderly settlement of international differences would be greatly strengthened if he were in a position in cooperation with other producing nations to control the shipment of arms." 72nd Cong. (1933). H. Rep. 2040, p. 4.

34 72nd Cong., 2nd Sess. S. J. Res. 229 and H. J. Res. 580.

35 Passage in the Senate was subsequently blocked by Senator Bingham's motion to reconsider. 72nd Cong., 2nd Sess. February 8, 1933. *Cong. Rec.*, pp. 3589-3591.

36 72nd Cong., 2nd Sess. (1933). Hearings on H. J. Res. 580, *Exportation of Arms or Munitions of War*.

37 For the text of the memorandum, see Edwin Borchard and William P. Lage, *Neutrality for the United States* (New Haven, 1937), pp. 305-307. The chief opponents of the resolution outside of the Committee were representatives of the aviation industry. Hearings, cited, pp. 26-28.

the world " but to " any American country." [38] The amended version, therefore, did not go as far as the President requested. It permitted the use of collective action in the laying of an arms embargo only in cases of international disputes arising in the Western Hemisphere. In other areas the President was denied that power.[39] Under pressure of domestic legislation the resolution did not come to a vote in the few remaining weeks of the short session.

When President Roosevelt took office in March, 1933, the nation's attention was riveted upon internal problems. Economic, financial, and relief measures took precedence over foreign affairs. However sharply these steps for internal recovery differed from those pursued during Mr. Hoover's administration, there was a marked degree of continuity in the matter of the arms embargo. Chairman McReynolds, sponsor of the arms embargo resolution in January, 1933, reintroduced the original text of that resolution on March 16, 1933. The hearings that followed shed no new light. The witnesses presented were primarily those in opposition to the resolution. The Democratic majority, both within the Committee and the House, was confident that it could put through the measure. Except for the memorandum of Mr. Green of the State Department, mimeographed and circulated among the Committee, no proponents of the administration uttered a word. The administration's cause was presented by the chairman and his Democratic colleagues on the Committee. That body's final report clearly showed a division along party lines. Seven of the eight Republican members of the Committee signed the minority report, Mr. Martin (Mass.) alone not attaching his name.[40]

38 72nd Cong., 2nd Sess. H. Rep. 2040. The resolution was reported out by a vote of fifteen to two.

39 The resolution did not contemplate the repeal of the 1922 resolution.

40 73rd Cong. H. Rep. 22 on H. J. Res. 93. There is no evidence in the Committee's files or minutes to indicate that Mr. Fish sought to limit the application of the resolution to " any American country " as he had done when the resolution was before the Committee in the previous Congress.

There is sufficient evidence to support the assertion that partisanship determined the fate of the resolution in the House as in the Committee. When Chairman McReynolds appeared before the Rules Committee to ask for a special rule on the resolution, he was willing to bring it up under a rule that would permit amendment of the resolution on the House floor. The Democratic leadership, however, insisted upon a rule, the effect of which, after the House debate, was to consider as ordered the previous question without an intervening motion except one to recommit. Chairman O'Connor of the Rules Committee bluntly told the Democratic members: [41]

As far as I know, everyone was elected as a Democrat, a part of the Democratic administration, pledged to the Democratic platform, agreeing to stand behind a Democratic President, and carry out that platform to fulfillment. . . . With all the Republican members on the Foreign Affairs Committee opposed to the resolution, they can put in that motion to recommit and offer the amendments which they would like to offer on this floor and have a roll call on all amendments. What is the use of making believe something that does not exist?

The principal Republican criticism was that the resolution was part of the administration's policy of supporting the British Government and the League of Nations against Japan. Despite Democratic denials, Republican apprehensions were confirmed in part by Norman Davis' speech in Geneva in which he stated his government's willingness that

Mr. Fish, speaking for the Republican minority, condemned the proposed embargo as an "act of war. It is nothing more than the old League of Nations proposal of picking the aggressor nation. . . . This is not the time for our Government to be pulling chestnuts out of the fire for the League of Nations. We have plenty to do at home, and should mind our own business. It is not difficult to imagine the resentment which would be aroused in the United States if Japan should lay an embargo on arms against us if we sent marines to Nicaragua or any other Central American country within our special sphere of influence."

41 *Ibid.* April 13, 1933. *Cong. Rec.*, p. 1694.

in the event that the states, in conference, determine that a state has been guilty of a breach of the peace in violation of its international obligations and take measures against the violator, then, if we concur in the judgment rendered as to the responsible and guilty party, we will refrain from any action tending to defeat such collective effort which these states may thus make to restore peace.[42]

Chairman McReynolds' concluding remarks in the debate were significant. " I insist the resolution be passed as it is. The administration is standing for it. . . ." By a vote of 254 to 109, largely on party lines, the resolution passed the House.

The Senate Foreign Relations Committee had not reported out the resolution when Mr. Davis made his speech. On May 30, however, that Committee reported with the important amendment that any embargo on arms shipment laid by the President be applicable to all belligerents and not merely to one of them.[43] Although the Democratic Party enjoyed a sizable majority in the Senate, the recalcitrant members of both parties would have been able to filibuster on the measure all summer to prevent its passage in a form other than that in which it was reported. Senator Pittman conveyed this information to the administration which reluctantly agreed to the amended version as a step in the right direction.[44] Not until February 28, 1934, did it pass the Senate.[45] But rather than urge the House to pass the amended form, Chairman McReynolds " let it die " on the Speaker's desk.[46]

[42] Department of State *Press Release*, May 22, 1933, p. 390. Although this statement was made before the Disarmament Conference, it served to strengthen the collective security policy of the League.

[43] 73rd Cong. S. Rep. 101.

[44] 73rd Cong. (1933-1934). Files, C. F. A.

[45] *Ibid.*, 2nd Sess. February 28, 1934. *Cong. Rec.*, p. 3390.

[46] *Cf.* remarks of Mr. McReynolds, 74th Cong., 1st Sess. Hearings on *National Munitions Act*, H. R. 8878, p. 17. He justified his conduct on the ground that the Senate amendment " was against the policy " of the Foreign Affairs Committee. The Senate had delayed its action too long. Any effect that the resolution's application against Japan may have had in early 1933 had been dissipated by the League's failure to act vigorously in the Far East.

For almost a decade the Committee had before it legislative proposals to prohibit the exportation of arms. It explored several approaches to the problem without benefit of executive guidance—at least until the last months of President Hoover's administration—and with no body of articulate public opinion behind it.[47] Then, within a little more than a year, developments in the Far East and in the field of disarmament gave new importance to arms embargo legislation. The request of President Hoover, followed by that of President Roosevelt, focused the Committee's attention upon a phase of the legislative proposals that theretofore had not been most prominent—that of presidential discretion. That the division of opinion on this point was not along abstract concepts of legislative power versus executive power, but along party lines, is not difficult to explain. When President Hoover made his request in January, 1933, for legislation, he was serving his last months as chief executive before turning over the presidency to President-elect Roosevelt. If the overwhelming Democratic majority was pledged to support the new President on the immediate and pressing domestic issues, it was certainly not disposed to challenge him on the more remote issues of foreign policy. When the Democratic chairman of the Committee, Mr. McReynolds, took up the cudgels for a Republican President, he was in reality pressing for a grant of power that the new Democratic President wanted.[48] By the time the Senate passed an amended version of

47 It was the contention of the United States Government, until the end of 1932, that the Federal Government was powerless to prescribe or enforce a prohibition upon private manufacture of arms; this was a power that resided within the states forming the Union. In November, 1932, this position was reversed. *Cf.* Manley O. Hudson, "The Treaty-Making Power of the United States in Connection with the Manufacture of Arms and Ammunition," *Amer. Jour. of Inter. Law*, XXVIII (October, 1934), pp. 736-739.

48 73rd Cong., 1st Sess. (1933). Hearings on H. J. Res. 93, *Exportation of Arms or Munitions of War*, p. 24, where there appears a letter written by Lord Robert Cecil to the *London Times*: "On Jan. 11 the Democratic President-elect of the United States, Mr. Roosevelt, said: 'I have long been in favor of the use of embargoes on arms to belligerent nations, especially to nations, which are guilty of making an attack on other nations . . . that is, against aggressor nations.'"

the House arms embargo resolution, the administration saw some hope of achieving international accord on the subject. On May 18, 1934, President Roosevelt called upon the Senate to give its advice and consent to the Geneva Convention of 1925.[49] At the end of that month Mr. Davis asked the Disarmament Conference to consider the international traffic in arms.[50] But these small gestures were not sufficient to stem the tide of international restlessness that was slowly engulfing Europe and Asia.

[49] " The private and uncontrolled manufacture of arms and munitions and the traffic therein has become a serious source of international discord and strife. It is not possible, however, effectively to control such an evil by the isolated action of any one country. The enlightened opinion of the world has long realized that this is a field in which international action is necessary." Department of State *Press Release*, May 19, 1934, p. 293.

On April 19, 1934, the Senate had set up a special committee to investigate the traffic in arms and munitions, popularly called the Nye Committee. 73rd Cong., 2nd Sess. April 19, 1934. *Cong. Rec.*, p. 6896.

[50] Mr. Davis to the Conference, May 29, 1934: " The American people and government are convinced that by some means the production and traffic in engines of death, and the profits resulting therefrom, must be controlled or eliminated... My Government is ready to join in measures for suppressing this evil and is prepared to negotiate in connection with disarmament a treaty that would deal drastically with this problem." Department of State *Press Release*, June 2, 1934, p. 333.

Without debate the House and Senate passed a resolution empowering the President to proclaim an arms embargo against Paraguay and Bolivia "after consultation with the governments of other American Republics and with their cooperation, as well as that of such other governments as he may deem necessary." 73rd Cong. Pub. res. 28.

CHAPTER VII
NEUTRALITY

By 1935 the collective security structure of the post-war period showed signs of crumbling at many points. In the Far East the Japanese penetration of China gave no indication of abating. In Europe armament programs replaced disarmament proposals. Germany, under Hitler, was ambitiously striving to regain her place in the sun. Italy was going through the motions of arbitrating her dispute with Ethiopia at the same time that she was pouring troops into East Africa. France, casting about for further security, entered into a pact of mutual assistance with the Soviet, while England, apprehensive of naval rivals, signed a naval agreement with Germany. These were only the more obvious signs that betokened troubled times.[1]

These portentous events were not the only source of concern for the American people. The Senate's Special Committee on the Investigation of the Munitions Industry (the Nye Committee) was in the process of untangling the intrigues and ramifications of the munitions industry and publicizing the abnormal profits of some manufacturers. In the spring of 1934, Charles Warren brought out a provocative article, titled " Troubles of a Neutral," a study of the difficulties that confronted the United States from 1914 to 1917.[2] Although it lacked the dramatic qualities of the materials unearthed by the Nye Committee, it was a sober reminder that the desire to be neutral involved decisions on questions other than the arms embargo.

Before 1935 the arms embargo proposals were regarded as steps toward keeping war out of the world. The events of 1934 and 1935 gave a new meaning and emphasis to such proposals; they became one of a series of legislative suggestions for keep-

1 The best concise analysis of the changing international scene and the effects upon American foreign relations may be found in Shepardson, *The United States in World Affairs, 1934-1935* (New York, 1935).

2 *Foreign Affairs*, vol. XII (April, 1934), pp. 377-394. *Cf. Fortune*, March, 1934.

ing the United States out of war. Credits to belligerents, travel
by Americans in war zones, the use of ports by submarines, and
the shipment of raw materials to belligerents commanded congressional attention—all for the purpose of maintaining what
was popularly called neutrality. As a further safeguard against
American involvement Congress seriously considered measures
that, it was claimed, would take the profits out of war.[3]

By way of explanation it is appropriate to state at this point
that this chapter does not aim to recount the circumstances,
domestic and international, surrounding the passage of the successive neutrality bills. Those have been described and analyzed
by others.[4] The objective is narrower—to examine the part
played by the Committee on Foreign Affairs and by the House
of Representatives in shaping the various neutrality laws. The
attempt to achieve this objective accounts for the over-weighted
and detailed presentation of materials pertaining to the Committee and the House.

In the belief that the general reader will have occasion to
refer, from time to time, to the successive neutrality acts a summary of the principal features of each of them is set forth.

I. The Joint Resolution of August 31, 1935.

    1. The President " shall " impose an arms embargo " upon the
       outbreak or during the progress of war." The President
       " may " extend the embargo to other states as they become
       involved in the war. These provisions expired on February
       29, 1936.

    2. A National Munitions Board was set up to register muni-
       tions manufacturers and to license munitions exports.

    3. When an arms embargo is imposed, American vessels can-
       not carry munitions to belligerents or to neutral ports for
       reshipment to belligerents.

3 *Cf.* 74th Cong., 1st Sess. (1935). H. R. 5529 (the McSwain bill).

4 See the annual volumes edited by Whitney H. Shepardson, *The United
States in World Affairs, 1931-*. Edwin Borchard and William P. Lage,
Neutrality for the United States (New Haven, 2nd ed., 1940) ; Allen W.
Dulles and Hamilton F. Armstrong, *Can America Stay Neutral?* (New
York, 1939).

4. The powers delegated to the President included the right:

   a. To withhold protection from American citizens traveling on any vessel of any belligerent nation " whenever, during any war in which the United States is neutral, the President shall find that the maintenance of peace between the United States and foreign nations, or the protection of the lives of the citizens of the United States, or the protection of the commercial interests of the United States, or its citizens, or the security of the United States, requires that the American citizen should refrain from traveling as " passenger " on such vessels;

   b. To prohibit the entrance of any foreign submarine during war into American ports or territorial waters except under conditions prescribed by the President;

   c. To require bond of vessels suspected of leaving an American port for the purpose of delivering up to any belligerent warship or supply ship, men or fuel, munitions or other supplies.[5]

II. The Joint Resolution of February 29, 1936.

   1. It amended and extended the resolution of August 31, 1935, to May 1, 1937.

   2. " Whenever the President shall find that there exists a state of war," the arms embargo shall be imposed; he " shall " extend this embargo when other states become involved.

   3. It provided for an embargo on loans and credits to belligererents.

   4. This act was not applicable to American republics engaged in war against a non-American state " provided the American republic is not cooperating with a non-American state."

     The effect of this resolution was to lessen the discretionary power of the President.

III. The Joint Resolution of January 8, 1937.

This statute, applicable only to Spain, was made necessary because the 1935 and 1936 acts were limited to international wars and not to civil wars. When civil war broke out in Spain in the summer of 1936, the President had no statutory authority to prohibit the shipment of arms to either faction in that country.

---

5 Raymond L. Buell, " The New American Neutrality," *Foreign Policy Reports*, vol. XI, no. 23 (January 15, 1936), pp. 279-280.

This statute was rushed through Congress immediately after it convened in 1937.

IV. The Joint Resolution of May 1, 1937.

1. Mandatory Provisions. " Whenever the President shall find that there exists a state of war . . . the President shall proclaim such fact, and it shall thereafter be unlawful " :

a. To export " arms, ammunition or implements of war " to any belligerent states named in such proclamation, or to any neutral state for transshipment to such belligerent.

b. To " purchase, sell or exchange bonds, securities or other obligations of the government of any belligerent state," or any political subdivision, or person or faction acting on behalf of such state. The President could exempt ordinary commercial credits and short-time obligations.

c. " To carry any arms, ammunition, or implements of war " on any American vessel to any belligerent state, or to any neutral country for transshipment to a belligerent.

d. For any citizen of the United States to travel on any belligerent vessel, except under such rules and regulations as the President may prescribe.

e. For any American vessel engaged in trade with belligerents " to be armed, or to carry any armament, arms, ammunition, or implements of war " except such small arms as the President may designate.

2. Discretionary Provisions. In his discretion the President may invoke the following measures :

a. To apply the arms embargo in cases of civil strife.

b. To prohibit American vessels from carrying " certain articles or materials " in addition to arms and ammunition, and requiring American citizens to transfer " all right, title and interest " in any articles to a foreign government or agency before shipment to a belligerent nation. This clause, popularly called " cash-and-carry," was effective to May 1, 1939. Since Congress failed to extend it before its expiration, its effectiveness ended on that date.

c. To prohibit the use of American ports as a base of supply for belligerent states.

   d. To forbid submarines and armed merchant vessels of
      foreign states from entering American ports or terri-
      torial waters.
3. Like the 1936 act, it does not apply to American republics
   engaged in war with a non-American state, " provided the
   American republic is not cooperating with a non-American
   state or states in such war."
4. Provision is made for a National Munitions Control Board
   with authority to license the manufacture and export of
   arms, ammunition and implements of war.[6]

V. The Joint Resolution of November 4, 1939.
   1. Whenever the President " *or the Congress by concurrent
      resolution,* shall find that there exists a state of war between
      foreign states, *and* that it is necessary to promote the secur-
      ity or preserve the peace of the United States or to protect
      the lives of citizens of the United States," the President
      shall issue a proclamation naming the states involved. The
      arms embargo provisions of the 1937 Act, applying to both
      war and civil strife, are eliminated. Thus a state of war may
      be recognized without the necessity for applying the act.
   2. Whenever the President has issued such a proclamation:
      a. It is " unlawful for any American vessel to carry any
         passengers or any articles or materials to any state named
         in the proclamation."
      b. It is unlawful to export or transport to any belligerent
         " any articles or materials . . . until all right, title, and
         interest therein shall have been transferred." By special
         exemptions embodied in the law, trade with certain areas,
         presumed to be relatively safe, may continue in American
         vessels and without prior transfer of title, except for
         munitions.
      c. And subsequently finds " that the protection of citizens
         of the United States so requires," he shall proclaim com-
         bat areas into or through which no American citizen or
         vessel may proceed. The President may modify or extend
         combat areas.

6 *Cf.* William T. Stone, " Will Neutrality Keep U. S. Out of War? ",
Foreign Policy Reports, vol. XV, no. 4 (October 1, 1939), p. 168.

   d. It is unlawful for an American citizen to travel on a
      vessel of a belligerent state.
   e. It is unlawful for an American vessel to be armed.
   f. It is unlawful for Americans to "purchase, sell or ex-
      change bonds, securities, or other obligations" of gov-
      ernments named in the proclamation; or to "make any
      loan or extend any credit" to them.
3. The President has discretion:
   a. To restrict the use of American ports by foreign or
      domestic vessels.
   b. To proclaim restrictions applicable to the use of the ports
      and territorial waters by submarines and armed merchant
      vessels.
4. Provision is again made for the National Munitions Control
   Board.
5. It is unlawful for foreign vessels to use the American flag
   or any distinctive signs or markings.
6. Again, this act is not applicable to an American republic engaged in war against a non-American state, provided the
   American republic is not cooperating with a non-American
   state.[7]

At the beginning of July, 1935, the Committee approached
the larger problem of American neutrality from two angles.
Both Congressmen Kloeb and Maverick introduced measures
to prohibit the granting of credits to belligerents. After brief
hearings on these measures, the Committee reported out that of
Mr. Kloeb which simply prohibited the making of loans or the
extension of credit to any belligerent government or its nationals.[8] At the same time the Committee also had before it
Chairman McReynolds' bill to establish a national munitions
control board, pursuant to the 1925 treaty ratified by the President only the month previous.[9] Some members felt that, since

7 *Cf.* David H. Popper, "American Neutrality and Maritime Rights,"
Foreign Policy Reports, vol. XV, no. 20 (January 1, 1940), pp. 248-249.

8 74th Cong. H. R. 7125 (Mr. Kloeb) and H. J.. Res. 259 (Mr. Maverick).
The hearings on these measures were titled *American Neutrality Policy.*

9 H. R. 8788. H. Rep. 1602. This bill was drafted by Mr. Joseph C. Green
of the Department of State.

the treaty provisions were not operative in time of war, the President's authority under the proposed law to proclaim " from time to time a list of articles which shall be considered arms, ammunition, and implements of war " whose export or import required a license from the board, would permit him to discriminate during the course of a war by altering the list of articles. To prevent this, Mr. Tinkham (R., Mass.) offered an amendment, providing that no licenses should be issued to persons for the export or import of arms, etc. to or from " any country engaged in armed conflict in which conflict the United States is not a party." By a vote of three to nine the Committee rejected the amendment and reported the bill favorably.[10] By the end of July, 1935, therefore, the House had reported out two separate measures, one to deal with loans and credits to belligerents, the other to control the arms trade.

In place of these piecemeal proposals the President and the State Department, recognizing the pressure of public opinion for some legislation, preferred an omnibus bill, more tempered in content, and giving the President discretion in its application. Such a measure was introduced by Chairman McReynolds on August 17, with the intention of letting it lie over until the next session of Congress.[11] The McReynolds resolution accorded the President the widest discretion not only in the application of the arms embargo, but also in prohibiting (1) American vessels from carrying munitions; (2) the use of American ports as bases of supplies; (3) the use of the American flag on vessels of belligerent nations; (4) submarines from entering American waters; (5) financial transactions with belligerent governments; and (6) travel by American citizens on belligerent vessels. The leadership of the House would have supported Mr. McReynolds' desire that no action be taken in the last days of that session, had not a number of senators pressed for legislation. Under a threat to delay adjournment by a filibuster, the Senate Foreign Relations Committee reported out a measure providing

10 74th Cong. Minutes, C. F. A.
11 *Ibid.* H. J. Res. 386.

for a mandatory embargo on war materials to all belligerents. The following day, August 21, with almost no debate, the measure, popularly called the Pittman resolution, was passed.[12] The first reaction of the Foreign Affairs Committee, to whom the resolution was referred when it reached the House, was unfavorable; fifteen Democrats voted that it should not be reported out while five Republicans and one Democrat voted that it should.[13] The Democratic opposition centered around the mandatory provisions of the arms embargo. Said Mr. McReynolds: "One thing is sure. The Committee will never report out the Senate bill. I am opposed to the mandatory embargo features."[14] It was realized immediately, however, that the Senate's insistence would force the House to act. At a White House conference, attended by Secretary Hull, Assistant Secretary Moore, and Mr. McReynolds, the President suggested a compromise which Mr. McReynolds presented to his Committee. The compromise proposed that the mandatory embargo provisions of the Senate resolution be limited in application until February 29, 1936.[15] The Committee accepted this amended version of the Senate resolution, fourteen Democrats voting for its adoption as against five Republicans. On August 23, the House speedily adopted the amended Senate resolution, followed the next day by similar action in the Senate.[16] Although in

12 *Ibid.* S. J. Res. 173. H. Rep. 1883.

13 *Ibid.* Minutes, C. F. A.

14 *The New York Times*, August 22, 1935.

15 Senator Pittman contended that the provisions regarding credits to belligerents were too involved to be handled in the short time that remained. They were therefore dropped from the resolution.

16 The resolution passed the House under suspension of the rules, thereby permitting only forty minutes debate. Mr. Martin (R., Mass.), a member of the Committee, stated that he understood the situation. "The President ...is opposed to mandatory legislation. He would like to have it left discretionary, but we find that in the compromise he will accept the mandatory feature until March 1. At this late hour of the session we can do nothing else than accept the legislation. The alternative would be no legislation." 74th Cong., 1st Sess. *Cong. Rec.*, p. 14357.

accord with the "wholly excellent" purpose of the legislation, President Roosevelt, in appending his signature to it, pointed out that "more complete consideration" would have to be given the arms embargo provisions before February 29, 1936.[17] Even though the Democratic party enjoyed a large following in the Senate, the Senate rules made it difficult for the President —through his supporters—to exert any considerable influence over that body. Instead, the President worked quietly through his supporters in the House to dilute the Senate resolution by the insertion of a time limit, hoping that when the provision expired, public opinion would rally behind his stand on the issue.

When Congress reexamined the problem of neutrality legislation in January, 1936, it had to take account of the unhealthy state of European affairs and American reaction to them.[18] The administration bill, introduced by Senator Pittman and Representative McReynolds in their respective bodies, did not propose to remove the mandatory embargo on arms shipments. It gave additional power to the President to embargo other "articles or materials used in the manufacture of arms, ammunition, or implements of war, or in the conduct of war" to the belligerents beyond the average amount exported to them for the three years preceding his proclamation. This was the much discussed section four of the bill.[19] Provision was also made for prohibition on

17 Department of State *Press Release*, August 31, 1935, pp. 162-163.

18 Whatever hopes the administration may have entertained for a shift in congressional opinion prior to the opening of Congress were dashed by the inept handling of the Italian-Ethiopian dispute by the League and the Great Powers, notably England and France. The Hoare-Laval plan for partition of Ethiopia turned public opinion away from any venture which sought to support a policy of cooperation.

19 H. J. Res. 422. Section 4 (a) provided: "Whenever, during any war in which the United States is neutral, the President shall find that the placing of restrictions on the shipment from the United States to belligerent countries of certain articles or materials used in the manufacture of arms, ammunition, or implements of war, or in the conduct of war, will serve to promote the security and preserve the neutrality of the United States, or to protect the lives and commerce of nationals of the United States, and

loans and credit to belligerents; and commercial transactions could only be made, when the President so proclaimed, at the risk of the American trader.

The Committee labored over the resolution throughout most of January, 1936, holding hearings and then attempting to perfect its language.[20] Opponents of the measure directed most of their fire at section four. It was feared that this section was a subterfuge to permit the administration to regulate " the entire foreign trade of the United States " and to impose economic sanctions against so-called aggressors. Representatives of Italian-American organizations and congressmen with constituents descended from Italian immigrants were particularly outspoken against this section since its application during the Italo-Ethiopian war, then in progress, would have adversely affected Italy.[21] When this section was reached in the Committee's de-

shall so proclaim, it shall thereafter be unlawful to export, or attempt to export, or cause to be exported, or sell for export, such articles or materials from any place in the United States to any belligerent country named in the proclamation, or to any neutral country for transshipment to or for the use of any such belligerent country in excess of a normal amount, in quantity and kind, of exports from the United States to the respective belligerent countries prior to the date of the proclamation, such normal amount to constitute the average of shipments during a previous period of years to be determined by the President: Provided, That no restriction or prohibition imposed under this section shall under any circumstances be applied to food, medical supplies, or clothing and processed or partly processed clothing materials of a distinctively nonmilitary character." The President was empowered to enumerate the articles to be restricted and to modify or to revoke the list as well as to extend it to other countries entering the war. This proposal was in line with the pronouncements of disapproval made by Secretary Hull in November, 1935, on trade with Italy. See Department of State *Press Release*, November 16, 1935, p. 385.

20 Hearings on the resolution were titled *To Maintain the Neutrality of the United States in the Event of War or Threat of War between or among Foreign Nations.*

21 *Cf.* testimony of Representative Healey (D., Mass.), p. 171. " I believe it will be freely admitted that the banning of the shipment of these articles will more adversely affect Italy than it will Ethiopia in the present conflict. If that fact is admitted, then I question the wisdom of the enactment of this section of the bill under consideration."

liberations, a minority member offered the following amendment in place of the language of the resolution: [22]

> During any war in which the United States is neutral, the President shall proclaim it to be unlawful to export, or attempt to export, or cause to be exported, or sell for export, articles or materials used in the manufacture of arms, ammunition, or implements of war, or in the conduct of war, from any place in . . . (the United States to any belligerent country . . .)

The intent was obvious—to make this section as mandatory as that on arms. By a strict party vote, the amendment was rejected, fifteen to five. When Mr. Fish, ranking minority member, took the House floor to explain " the viewpoint of the Republican Party " on the resolution, he left no doubt that that section was regarded as a party measure. " We do not propose to give any additional power whatever to the President of the United States, discretionary or otherwise, to involve us in foreign entanglements." [23]

The protracted hearings and debates before the two committees, particularly in the Senate, indicated that any change in the neutrality law would have hard sledding. Moreover, it was broadly hinted that the alienation of Italo-Americans might have important repercussions in the fall election.[24] The Democratic forces in both Houses, therefore, readily accepted the compromise measure drafted by Representative Kloeb which extended the existing law with three amendments until May 1, 1937. The resolution's amendments have been summarized: it forbade the granting of loans and credits to belligerents; it made mandatory the existing discretionary power of the President to extend the arms embargo to additional states as they became involved in any war; and it exempted from the operation of the law any American republic at war with a non-

---

22 74th Cong. Minutes, C. F. A.

23 74th Cong., 2nd Sess. February 6, 1936. *Cong. Rec.*, p. 1613.

24 *Cf.* Charles Warren, Congress and Neutrality, in *Neutrality and Collective Security*, edited by Quincy Wright (Chicago, 1936), p. 140 f.

American state and not cooperating with a non-American state or states in such war.[25] The resolution was put through the House under suspension of the rules, allowing no amendment on the floor and only forty minutes of debate. To the Republicans this was a token of victory, since, by it, they secured their major objective—a check upon the extension of the President's powers. To the President's supporters it was a compromise, the best that could be achieved " under the circumstances existing." [26]

The Seventy-fifth Congress was less than twenty-four hours old when it was called upon to enact legislation prohibiting the shipment of arms to the various factions engaged in civil war in Spain. That war had begun the previous summer, shortly after Congress had adjourned. The statutes over which Congress had labored in 1935 and 1936 were applicable to international wars and not to civil wars. The desire of certain Americans to take advantage of this hiatus in the law led the President to request immediate action by Congress. So urgent was the need that Mr. McReynolds, acting under a special rule, brought up the resolution in the House before it had been printed; it was never referred to the Foreign Affairs Committee. While the House was discussing it, the Senate sent over an identical resolution except for the preamble. To save time the House passed the Senate's resolution and dispatched it to the President who signed it.[27]

25 Whitney H. Shepardson, *The United States in World Affairs, 1936* (New York, 1937), p. 143.

26 Remarks of Chairman McReynolds, February 17, 1936. *Cong. Rec.*, p. 2241.

27 75th Cong. Pub. Res. 1. Shortly after the Spanish civil war began, the State Department sent the following instructions to American consular and diplomatic representatives in Spain. " It is clear that our neutrality law with respect to embargo of arms, ammunition and implements of war has no application in the present situation, since that applies only in the event of war between or among nations. On the other hand, in conformity with its well-established policy of non-interference with internal affairs in other countries, either in time of peace or in the event of civil strife, this govern-

The respective committees in each House then began discussions on the whole subject of neutrality in anticipation of the law's expiration on May 1, 1937. To say that congressmen were perturbed would be an understatement. No fewer than twenty-two measures were sent to the Foreign Affairs Committee, covering all phases of neutrality. All of them were pigeonholed except that introduced by Chairman McReynolds.[28] Except for the inclusion of provisions pertaining to civil wars and the omission of those dealing with the National Munitions Control Board, the McReynolds resolution was identical with the amended resolution of the previous Congress over which the Committee had wrangled so vehemently before accepting the Senate compromise.[29] Although Mr. McReynolds insisted that his resolution was prepared without the assistance of the State Department, the discretionary power it conferred upon the President was more in accord with administration desires than a comparable resolution sponsored in the Senate by Mr. Pittman.[30] "Technicians" from the Department, however, ap-

ment will, of course, scrupulously refrain from any interference whatsoever in the unfortunate Spanish situation...." Department of State *Press Release*, August 15, 1936, p. 152.

28 75th Cong., 1st Sess. H. J. Res. 147.

29 *Supra*, pp. 205-206.

30 75th.Cong., 1st Sess. H. J. Res. 147 and 242. *Cf.* hearings on these resolutions, titled *To Maintain the Neutrality of the United States*, p. 34. The Pittman resolution was S. J. Res. 51.

In an address delivered at Chautauqua, New York, the previous August, President Roosevelt had made a studious plea in behalf of greater executive discretion. "... The effective maintenance of American neutrality depends today, as in the past, on the wisdom and determination of whoever at the moment occupy the offices of President and Secretary of State.... In spite of every possible forethought, international relations involve of necessity a vast uncharted area. In that area safe sailing will depend on the knowledge and the experience and the wisdom of those who direct our foreign policy. Peace will depend on their day-to-day decisions." Department of State *Press Release*, August 22, 1936, pp. 167, 168.

Doubtless Congress had been impressed by the sweeping terms of the Supreme Court decision in the Curtiss-Wright case, handed down in December, 1936. The Court recognized "the very delicate, plenary and

peared before the Committee to assist the members in laying down principles Congress wanted the President to follow, leaving to the latter " the day-to-day decisions that the carrying out of that policy will require.[31]

The House measure retained the arms embargo and the prohibition on credits of the earlier bills, and extended them to cases of civil war. " The country is sold on that and also the Congress and we can't back water on that," said Mr. McReynolds.[32] The so-called commodities section, restricting " the shipment of certain articles or materials " in addition to arms, was the most debated portion of the resolution, both within the Committee and the Congress. The McReynolds resolution, in section four, again proposed a normal quota, determinable by the President, beyond which belligerents could not purchase materials. Section nine further empowered the President, during a period of American neutrality, to proclaim that commercial transactions with belligerents were undertaken at the risk of American individuals. But the Committee had misgivings, shared by the chairman, over the administration of a quota system and the dangers to which American shipping was exposed. At Mr. McReynolds' suggestion, and supported by the Department experts, those sections were stricken from the bill and replaced by the so-called " cash and carry " section, to be applied at the President's discretion, with " such limitations and exceptions " as he may prescribe.[33] Oddly enough, the Committee gave no heed to the relation of the cash and carry section to the administration's reciprocal trade program. In view of the exploratory conversations on this subject then in progress

exclusive power of the President as the sole organ of the federal government in the field of international relations—a power which does not require as a basis for its exercise an act of Congress ... " 299 U. S. 304.

31 Hearings, cited, p. 35. Statement of Mr. Joseph C. Green, chief, Office of Arms and Munitions Control, Department of State.

32 *Ibid.*, p. 34.

33 *Ibid.*, p. 14 f., 30 f.

with Great Britain, one would have expected that the shift to cash and carry would have evoked some comment.[34]

The amended McReynolds resolution was introduced as a new resolution, H. J. Res. 242, and reported out late in February, 1937. The majority report confined itself to a resumé of each of the sections of the resolution. The minority report, signed by Representatives Fish, Martin, Rogers, Allen, and Dondero, five of the seven Republican members of the Committee, took sharp issue with the majority, principally because the resolution " delegates excessive discretionary powers to the President to lay embargoes, tends to take away the constitutional power of the Congress to declare war, and discriminates in an intolerable and unfair manner against American shipping." [35] On this last point the minority was especially agitated, ignoring the difficulties arising from the attempted maintenance of the doctrine of the freedom of the seas during the period of American neutrality from 1914 to 1917.[36] Mr. Fish, author of the minority report, wrote:

For what reason has Congress appropriated huge sums, amounting to half a billion dollars annually, to build and maintain a Navy, except to protect our trade on the high seas? We have withdrawn, or are about to withdraw, from the Philippines, and now propose to sacrifice our American merchant marine for the benefit of other nations by keeping our own ships at home through the placing of discriminatory embargoes on them.

We might just as well keep our Navy in the Chesapeake Bay, or sink it and save a half billion dollars a year. What has become of the famous old American slogan of " Millions for defense, but not

34 During the debate on the House floor, Mr. Shanley, a member of the Committee, was one of the few to suggest the connection between section four and the reciprocal trade program. " The positing of this discretionary power in the President's hands in contradistinction to the mandates of the Pittman bill give him the opportunity to make his reciprocal trade policy coincide with his neutrality ideas." March 18, 1937. *Cong. Rec.*, p. 2386.

35 Representatives Tinkham and Eaton were the two Republicans who did not sign the report.

36 75th Cong., 1st Sess. H. Rep. 320, part 2.

a penny for tribute " ? Are American ships to be kept off the high seas by Presidential discrimination and through weakness and fear ? [37]

To offset the criticism that the 1935 and 1936 laws had been hurried through the House without time for adequate debate, the Rules Committee allotted ten hours for general debate on the 1937 resolution. That the administration did not intend to lose control on the floor was indicated when the chairman moved, as each section came up for amendment, that all debate be closed in a specified number of minutes, usually not more than thirty. Several members protested that this was a gag rule. While this was doubtless true, the fact was that the administration forces held their lines and only amendments approved by Chairman McReynolds passed.

Economic considerations weighed heavily with most of the representatives. Mr. McReynolds appealed especially to those from districts benefiting from commercial relations with Canada, insisting that the mandatory application of the law, in case Canada were a belligerent, would seriously injure American commerce. Subsequently he offered an amendment, accepted by the House, limiting the application of section four to " overseas." [38] Renewing his proposal that arms shipments were as dangerous in peace as in war, Representative Fish offered an amendment, prohibiting their exportation both in peace and war. He was careful to point out that he had omitted the word *munitions* from his amendment, a word which he understood

[37] When the resolution was open for amendment on the House floor, Mr. Fish moved to strike out section 4 (a) because it "discriminates against American shipping." The President was given "the discretionary power to wreck the American merchant marine." 75th Cong., 1st Sess. March 8, 1937. *Cong. Rec.*, p. 2389.

In contrast with this expression it is interesting to read Mr. Fish's reply to a query put to him by *The United States News*, May 10, 1937. " These provisions (cash and carry) will greatly restrict our neutral rights on the high seas, and I am in favor of that as the doctrine of freedom of the seas has involved us in practically all European wars in the last 150 years."

[38] 75th Cong., 1st Sess. March 8, 1937. *Cong. Rec.*, p. 2396.

to mean raw materials. " Then you would have a total embargo; you would have a Jeffersonian embargo and I am absolutely against that." [39] The amendment was defeated, 74 to 101. If the House was not willing to enact legislation prohibiting all trade with belligerents, neither was it desirous of reverting to the doctrine under which trade was conducted from 1914 to 1917. This was abundantly proved when Representative Ferguson's amendment to strike out all of section four " to save our trade . . . and our honor " mustered only twenty-nine votes. [40] There was a quiet recognition of the fact that cash and carry would not disrupt trade with those nations having the money to make purchases—that is, Great Britain and France—and, by their control of the seas, able to carry away the commodities they bought. The untried experiment of cash and carry therefore held out the hope of maximum trade at minimum risk. With the approval of Representatives McReynolds and Fish the House accepted Mr. Shanley's amendment to limit section four to May 1, 1939, when a new Congress could reexamine the whole policy. [41]

In the Senate the Pittman resolution gained the approval of the so-called neutrality bloc and was passed on March 3, 1937, by a vote of sixty-three to six. Since there were differences between the two resolutions, some of a fundamental nature, the two bills were referred to a conference committee. Three of the four representatives and two of the three senators of the conference committee were strong supporters of the administration. The minority members, Senator Borah and Representative Fish, were not in a position to make their views felt. Despite the fight put up by the mandatory bloc, the vote in both Houses had shown that those favoring greater discretion to the executive had surprising strength. In the conference committee, therefore, it was only a question of how far the Senate conferees, more

39 *Ibid.*, p. 2379.
40 *Ibid.*, p. 2391.
41 *Ibid.*, p. 2386.

sympathetic to the views expressed in the House resolution than in their own, could yield without losing too much support in the upper House.

The principal differences between the House and Senate resolutions may thus be summarized:

1. " Cash and carry " or commodities section. The Pittman resolution was, on the whole, mandatory and rigid whereas the McReynolds resolution was discretionary and flexible.[42] Subsection (a) of the McReynolds resolution empowered the President to provide " limitations and exceptions " for the transport of articles and materials in American vessels " overseas "—i. e. Canada was excepted. The Pittman resolution gave him no comparable power. Subsection (b)—the " cash " section—providing for transfer of title of goods to a belligerent, in the Senate resolution, became effective as soon as the President found a state of war or civil war to exist. The House resolution called for two proclamations, first, the general proclamation that war exists; second, if the President finds that the peace, security, and neutrality of the United States require restrictions on the exportation of commodities to belligerents or a state where civil war exists, he may issue another proclamation forbidding the exportation of those commodities.[43] Again the President was empowered to specify limitations and exceptions in the application of this second proclamation.

The Senate conferees accepted the House version of a double proclamation, but the broad phrase, " limitations and exceptions," was qualified by the addition of the words, " as to lakes, rivers, and inland waters bordering on the United States, or as to transportation on or over lands bordering on the United States." This narrowed the House resolution which would have permitted the President to prescribe " limitations and exceptions " on the shipment of articles " overseas," and not across the American boundaries.

2. "Arms, ammunition, and implements of war." The Senate resolution specified that those words would embrace the articles

42 See *Comparison of the Pittman and McReynolds Neutrality Bills. Confidential Committee Print*, March 23, 1937, p. 6.

43 *Cf.* Committee of conference report and statement by managers on the part of the House, H. Rep. 723, p. 11.

enumerated in the President's proclamation numbered 2163 of April 10, 1936. To forestall the inclusion of raw materials as " implements of war " the House conferees insisted upon the insertion of the words that " arms, ammunition, and implements of war " shall not include " raw materials or any other articles or materials not of the same general character as those enumerated in the said proclamation," and in the Geneva Convention of 1925.

3. Prohibition of travel by Americans on belligerent vessels. As in the case of cash and carry, the Senate resolution provided for the automatic application of prohibition on travel on belligerent vessels whenever the President proclaimed that there existed a state of war or civil strife. The House resolution provided for discretion on the part of the President in placing the prohibitions in effect.[44] The House conferees accepted the Senate's language.

4. Arming of American merchant vessels. The McReynolds resolution made no reference to this subject; the Pittman resolution prohibited the arming of such vessels. In the final bill American merchantmen engaged in commerce with any belligerent state or any state wherein civil war existed were prohibited from carrying any " armament, arms, ammunition, or implements of war, except small arms and ammunition." (Section 10).

For the Foreign Affairs Committee the 1937 legislation climaxed a two years' struggle to bring the legislative body more nearly into accord with executive views. A combination of circumstances determined the final form of the legislation. On the political side, the strength of the Democratic majority never left any doubt that, at least in the House, the administration forces could muster the votes despite some notable defections from their own ranks, for example, Representatives Ludlow and Maverick. The best the Republicans could hope for was confusion and division among the opposition. Confusion there was; but by telephone and personal conversations the majority leaders were able to check divisions. The task of convincing the doubting Democrats fell largely to Chairman McReynolds who, by argument, strategy, and compromise, pushed through

44 See *Comparison of the Pittman and McReynolds Neutrality Bills*, cited, p. 12.

his pet thesis of wide executive discretion. Executive restraint in the handling of situations arising out of the Spanish civil war had tempered congressional critics of the discretionary school of thought. There was a comprehension that a choice between the two basic policies did not offer two real alternatives. By passing no legislation, the executive was accorded the widest latitude in laying down a foreign policy. The converse—legislation—did not deny him discretion, but only limited his freedom of action. Decisions still had to be made at a number of points. All that Congress could do was to lay down a few specific restraints beyond which he could not go.[45]

45 In July, 1937, the Committee considered a resolution to amend the neutrality act in line with the terms of the Convention to Coordinate, Extend and Assure the Fulfillment of the Existing Treaties between the American States, and of other conventions, adopted at the Buenos Aires conference late in 1936. 75th Cong., 1st Sess. H. J. Res. 439. Cf. *Report of the Delegates of the United States of America to the Inter-American Conference for the Maintenance of Peace*, Buenos Aires, Argentina, December 1-23, 1936, p. 23, 131 f. This convention was not brought to the attention of the Committee when the neutrality resolution was under discussion because it had not yet been submitted to the Senate. (The Senate gave its advice and consent on June 29, 1937.) The 1937 neutrality statute was applicable to American countries engaged in war with each other. (Section 4). The Buenos Aires convention provided that the outbreak of hostilities or the threat of hostilities between two or more American states would result in consultation by the other American nations in an "endeavor to discourage or prevent the spread of prolongation of hostilities." The resolution before the Committee, therefore, proposed to except American republics engaged in war from the provisions of sections 1 (a) and (b) (the arms embargo provisions applicable in case of international war) ; 2 (cash and carry) ; 3 (financial transactions) ; 6 (prohibiting American vessels from carrying arms to belligerents) ; and 10 (prohibiting the arming of American merchant vessels)

> unless the President shall find, after consultation with the governments of other American republics and after consideration of all the circumstances, that application of the provisions of these sections, or any one or more of them, would tend toward the reestablishment of peace or the protection of the commercial or other interests of the United States and its nationals and shall so proclaim, whereupon the provisions of the section or sections invoked by the President's proclamation shall apply to the country or countries named therein subject to such limitation and exceptions as he may prescribe.

The unpublished hearings on this measure showed clearly that some members of the majority as well as of the minority had misgivings about the President's

Once the Committee had disposed of the neutrality resolution, it lapsed into a period of relative inactivity. Its discussions were confined to inconsequential items. Congress was not in session when the President delivered his " quarantine " speech in October, 1937; but it was in session when the *Panay* was sunk by the Japanese in December, 1937. Neither event, however, stirred to action the President's supporters on the Committee; they were more than willing to let him handle foreign affairs. All measures that gave any possibility of opening debate on foreign policy were pigeonholed by the chairman of the Foreign Affairs Committee. The more dauntless legislators who hoped to smoke out the administration through resolutions of inquiry had small consolation for their efforts; the resolutions were reported adversely.[46] In the House the majority leader's response to Mrs. Rogers' comments upon the " extremely unfortunate Neutrality Act " showed clearly the determination of the leaders to turn back criticism directed against the administration's foreign policy.

. . . If we are to remain neutral, . . . if we are to remain out of war, those of us in positions of responsibility should be very careful about our public utterances and leave these matters to the executive department; at least until Congress may be called upon to take some drastic action.[47]

The President's expeditious settlement of the *Panay* incident left congressional critics little opportunity for complaint and

application of the law, especially where it might be applied against one of two or more nations at war. The unneutral actions in which the President could indulge made it possible, in the view of one member, for him " to hold a big stick over South American countries all the time." In spite of the endorsement of the State Department, it was doubtful whether the measure could muster sufficient support in the Committee. Even had it been reported out, the sharp debate it certainly would have engendered on the floor would do much to vitiate the benevolent purposes contemplated by its enactment. Hence no further action was taken. Files, C. F. A.

46 75th Cong., 3rd Sess. H. Rep. 1651 on H. Res. 364; H. Rep. 1809 on H. Res. 417; H. Rep. 1831 on H. Res. 418.

47 75th Cong., 2nd Sess. Remarks of Mr. Rayburn, December 13, 1937. *Cong. Rec.*, p. 1416.

undoubtedly contributed to the small margin of victory in January, 1938, by which the House turned down the Ludlow war referendum resolution. Generalizations on the attitudes of congressmen toward this measure are risky. There was, however, a strong undertone of distrust of the President's objectives in foreign affairs. Unable to ascertain these objectives and incapable of formulating them, the logical move was to inform the President how far Congress would *not* go—a " thou-shalt-not " expression of policy. The Ludlow resolution was the high-water mark of congressional protest against President Roosevelt's foreign policy. Its defeat again evidenced the commanding position of the administration forces in the House. Secure in this knowledge, the executive branch moved cautiously, but steadily, toward a more positive part in international affairs. Secretary Hull pointed the direction when, on June 3, 1938, he asserted:

It is my firm conviction that national isolation is not a means to security, but rather a fruitful source of insecurity. For while we may seek to withdraw from participation in world affairs, we cannot thereby withdraw from the world itself. Attempts to achieve national isolation would not merely deprive us of any influence in the councils of nations, but would impair our ability to control our own affairs.[48]

The significance of the Secretary's remarks drew no comment from a Congress that was rushing to complete its program preparatory to adjournment.

[48] Address before the Tennessee Bar Association. State Department Publication 1190. Note, also, the remarks of Assistant Secretary of State Sayre: " ... When forces of lawlessness are abroad, supine inaction in effect means siding with the evil against the good; the strongest encouragement which can be given to lawless aggression is to make it quite clear that they have nothing to fear from those with power to withstand them. The United States cannot afford to be a cipher at this crucial moment of the world's history. We must be resolute and prepared if necessary to withstand the aggression of the lawless." Address on *American Foreign Policy*, June 6, 1938. State Department Publication 1186.

The cash and carry provisions of the 1937 neutrality law expired on May 1, 1939. Even had Congress been disposed to permit the expiration to pass unnoticed in order to avoid another struggle on neutrality, President Roosevelt's message to the new Congress hinted that the subject would be opened up. He referred to the neutrality legislation as " laws that may operate unevenly and unfairly—may actually give aid to an aggressor and deny it to the victim " [49] But no move was made by the administration to tackle the revision of the neutrality law until early March, 1939, when the President stated his opposition to the neutrality legislation in the course of a press conference. Some question attaches to the delay in raising this matter. One thought was that the conclusion of the Spanish civil war (Great Britain and France recognized the Franco regime on February 27) removed that contentious issue from any congressional debate. More to the point, in explanation for this cautious procedure, was the desire of the President to be certain that the new Congress, with a smaller Democratic majority, would support him when the neutrality question came to a vote. Failure to gain legislative approval would do much to impair his standing vis-à-vis the " aggressor " nations.[50]

49 76th Cong., 1st Sess. January 4, 1939. *Cong. Rec.*, p. 75. By 1939 the President had embarked upon a positive foreign policy that had as its objective the postponement or avoidance of war " by tipping the balance of force in Europe against the axis powers and in favor of Britain and France." *Cf.* William T. Stone, *Foreign Policy Bulletin*, vol. XVIII, 16, February 10, 1939. In his message to Congress he stated that " there are many methods short of war, but stronger and more effective than mere words, of bringing home to aggressor governments the aggregate sentiments of our people." The country was given a startling illustration of what this policy meant when it was revealed, late in January, 1939, that aircraft were being sold to France. This revelation was followed by a secret meeting between the President and the Senate Military Affairs Committee at which it was alleged that the President placed the American frontier " on the Rhine " or " in France." The President vigorously denied having made this statement. *Cf. The New York Times*, January 24, 1939–February 4, 1939, inclusive.

50 *Cf.* W. H. Shepardson, *The United States in World Affairs, 1939*, p. 72.

Congressional reaction to the disturbed trends in Europe and the Far East again took the form of a rush of bills and resolutions aimed to prevent American involvement in any conflict. By April, 1939, no less than sixteen measures were before the Foreign Affairs Committee The Committee responded to this display of public and congressional uneasiness and confusion by holding hearings during April and early May. Though these were the most lengthy yet held on the general subject of neutrality, they were also the most inconclusive. In reality sixteen different measures were under examination at one time with no one of them commanding the attention of any large number of witnesses. Some witnesses added to the confusion by talking in the most general terms without reference to any one of the measures. As an outlet for public expression the hearings served their purpose; as an aid to the Committee in accepting one of them or in drafting a new measure, they failed. In the plethora of discussion one theme was dominant—that the retention of the arms embargo was the best assurance to American peace.

The Committee then turned its attention to official witnesses by inviting the Secretary of State, of War, of the Navy, and of Commerce to appear. From the examination of these gentlemen it was hoped that an agreement could be reached on details of a new bill. It was believed that Mr. Bloom, acting chairman of the Committee, would introduce a measure proposing the removal of the arms embargo.[51] Since such a proposal would give rise to acrimonious debate, the members were especially anxious to have Secretary Hull explain the administration's views. When Mr. Bloom demurred in requesting the Secretary's appearance, the Committee unanimously voted that a subcom-

---

51 Some inkling of the contents of such a bill was revealed in the resolution introduced in the Senate in March by Senator Pittman, the chief feature of which was the repeal of the arms embargo section. Although he denied that the measure had been prepared by, or in consultation with, the State Department, the resolution included the chief objectives of the administration's neutrality program. *The New York Times*, March 19, 1939. During the illness preceding Mr. McReynolds' death, in July, 1939, Mr. Bloom was acting chairman.

mittee of five wait upon the Secretary.[52] There is no record of its labors. Small groups of Democratic members, however, did meet with the Secretary to exchange views on the content of the proposed legislation as well as the parliamentary details to expedite its passage.[53] After these exploratory talks the Secretary adopted the unusual policy of inviting members of the Committee, minority and majority, to his apartment to explain his views. Two minority members, Representatives Fish and Tinkham, were not included in the invitation. As persistently bitter critics of the administration's foreign and domestic policies, " Mr. Hull decided that their presence would not make for a peaceful exchange of views." [54]

These private conversations were followed by an open letter from Mr. Hull to Senator Pittman and Representative Bloom, setting forth a six-point program that would be " the most effective legislative contribution at this time toward keeping this country out of war." [55] These points were:

1. To prohibit American ships, irrespective of what they may be carrying, from entering combat areas;

2. To restrict travel by American citizens in combat areas;

3. To provide that the export of goods destined for belligerents shall be preceded by transfer of title to the foreign purchaser;

4. To continue the existing legislation respecting loans and credits to nations at war;

5. To regulate the solicitation and collection in this country of funds for belligerents;

6. To continue the National Munitions Control Board and the system of arms export and import licenses.

52 The members were Messrs. Bloom, Kee, Shanley, Eaton, and Vorys.

53 *The New York Times*, May 25, 1939.

54 *Ibid.* May 27, 1939. Mr. Bloom alleged that Mr. Tinkham threatened to divulge to the press any remarks the Secretary might make in executive session, should the latter appear before the Committee. *Ibid.* May 26, 1939. The other cabinet officers did not meet with the Committee.

55 Department of State *Bulletin*, June 3, 1939, p. 477.

These points, already incorporated in Senator Pittman's resolution of March, appeared in the joint resolution introduced two days later—May 29—by Mr. Bloom.[56]

The history of the Bloom resolution, until it passed the House a month later, was turbulent and bitter, marked by inept leadership and poor judgment. In an endeavor to retain the principal features of the measure the executive sessions of the Committee, for the first time in more than a score of years, possibly longer, were conducted under the five-minute rule, thus restricting the members' freedom of discussion at the one point in the legislative process where discussion can be, and should be, most full. For five years the House had labored under the impression that the arms embargo was the main safeguard against war; now the Bloom bill proposed to remove that very provision. Mr. Luther Johnson, second ranking majority member, summed up the reasons for repeal in the following words:

It is not the sale of arms. It is the transportation and delivery of arms and goods that will likely involve us in war. Further, I point out that the arms embargo that we have had has been difficult of enforcement. Representatives of the State Department . . . said it was difficult in most instances to know whether or not arms were intended for shipment to belligerent nations or not. . . . If we repeal that provision now we stand upon international law and international right, and no one can claim that international law is unneutral.[57]

He then reverted to an argument advanced earlier by Mr. Barton (R., N. Y.) that

if war should break out and if conditions should arise under which the American people should demand the repeal of the arms embargo on account of the conditions then existing, repeal after war had broken out would be an unneutral act.

There was a deeply rooted suspicion that the repeal of the arms embargo would lead, by indirection, to American support of

56 76th Cong., 1st Sess. H. J. Res. 306.
57 76th Cong., 1st Sess. June 29, 1939. *Cong. Rec.*, p. 8324.

those powers favored by the President. Moreover, other sections of the Bloom resolution, notably that giving the President power to define areas of combat operations, were interpreted as granting the power to select the aggressor.[58] All the pressure of the House Democratic leaders was not sufficient to allay the suspicions of their own members. In such an atmosphere one can readily understand the strength given Mr. Vorys' (R., Ohio) amendment restoring the embargo on arms and ammunition but omitting any reference to implements of war. This compromise appealed to those who saw a danger in the traffic in lethal weapons; at the same time, it assured the continuation of trade in all other commodities. By a teller vote of 159 to 157 the amendment was adopted. This was later confirmed by a roll call vote, 214 to 173.[59]

The legislators' perplexities on neutrality were multiplied by the extraordinary procedure of the majority members of the Foreign Affairs Committee in presenting the resolution to the House. Reference has already been made to the section dealing with areas of combat operation, one of the six points recommended by Secretary Hull.[60] The majority's report endorsed

58 *Ibid.* June 28, 1939. *Cong.* Rec., p. 8160, remarks of Mr. Wadsworth.

59 *Ibid.* June 30, 1939. *Cong. Rec.*, pp. 8511-8512. The Vorys amendment provided that "whenever the President shall have issued a proclamation under the authority of section 1 (a) it shall thereafter be unlawful to export, or attempt to export, or cause to be exported, arms or ammunition from any place in the United States to any belligerent states named in such proclamation."

60 Section 3, titled Areas of Combat Operations, read: "(a) Whenever the President shall have issued a proclamation under the authority of section 1 (a), and he shall thereafter find that the protection of citizens of the United States so requires, he shall issue a proclamation, whereupon it shall be unlawful, except under such limitations not inconsistent with the purposes of this joint resolution as the President may prescribe, for citizens of the United States or vessels flying the flag of the United States to proceed through any areas defined from time to time by the President to be areas of combat operations and so specified in his proclamation.

(b) The President may from time to time modify or extend his proclamation, and when the conditions which have caused him to issue his proclamation have ceased to exist he shall revoke the same and the provisions of this section shall thereupon cease to apply."

this section as one designed " to prevent the loss of American lives in time of war."[61] Opposition to this section developed among the minority, principally because it was a grant of power " without precedent in American history. With this power the President can effectively quarantine an aggressor from American ships and citizens by simply naming the aggressor as a ' combat area.' " [62] By a margin of one vote the Committee agreed to leave this section in the resolution. Yet, without explanation to the House, Mr. Bloom confounded many of his Democratic colleagues by offering an amendment to strike out this section. This was agreed to, to the satisfaction of the opposition and to the dilemma of the majority.

Section nine, titled "Arming of American Merchant Vessels Prohibited," did not appear in Mr. Bloom's resolution as introduced in the House.[63] While the resolution was before the Committee, Mr. Tinkham offered this section as an amendment. It was adopted on a roll call vote by a majority of one, the deciding vote being that of Mr. Richards (D., S. C.). In the House the majority members of the Committee asked that the amendment be defeated. In justification for this repudiation of a Committee amendment, it was claimed that the amendment, as adopted in the Committee, deleted that portion of the law which denied American vessels the right to carry any armament, arms, ammunition, or implements of war.[64] Through an error on the part of the clerk in preparing the bill for printing the deletion

61 76th Cong., 1st Sess. H. Rep. 856.

62 *Ibid.*

63 Section 9, essentially the same as section 10 of the 1937 law, read: " Whenever the President shall have issued a proclamation under the authority of section 1, it shall thereafter be unlawful, until such proclamation is revoked, for any American vessel engaged in commerce with any belligerent state, named in such proclamation, to be armed or to carry any armament, arms, ammunition, or implements of war, except small arms and ammunition therefor which the President may deem necessary and shall publicly designate for the preservation of discipline aboard such vessels."

64 For the debate on the Committee's procedure, see *Cong. Rec.*, June 30, 1939, p. 8490 f.

was not made. Hence, the Committee majority asked the defeat of its own amendment. This explanation was hotly disputed by Mr. Tinkham who upheld the amendment because it made impossible the mixing of " babies and bullets." [65] In view of the amendments already adopted by the House in Committee of the Whole, the question of deleting this particular section took on added importance. Mr. Chiperfield (R., Ill.) stated the point neatly:

With the Vorys amendment placing into this bill a limited arms embargo, it is entirely consistent to retain section 9, which prohibits American vessels from carrying such articles to belligerents. If, on the other hand, before final passage the Vorys amendment should be defeated, and with section 3, creating combat areas, already deleted, it is all the more important that we retain section 9 because it would then be the only provision in the entire bill that would prevent our vessels from carrying on this dangerous trade with belligerents.[66]

What about the congressmen who were trying to form an intelligent judgment on this intricate point? Accusations and counter-accusations, claims and counter-claims on what the Committee did and did not do gave them no assistance in resolving the issue. Mr. Cooley (D., N. C.) won a warm round of applause when he arose to castigate the Committee.[67]

Instead of bringing to us a bill which represents the considered judgment of the committee, we have before us a measure which is badly bungled and which is actually a crazy quilt, patched up here and there with committee amendments, some of which apparently

65 Mr. Kee (D., W. Va.), a member of the Committee, pointed out that on the day previous the Committee of the Whole had rejected an amendment offered by Mr. Bell (D., Mo.) which would have prohibited American vessels from transporting " any articles or materials " to any state named in the President's proclamation. He intimated, however, that the majority members would not oppose an amendment making it unlawful for such vessels to be armed. *Ibid.*, p. 8491.

66 *Ibid.*, p. 8491.

67 *Ibid.*, p. 8496.

the majority of the committee approve and some of which apparently a majority of the committee disapprove. Who can tell by the actions and speeches of the members of the committe just what the judgment of the committee is? The members of the committee cannot even now agree as to what transpired in the committee room or upon the action taken by the committee before reporting the bill. A very important committee amendment has been offered and, although it has been stated on the floor of this House many times during the course of the debate on this measure that the majority members of the committee voted unanimously for a favorable report of the measure we are now considering, we now see majority members of the committee repudiating and disowning the important committee amendment which has been offered. . . . The committee stands before us in a hopeless and helpless position. . . .

The vote was taken during dinner hour when attendance was small. But the appeal of the Committee was successful in securing the defeat of its own amendment by a vote of 49 to 89.

After the House, in Committee of the Whole, had finished amending the Bloom resolution, Mr. Johnson, a Committee member, arose to offer a substitute amendment. This struck out everything after the enacting clause and inserted a new resolution, the chief feature of which was the absence of the Vorys limited arms embargo amendment.[68] Nor was reference made to the use of American vessels as transports of supplies to belligerents or to their arming. Although it had been intimated that such an amendment would be offered, none of the minority and few of the majority had seen it. The only copy available was that on the clerk's desk. The short, but sharp, debate was not over the procedure, which was technically correct, but over the absence of the arms embargo provision. This was the one

68 This procedure, seldom used, was supported by the precedents of the House. " Substitutes for an entire bill may be offered following the reading of the first paragraph or at the conclusion of the reading of the entire bill. A substitute offered after the reading of a bill has been concluded is in order regardless of whether it includes language stricken from the bill or inserted in the bill when read for amendment." Cannon's *Precedents*, VIII, sec. 2904.

issue over which the administration forces were unable to exert their influence. Mr. Johnson won a momentary victory when, on a division vote, his amendment was adopted, 173 to 148. But a teller vote resulted in its rejection, 176 to 180.[69] This action was confirmed when, upon a roll call on the Vorys amendment, the House voted, 214 to 173, to retain that amendment in the resolution it sent to the Senate. The final vote on the Bloom resolution was 200 to 188.[70]

The main features of the Bloom resolution, as it passed the House, have been summed up as follows:

1. Authority for Congress, by concurrent resolution, as well as for the President, to proclaim the existence of a " state of war," thus bringing the act into effect.
2. An embargo on " arms and ammunition " to all belligerents, apparently permitting export of " implements of war " forbidden under the 1937 neutrality law.

69 June 30, 1939. *Cong. Rec.*, p. 8511.
70 The members of the Foreign Affairs Committee voted as follows:
    1. The Vorys amendment.
        Yea: 1 Democrat (Pfeifer); 8 Republicans (Chiperfield, Corbett, Eaton, Fish, Rogers, Schiffler, Tinkham, Vorys).
        Nay: 13 Democrats (Allen, Arnold, Bloom, Burgin, Ford, Hennings, Izac, Jarman, Johnson, Kee, Mouton, Richards, Shanley); 2 Republicans (Barton, Stearns).
    2. Motion to recommit the Bloom Resolution to the Foreign Affairs Committee,
        Yea: 2 Democrats (Arnold, Pfeifer); 10 Republicans (Barton, Chiperfield, Corbett, Eaton, Fish, Rogers, Schiffler, Stearns, Tinkham, Vorys).
        Nay: 12 Democrats (Allen, Bloom, Burgin, Ford, Hennings, Izac, Jarman, Johnson, Kee, Mouton, Richards, Shanley). No Republicans.
    3. Motion to pass the Bloom Resolution.
        Yea: 11 Democrats (Bloom, Burgin, Ford, Hennings, Izac, Jarman, Johnson, Kee, Mouton, Richards, Shanley); 3 Republicans (Barton, Fish, Vorys).
        Nay: 3 Democrats (Allen, Arnold, Pfeifer); 7 Republicans (Chiperfield, Corbett, Eaton, Rogers, Schiffler, Stearns, Tinkham).
    Mr. McReynolds was absent from all roll calls.

3. Embargo on loans and credits retained without change from existing act.

4. Restriction of travel by American citizens on belligerent vessels; provision for " transfer of title " ; continuation of Munitions Control Board, etc., retained from existing act.[71]

When the Bloom resolution reached the Senate, it was referred to the Foreign Relations Committee. There it was only one of several bills and resolutions looking to neutrality revision. No one of them commanded sufficient support to bring it before the Senate. By a vote of twelve to eleven, on July 11, the Committee agreed to shelve the question until the next session of Congress. Even a special message from President Roosevelt on July 14, was of no avail. On August 5, Congress adjourned. Less than four weeks later, when war broke out in Europe, the State Department used the occasion to focus attention upon the neutrality problem as it affected the United States. The covering statement handed to the press with the President's two neutrality proclamations of September 5 was significant.[72] After explaining that the first of these was issued in accordance " with our activities as a neutral under the rules and procedure of international law and those of our domestic statutes in harmony therewith," it noted that the second was based upon the act of May 1, 1937. In anticipation of charges that it was unneutral to change the law once war had begun, the statement concluded:

Several proposals for modifying that act were made during the last session of Congress and are still pending. It was generally understood in Congress at the close of the last session that final action on these proposed modifications would be taken at the next session of Congress.

71 William T. Stone, " Will Neutrality Keep U. S. Out of War? " *Foreign Policy Reports*, vol. XV, no. 14 (October 1, 1939), p. 172. The grant of authority for Congress as well as for the President was an amendment by Mr. Barton. It is extremely doubtful whether a concurrent resolution (which does not require the President's signature) has any binding force upon the President.

72 Department of State *Bulletin*, September 9, 1939, p. 203.

On September 29, eight days after the President called Congress into special session, Chairman Pittman reported from the Senate Foreign Relations Committee a substitute for the Bloom resolution.[73] Two observations may be advanced on this substitute resolution. First, it was more nearly in accord with the Hull program than was the Bloom resolution. Second, by renouncing some of the rights upon which the United States had hitherto rested its neutrality policy, it left the isolationist bloc with little complaint except the repeal of the embargo provisions. Section 3, permitting the President to designate combat areas, renounced the doctrine of freedom of the seas. Section 5 (a) prohibited United States citizens from traveling on belligerent ships; the Bloom resolution permitted passage at their own risk. Section 6 forbade the arming of American vessels, the Tinkham amendment which had been eliminated by the House at the Committee's request. After a debate which promised to be the debate of the century, but soon settled down to desultory and repetitious remarks, the Senate, by a vote of 63 to 30, passed the Pittman substitute with some slight modifications designed to tighten up the resolution.

The measure then returned to the House, but not to the Foreign Affairs Committee. Since the Pittman resolution was in the nature of a substitute to the Bloom resolution, the procedure was to refer it to a conference committee. The strategy was obvious. In a conference committee weighted with proponents of the Pittman substitute, speedy and effective action could be

73 76th Cong. S. Rep. 1155. In his message the President declared that the embargo provisions are "most vitally dangerous to American neutrality, American security, and American peace." Through a repeal of these provisions and a return to international law, he sought the "reenactment of the historic and traditional American policy which, except for the disastrous interlude of the Embargo and Nonintercourse Acts, has served us well for nearly a century and a half." Along with the repeal of the embargo "certain other phases of policy reinforcing American safety should be considered." The "other phases" were essentially those embraced in Secretary Hull's six-point program of the previous May. *Ibid.*, H. Doc. 474.

expected. The Rules Committee, although it contained Democrats who had opposed the President on domestic measures, reported out a rule requesting a conference of the two Houses. While admitting the regularity of the procedure, several opposition members called it a vicious gag rule. Representative Fish, also a member of the Rules Committee, wanted a rule that would send the measure back to the Foreign Affairs Committee for further study, then bring out the Committee's findings for twelve hours of general debate and twelve hours of debate under the five-minute rule.[74] By reverting to procedure under the five-minute rule it was his apparent hope that the House would reinsert the Vorys amendment providing for a limited arms embargo, thus binding the House conferees. By a vote of 237 to 177 the House adopted the resolution as reported by the Rules Committee.

Immediately upon its adoption, Mr. Shanley, a Democratic member of the Foreign Affairs Committe, submitted a motion to instruct the conferees. His motion provided for the immediate application of an embargo on arms, ammunition, or implements of war upon the President's issuance of a proclamation declaring a state of war to exist. By restoring " implements of war " Mr. Shanley's motion went further than the proposed Vorys amendment. As an amendment to the Shanley motion, Mr. Vorys offered his original amendment which the House had adopted the previous spring. In the interim, however, forty-six members—thirty-two Democrats, thirteen Republicans, and one Farmer-Laborite—shifted their position and helped defeat the Vorys, and ultimately the Shanley, amendment by a vote of 179 to 245.[75] Confident of the outcome, administration leaders permitted the members to unburden themselves. Sincerity rather than clarity marked the forensic efforts of the members. The word *neutrality* confused some and entranced

74 *Ibid.* October 31, 1939. *Cong. Rec.*, p. 1102.

75 *Cf. The New York Times*, November 5, 1939. November 2, 1939. *Cong. Rec.*, pp. 1343-1344.

all.[76] After two days of running debate, during which it was freely admitted that the speeches would change no votes, the House defeated all pending motions and the Speaker appointed five conferees—Messrs. Bloom, Johnson, Kee, Fish, and Eaton —to meet with the Senate conferees. The measure to which the conferees agreed and which they submitted to their respective bodies was the Senate substitute (with slight amendments)— a measure that had never been brought before the House.[77] On November 2 it passed the House, 243 to 172, and a day later the President signed it.[78]

In 1935, and again in 1937, neutrality legislation originated in the Senate. A sizable minority of that body, impressed by the slow drift of the country toward what it believed to be a war policy, was able to check the administration's demands for a free hand in the application of the law. The House Committee on Foreign Affairs assumed the function of diluting the mandatory provisions of those earlier proposals to conform more nearly with the President's wish for greater discretionary power. Controlled by a leadership that was in agreement with the President on foreign affairs, the House followed the recommendations of its majority on the Foreign Affairs Committee.

In 1939, however, the procedure was reversed; the House initiated the legislation and passed it on to the Senate. To press for the removal of the arms embargo section at the very time the law was to undergo its first severe test was regarded by many congressmen as a gamble. Repeal, it was felt, was tantamount to renouncing a policy of neutrality. The haphazard way

76 Some members confined their thought on the subject to the limits of a dictionary definition. *Cf.* Mr. Schiffler's citation of Fiore's *International Law Codified. Ibid.*, p. 1319; Mr. Dondero's citation of Bouvier's *Law Dictionary and Encyclopedia*, October 31, 1939, p. 1128.

77 H. Rep. 1475.

78 Of the twenty-five members of the Foreign Affairs Committee fourteen voted yea—thirteen Democrats and one Republican—and nine voted nay—one Democrat and eight Republicans. One Democrat and one Republican did not vote. November 3, 1939. *Cong. Rec.*, p. 1389.

in which the Committee reported out the 1939 measure did nothing to reassure the members that support of the Committee's resolution was best for the country or even for themselves. Before 1939 the House had had the advantage of the extensive debates in the Senate; now the members were asked to make a vital decision on this problem without an adequate understanding of the implications of their decision.[79] It was this uneasiness, supported by spontaneous messages from constituents, that led to the adoption of the Vorys amendment. The Senate debate, conducted after the European war had begun, was closely followed by the House. The safeguards inserted by the Senate, in which certain rights were renounced, offset the elimination of the arms embargo section. The overwhelming majority by which the Senate amendment passed that body was reassuring to members in the lower House, many of whom were unfamiliar with the ramifications of neutrality legislation. Even though the House did not have the opportunity to debate the Senate substitute, the rejection of the Vorys amendment as part of the instructions to the House conferees was an indirect endorsement of the Senate's substitute.

Finally, some attention must be given to the political complexion of the House vote. Professions of non-partisanship notwithstanding, a break-down of the final roll call on agreeing to the conference report (which meant accepting the Senate version) found twenty Republicans voting for the report as against 140 in opposition to it. Thirty Democrats voted against the report and 221 for it. Thus, the ratio of Democrats was seven to one for the report while that of the Republicans was one to seven. By his quick application, in September, 1939, of the 1937 neutrality law the President weakened the position of those who feared the use, or abuse, of discretionary power. This probably explains the scant appearance of the argument, advanced in the June debates on the Bloom resolution, that to

79 Mr. Kennedy (D., N. Y.) expressed the thoughts of others when he expressed regret that the Senate had not first debated the neutrality measure. 76th Cong., 1st Sess. June 28, 1939. *Cong. Rec.*, p. 8173.

increase the President's powers endangered American neutrality. The opposition therefore directed its fire against the elimination of the arms embargo provision which became the symbol of the extension of executive power. The administration supporters, however, had to engage in some mental gymnastics to explain their position. Upon them fell the burden of proving that what had hitherto passed as neutrality was, in fact, legislation to keep the United States out of war. That, after all, was what the Senate substitute proposed. The presence of the embargo section had failed to deter the outbreak of war. Its deletion, therefore, was nothing but a return to the " true neutrality " previously followed by this country. By an elaboration of these arguments both groups were able to convince themselves of the correctness of their positions without subjecting themselves to charges of partisanship. At the expense of straining their dialectics they satisfied their consciences.[80]

By the end of 1940 Britain's need for supplies to carry on the war could not be satisfied under the cash and carry provisions of the 1939 Neutrality Act. Committed to a policy of " all out " aid to Britain, the President reflected, in December, 1940, on how best to increase American aid to that country. " If we take over not all but a large part of future British war orders," he told the press in mid-December, " when they come off the production line and come to an arrangement for their use by the British and get repaid in kind when the war is over, that would be satisfactory. We would leave out the dollar mark in the transaction . . . substituting a gentleman's agreement to pay in kind." [81] At the end of the month and again in his message to Congress in January, he followed the same line of thought.[82] To suggest an alteration in the " carry " part of the

80 Cf. 76th Cong., 2nd Sess. October 31, 1939. Remarks of Mr. Bloom and Mr. Allen, Cong. Rec., pp. 1119-1120. See also, The New York Times, article by Arthur Krock, September 24, 1939; October 28, 1939.

81 The New York Times, December 17, 1940.

82 Ibid. December 31, 1940. Also, 77th Cong., 1st Sess. Messages to Congress, January 6, 1941. Cong. Rec. (daily ed.), p. 53.

law contained too much political dynamite; that would open the way to those incidents on the high seas that preceded American entry into the war in 1917. It was easier to ask for a change of the " cash " requirements. If the problem was presented as one of defense of this country, Congress would hardly balk; it had gone along with him on the whole defense program. It remained, therefore, to work out a legislative proposal that linked the defense of this country with that of Britain.

The bill that incorporated these ideas was popularly known as the Lend-Lease Bill.[83] The heart of the bill was section 3. It empowered the President to authorize the Secretary of War, the Secretary of the Navy, or the head of any other department or agency of the Government, to manufacture or procure, dispose of and repair defense articles, and to communicate defense information, to or for the benefit of those nations the defense of which is vital to the defense of the United States, notwithstanding the provisions of any other law.[84] Although it was offered as a defense measure, only Democratic members of Congress had met with members of the executive branch to draft the bill. When it was introduced, the minority leader, Mr. Martin, remarked on the absence of Republican legislators among its draftsmen, an indication that the minority intended to fight its passage.[85]

The bill was referred to the Foreign Affairs Committee, although not without a challenge from the Military Affairs Committee.[86] Never before had the Committee had before it such a galaxy of personalities. Four members of the cabinet, followed by a number of private citizens, gave testimony for and against the bill. Doubtless the presence of such distinguished company, coupled with the wide press coverage, stimulated some of the Committee members to extraordinary efforts to draw fanciful

83 77th Cong., 1st Sess. H. R. 1776.

84 *Ibid.* H. Rep. 18, p. 3.

85 *Ibid.* January 10, 1941. *Cong. Rec.* (daily ed.), p. 117.

86 *The New York Times*, January 12, 1941.

conclusions from the slightest statements.[87] This was particularly true of Mr. Fish and Mr. Tinkham whose questions often degenerated into speeches and hypothetical statements, not capable of evoking enlightening answers. On several occasions the members turned from the witness on the stand to argue among themselves on the relevance or irrelevance of questions. Mr. Eaton protested in vain "against this intercommittee [sic] warfare being substituted for a discussion of the greatest crisis that has ever confronted the world." [88] Mr. Fish took it upon himself to invite witnesses who were opposed to the bill, a procedure which brought him into conflict with Chairman Bloom. Rather than lay themselves open to accusations of throttling the opposition, the majority members authorized invitations to those whom Mr. Fish had already asked. Mr. Fish went further; he invited Admiral Stark, General Marshall, and General Brett to appear. These gentlemen were willing to come on two conditions: that the Committee extend the invitation and that their testimony be heard in executive session. The latter condition would have defeated Mr. Fish's purpose of publicizing the defense measures thus far taken. The Committee, voting strictly on party lines, upheld the chairman's decision not to invite them to testify in open hearing. Subsequently they testified in executive session.[89]

Even before the Committee had concluded its hearings, the majority members gave evidence of offering amendments to meet, in part, the criticisms of the minority. By this means it was hoped to allay some of the fear felt by those who otherwise were willing to aid Britain. The majority members therefore offered

87 77th Cong., 1st Sess. Hearings on H. R. 1776, *Lend-Lease Bill. Cf.* the colloquy between Secretary Stimson and Mr. Tinkham, p. 107 f. At the conclusion of the hearing Chairman Bloom stated: "Especially do we (the Committee) wish to thank the members of the press, who have been very courteous to all of us. . . . We want to thank the photographers and the movie people and the commentators. You have been very thoughtful and helpful. . ." P. 680.

88 *Ibid.*, pp. 117-118.

89 *The New York Times*, January 25, 1941. Hearings, cited, pp. 479-480.

four amendments: (1) no defense article shall be disposed of " except after consultation with the Chief of Staff of the Army or the Chief of Naval Operations of the Navy, or both," an amendment designed to prevent the President from transferring any part of the navy to Great Britain; (2) a time limit, setting June 30, 1943, as the terminal date of the powers granted to the President; (3) a statement that " nothing in this Act shall be construed to authorize or to permit the authorization of convoying vessels by naval vessels of the United States," inserted to meet the criticism that the President might interpret the act to modify the " carry " provision of the Neutrality Law; and (4) a provision calling upon the President for " a report of operations under this Act except such information as he deems incompatible with the public interest to disclose " at least every ninety days.[90] The Republicans found these amendments only partially satisfactory, contending that they did not go far enough. They were particularly concerned about the absence of any restriction on the financial obligations that could be incurred under the act, suggesting a maximum of two billion dollars.[91]

The report of the minority members of the Committee opened with the statement: " We are for all aid to Britain short of war, and short of sacrificing our own defense and our own freedom." Upon the first part of that statement they were in agreement with the majority. Consequently the debate in the House centered around defining " our own defense and our own freedom "—which was putting in another form the question of presidential powers. The interpretation placed upon these words was resolved almost entirely in terms of party affiliation. With one exception the Democratic majority in the House voted down all amendments not favored by the House leaders. The one exception was the Dirksen amendment, slipped through the Committee of the Whole when sixty-five Democrats were at lunch. This amendment gave Congress the power, by con-

90 77th Cong., 1st Sess. H. Rep. 18.

91 *Ibid.* Minority views, p. 13. The seven amendments proposed by the minority may be found on pp. 14-15.

current resolution, to rescind at any time any or all of the powers given to the President under the terms of the Lend-Lease bill.[92]

Despite the prohibition on convoys there was still some uneasiness even among the Democrats that the Neutrality Act of 1939 would be circumvented if the President thought it necessary to do so. To placate further these individuals, Mr. Bloom secured the acceptance of an amendment providing that " nothing in this Act shall be construed to authorize or to permit the authorization of the entry of any American vessel into a combat area in violation of section 3 [combat areas] of the Neutrality Act of 1939." [93] During the 1939 debate in the House on the Neutrality Bill this section had been stricken out because of Republican criticisms that it enabled the President to pick the aggressor!

The bill did not contain any limit on the amount of equipment and other material the President could lend or lease. Mr. Wadsworth, a Republican who warmly supported the bill, proposed that it be amended to place some limit " on the amount authorized to be appropriated." [94] The warm response his proposal received on both sides of the aisle made the majority leaders reconsider their refusal to name any sum as a limit for the leasing or lending of supplies.[95] Cloakroom polls convinced the leaders that there was a strong sentiment for retaining control of the purse strings. Speaker Rayburn finally consented to an amendment which, in its final form, stipulated that " the value of defense articles disposed of in any way (under authority of this act) and procured from funds *heretofore* appropriated, shall not exceed $1,300,000,000." Thus Congress kept a small measure of financial control—at least on the down payment.[96]

92 *The New York Times*, February 7, 1941.

93 77th Cong., 1st Sess. February 7, 1941. *Cong. Rec.* (daily ed.), p. 787.

94 *Ibid.* February 4, 1941. *Cong. Rec.* (daily ed.), p. 579.

95 *The New York Times*, February 5, 1941.

96 77th Cong., 1st Sess. February 8, 1941. *Cong. Rec.* (daily ed.), p. 821.

The final vote in the House on passage of the bill was 260 to 165. The yeas consisted of 236 Democrats and 24 Republicans; the nays, 135 Republicans, 25 Democrats, and five from minor parties. While this was a sizable vote of confidence in the President—principally by his political cohorts—it indicated that the country was not as united as many had believed. The inclusion of the restrictive amendments was further indication that there was some suspicion of the foreign policy of the President.

Notwithstanding the wide publicity marking the Senate debates, the Senate contributed relatively little to the bill. Its principal accomplishment was the perfection of the bill. There, too, the leaders were able to beat down the amendments they did not favor and secure the adoption of those they wanted. In all, the Senate adopted eight amendments, the most important of which were those keeping control of the purse in the hands of Congress. Senator Byrd secured the inclusion of an amendment specifying that future expenditures under the act must be authorized for that purpose and cannot be taken from the sums appropriated for the regular activities of the government. Senator Byrnes' amendment limited the President's power " to . . . place in good working order " any defense article " to the extent to which funds are made available therefor, or contracts are authorized from time to time by the Congress, or both . . ." With these amendments, and some of lesser importance, the Senate passed the bill, 60 to 31.[97]

97 Senator Connally put through an amendment to modify the Dirksen amendment that the House had approved. The Connally amendment, which appears in the act, provided that Congress, by concurrent resolution, could revoke the powers delegated to the President only if it declared that they are no longer necessary to promote the national defense. Section 3 (c).

Senator Ellender's proposed amendment restricting the use of the armed forces outside the Western Hemisphere drew such unexpected support that the Senate leaders did not wish to risk a vote on it. Instead, they offered a compromise acceptable to the administration as well as to the supporters of the Ellender amendment. It appears as section 10 of the act. " Nothing in this Act shall be construed to change existing law relating to the use of the land and naval forces of the United States, except insofar as such

When the bill returned to the House, the leaders were concerned with securing the quickest action on it in order to submit it to the President. The usual technique of submitting it to a conference committee to reconcile the divergent views of both Houses was ruled out, principally because the minority leaders in the House found the Senate amendments acceptable. The Rules Committee reported out a rule providing that "all Senate amendments be . . . agreed to." By unanimous consent debate on the rule was limited to two hours. Thus, the House, in the two hours available, did not debate the bill, but the Senate amendments thereto. The Republicans who had strenuously contested its original passage found the Senate amendments an improvement over the bill that the House had passed. Not wishing to be saddled with the accusations of impeding the defense of the country, many of them announced their support of the amended bill. The final vote was 516 to 71, a loss of almost a hundred opposition votes.[98]

Whatever the constitutional weaknesses of the Lend-Lease bill, psychologically it was sound. It was presented as a defense measure to supplement the accelerated defense program upon which the country embarked. Congress, throughout 1940, had responded to executive requests for grants of money and power to insure the safety of the nation. This bill therefore was another step in a long range program of domestic security. Taking advantage of the popular enthusiasm for such a program, the administration, as part of that program, removed by indirection one feature of the neutrality acts to which it was always opposed. Large sections of Congress had always protested against the executive's requests for discretion in selecting

use relates to the manufacture, procurement, and repair of defense articles, the communication of information and other noncombatant purposes enumerated in this Act."

In the Senate 49 Democrats, 10 Republicans, and one Independent voted affirmatively. The opposition comprised 13 Democrats, 17 Republicans, and one Progressive.

98 77th Cong., 1st Sess. March 11, 1941. *Cong. Rec.* (daily ed.), p. 2229.

the aggressor nations. The Lend-Lease bill accorded the President this power by proceeding in the opposite direction—the President was given the power to select the nations that were the victims of aggression, or to use the language of the bill, those " whose defense the President deems vital to the defense of the United States."

It may be argued whether the cash part of the " cash and carry " requirements of the 1939 neutrality act is untouched by the terms of the Lend-Lease law since the 1939 act is applicable to private citizens and not to the United States Government. The distinction, if there is one, becomes less important, however, when one considers that the Government, as part of the defense program, has secured a wide degree of control over private enterprise and encouraged its expansion through the use of subventions. What a private citizen cannot do because of the law can be done for him, indirectly, by the Government's command over a large area of the industrial life of the nation. This line of reasoning was followed by Secretary Hull in explaining the effect of the Lend-Lease bill upon the Johnson act.

This act [the Johnson act] would not appear to be involved for the reason that it does not apply to this Government, or to a public corporation created by or in pursuance of special authorization of Congress, or to a corporation in which the Government has or exercises a controlling interest, as, for example, the Import-Export Bank.[99]

He offered a similar explanation in regard to section 7 of the 1939 neutrality law, which prohibits the extension of loans or credits to a belligerent government. As a further assurance that the aid extended by the President to foreign governments would not be challenged on the ground that the Lend-Lease bill conflicted with earlier statutes, the grants of power under which he can act are given him " notwithstanding the provisions of any other law."

99 Hearings on *Lend-Lease Bill*, pp. 8-9.

However willing the administration found Congress in yielding on the financial question—it must be admitted that the House was surprisingly indifferent to protect its time-honored function of watchdog of the Treasury—Congress was concerned lest, by implication, the " carry " part of the neutrality law be altered. Administration leaders recognized this concern and therefore did not oppose the inclusion of several sections of dubious value. The prohibition on the convoying of vessels by naval vessels does not deprive the President of his constitutional role of commander-in-chief of the navy. The further restriction that the act should not be interpreted so as to permit American vessels to enter combat areas overlooks the fact that such areas are established by the President who may modify, extend, or eliminate them at his discretion. " The interest of national defense " may be a compelling reason therefore for his failure to observe these sections of the law.

Finally, a word should be said about the political scene. From the moment the Lend-Lease bill was presented to Congress, it was evident that it would be debated and voted upon, particularly in the House, on party lines. For one thing, the Democratic ranks were closed. Whatever the degree of opposition on the part of Southern congressmen to the President's domestic program, on foreign affairs they stood strongly behind him. Moreover, President Roosevelt's reelection was interpreted as an endorsement not only of the objective of his foreign policy —aid to the democracies—but also of the methods he was using to reach that objective. The Republicans, as a party, were embarrassed and divided on the issue of foreign policy. Mr. Willkie, although standing for aid to Britain, was critical of the President's conduct of foreign policy. Most of his competitors for the Republican nomination, and many Republican congressmen too, were essentially isolationists. The President's drive to make good on his promise of aid to Britain, therefore, put before the Republicans a difficult problem. If Britain was to be given assistance, it could only be done by modifying some of the mandatory features of earlier legislation and placing in the President's hands, as other defense measures had done, a large degree of discretionary power. Had the administration put forward a bill for repeal of the neutrality law, the Republicans could have raised the issue of war. But the administration's skill in presenting the Lend-Lease bill as a defense measure put them in a hole. To oppose it would open them to the charge of impairing the defense program of the country. To support it would be a volte-face. More important, they had no alternative program to offer. Unable to count upon the support of dissident Democrats, their only choice lay in tempering the extraordinary powers the bill conferred upon the President. Even on that point they were not always able to get up a good fight since the administration forces, in an effort to eliminate internal disagreement, agreed to insert into the bill several amendments that were regarded as checks upon the President. Having registered their opposition when the bill was submitted to the House, many Republicans, sensing the drift of popular sentiment, welcomed the opportunity to shift their position when the Senate's amendments were submitted to the House.

Thus, after years of labor in time of peace to build up a statutory barrier against war, the presence of war and the problems it created raised grave doubts in the minds of legislators as to their capacity to deal effectively with the conditions created by war. On two occasions, in 1939 and in 1941, they removed some of the restrictions placed upon the executive. More than at any time since 1935, Congress showed a willingness to be led, rather than to lead.

CHAPTER VIII
CONCLUSIONS [1]

IT may not be without significance that the legislative committees charged with discussing international questions are called *Foreign Relations* in the Senate and *Foreign Affairs* in the House. I am not able to offer any evidence that the choice of the words *Relations* and *Affairs,* when the two committees were established, was marked by any debate or by a perception of a restrictive meaning. Neither committee, however, chose to describe itself as a Committee on *Foreign Policy.* This elusive term suggests conduct, purpose and continuity in international matters, elements most closely associated with the executive office. An appeal to semantics therefore offers some tenuous support for the relative quiescence of the legislature in foreign affairs.

" Domestic policy and foreign policy are seldom wholly diverse, and foreign policy is in the main profoundly influenced by local interests and ideals." [2] That a distinction should ever have been entertained is understandable. Attention to domestic issues is the cardinal rule of politics. In the popular mind international affairs vacillate between two categories as distinct as black from white. These are peace and war. When the nation is at peace, foreign policy seems relatively remote. It is the work of an initiated few who understand the passwords and ritual. The significance of the day to day decisions of the executive organ which collectively give shape and substance to our foreign policy is lost in the tangle of national and local issues. Many see the deeds; few understand their import. When war is imminent or present, the focus is sharpened. The test of each

1 No attempt is made in this chapter to offer observations pertaining to congressional activities beyond foreign affairs.

2 John Bassett Moore, *Principles of American Diplomacy* (New York, 1905), vii.

decision and of each measure is the strength it gives to the successful prosecution of the conflict.[3]

One need not recite here the historical factors in American history that have given rise to this dichotomy in popular thought between domestic and foreign matters. The significance for this study lies in the fact that congressional organization by its committee system has given support to this division. Rule XI, paragraph 11, of the House Rules, gives to the Committee on Foreign Affairs jurisdiction on " all proposed legislation " relating " to the relations of the United States with foreign nations." At first glance this appears to confer on that Committee the widest latitude. But a reading of the Notes and Annotations attached to that paragraph (and which I have quoted on page 21) and of the balance of the Rule defining the jurisdiction of other standing committees, makes it clear that the Foreign Affairs Committee has very circumscribed powers. Emphasis may be given this point by noting the jurisdiction that is *not* conferred upon it. It does not consider, of course, the naval or military establishments of the nation; it does not pass upon immigration; it does not consider economic measures except those incidental to more basic legislation as, for example, the cash and carry provisions of the neutrality act. (For a brief period in the late nineteenth century the Committee did handle measures dealing with commercial and reciprocal treaties, measures now referred to the Committee on Ways and Means.)

3 Norman Angell relates the following: " Chatting the other day with a journalist friend of mine, I asked him why the newspapers hadn't paid more attention since the Lusitania went down, to alternative methods of action, something other than war, the future foreign policy of the United States, things very relevant to the problem which was presented to us on the morning after the Lusitania was sunk, nearly a year ago. He said, ' It is impossible copy. Our people are not interested in it, save when they think that there is going to be a war the day after tomorrow. For forty-eight hours it would make good copy. From the moment the danger of war had passed, it would cease to be good copy.' " Norman Angell, " Public Opinion in Foreign Policies," *Annals of the Academy of Political and Social Science,* vol. 66, July, 1916, pp. 137-138.

Nor does the Committee pass upon proposals pertaining to foreign commerce. Each of these subjects is within the jurisdiction of some other committee. In the case of economic measures affecting foreign policy there is frequently further legislative diffusion; any one of several committees may handle bills in that sphere. Thus, the Committee on Banking and Currency considered the establishment of the Export-Import Bank; the Committee on Coinage, Weights and Measures passed upon the Foreign Exchange Stabilization Fund; and the Committee on Ways and Means reported out the Reciprocal Trade Agreements Act.

Each legislative proposal enacted into law stands as an authorization. If the law involves an expenditure—and most laws do—another law, carrying an appropriation is necessary. Only the Committee on Appropriations has jurisdiction at this point. It reserves the right to alter, and may even refuse, the requisite sum. An authorization, said President Roosevelt, is like a New Year's resolution that may or may not be kept. Topping all these committees, of course, is the final judgment of the House itself. In the Senate a similar procedure is followed; and when decisions different from those of the House are reached, a conference committee reconciles the divergent views. Thus, bit by bit, the legislature gives direction and meaning in some degree to foreign policy. But at no point in the legislative process is provision made for an examination of the structure which Congress has, in part, created. Certainly the Committee on Foreign Affairs has never drawn up a balance sheet of American foreign policy. The House Rules do not encourage it to undertake so comprehensive a survey. The integrated picture that cannot be secured within the House is not supplied by the executive branch. Alone among the executive departments, the State Department makes no annual report to Congress. The reasons for this exception are readily apparent; the result is that the Foreign Affairs Committee lacks a perspective which makes possible an intelligent understanding of the direction of policy.

Congressional attention to foreign affairs is no more continuous than it is concentrated. At scattered intervals throughout a congressional session bills and resolutions are introduced, considered, and debated that bear, directly or indirectly, upon foreign affairs. The annual appropriation bills give both the Committee on Appropriations and the House an opportunity to make inquiries into policy. But a careful reading of the bulky hearings and the lengthy debates shows a far greater concern for detail of expenditure than for policy objectives. The attempted deletion of the appropriation for an ambassador to Russia stands out as a recent, but relatively rare, exception to this generalization.[4] The criticisms expressed by the House on that occasion were directed more against Russian foreign policy than American foreign policy. By forcing the withdrawal of the American ambassador the House hoped to impress upon the Russian Government its displeasure with the direction of Soviet policy. It is difficult to attribute any constructive purpose to this expression of indignation.

Apart from appropriation bills which follow an annual cycle, legislative ventures in foreign affairs trace their origin to the course of international events and the degree of popular reaction they evoke. One could make a reasonably accurate chart of the drift of international affairs solely by reference to the amount of space devoted to them in the *Congressional Record*. To evaluate congressional influence on foreign policy by this criterion is of little worth. A better yardstick is the translation of these words into legislation capable of dealing with rapidly moving events beyond legislative jurisdiction. It is a task quite unlike that which confronts Congress in domestic affairs.

For one thing, Congress never has before it a complete array of information. The executive is the sole repository of the details that fashion our foreign relations. He may release such information as he decides. Whatever the amount, one may be certain that it will serve to bolster his policy. Two important consequences arise from this situation. The President always

4 *Supra*, p. 129 f.

holds a trump card. Each attack upon his policy may be countered by the revelation of additional details. Congressional critics, deprived of a similar advantage, lean more heavily upon the columns of the press and the discourses of commentators, and opinions more easily pass as facts. One need only offer in evidence the greater volume of this material found in the *Congressional Record* and the interpretations placed upon it by congressmen. Almost no recognition has been given to the role of the journalist in the formulation of congressional judgment on foreign affairs.[5]

There are those in Congress who seek to contest the President's foreign policy. But the sufficiency of his powers makes him an elusive opponent. Until such time as he seeks to supplement his powers by legislation, congressional critics must confine their jousting to straw men and content themselves with the scattered cheers of a few partisans. Once a measure is presented to Congress, his opponents are able to concentrate their attack.

The contest is not between equals. The offensive rests with the President and his cohorts in Congress. The element of time is important, for the moment of introduction of a bill as well as its contents may catch the opposition off guard. The President's forces have access to authoritative information upon which they may draw as circumstances require. The sharper the clashes, the more likely they are to be publicized. And no one can compete with the President in securing publicity.[6] In the committees and on the floor his followers press for tactical advantages. Points of order, time limitations and roll calls are

5 Senator Bone, during the debate on the Selective Compulsory Military Service bill, observed: "I learn of pronouncements by the State Department by reading the Washington daily press. The Senate is not dignified by having them transmitted directly to us, although I, as a Senator, would be compelled to vote on a proposed declaration of war." 76th Cong., 3rd Sess. August 21, 1940. *Cong. Rec.*, p. 1067.

6 *Cf.* Lindsay Rogers, *The American Senate* (New York, 1926), p. 214 f.

only a few of the stratagems in which they may indulge if the contest promises to be close.[7]

The rules of the contest require that each party attribute to his opponent only the highest of purposes. A reference, even an allusion, to partisanship is met with an air of righteous indignation by the accused. I cannot recall a single instance where a member of Congress announced his position on foreign policy solely on the basis of party allegiance. Yet an analysis of the discussions and debates, within the Committee on Foreign Affairs and the House itself, makes pretty clear the fact that the line—admittedly somewhat jagged—dividing proponents and opponents is the party line. The arguments advanced are largely rationalizations of predetermined judgments. Witness the Democratic opposition to President Coolidge's Nicaraguan policy in 1927 and the Republican opposition to the neutrality legislation of the late 1930's. When, in the winter of 1912, the Committee investigated the acquisition of the Panama Canal, it was not motivated primarily by the inability of the United States and Colombia to reach an amicable settlement of their differences. The Democrats who had captured the House in 1910 were laying the groundwork for attacks against Taft and Roosevelt, preparatory to the presidential election in 1912.[8]

The application of the neutrality legislation of the late 1930's was made contingent upon future events outside the immediate control of the United States but vitally affecting its interests. This called for the exercise of presidential discretion, a power which the President's opponents were unwilling to grant him. To have put the argument on the same plane of partisanship as had marked debates on domestic issues, would have cost the

7 How President Wilson used his influence in the House to defeat the McLemore resolution is told by Charles C. Tansill, America Goes to War (Boston, 1938), chap. XVII. See, supra, p. 13, ft. 8.

8 62nd Cong., 1st Sess. H. Res. 32 (Rainey resolution). The hearings are titled The Story of Panama. For the political background, see Henry F. Pringle, Theodore Roosevelt (New York, 1931), pp. 315-338; the same author's Life and Times of William H. Taft (New York, 1939), p. 815 f. Also, Philip C. Jessup, Elihu Root, cited, p. 521 f.

opposition much public support and respect. The issue was elevated to the dignity of a conflict between the executive and legislative organs in which the latter presumed to be a more sensitive barometer of public sentiment.[9] On the other hand, the President's proponents found the extraordinary conditions of the world demanding a greater concentration of powers in his hands.[10] That the grant of discretionary power was not a novel one is attested to by the Supreme Court in the Curtiss-Wright decision.

Practically every volume of the United States Statutes contains one or more acts or joint resolutions of Congress authorizing action by the President in respect of subjects affecting foreign relations, which either leave the exercise of the power to his unrestricted judgment, or provide a standard far more general than that which has always been considered requisite with regard to domestic affairs.[11]

Not all opposition is narrowly partisan. Some of it does center around the recurring conflict of powers between the executive and the legislature. Such was the issue involved in the rejection by Congress of Secretary Mellon's request for complete power for the Treasury Department to deal with the debtor nations.[12] Despite a large Republican majority in both Houses

9 Cf. the remarks of Mr. Mott, 76th Cong., 1st Sess. June 28, 1939. Cong. Record, p. 11356: "Let us take it and consider it and debate it and vote upon it for exactly what it is—a bill demanded by the President and prepared under the order of the President to put a new and novel foreign policy invented by the President into actual and immediate operation..."

10 Cf. the remarks of Mr. Jarman, ibid., p. 11330: "Everyone of us fully realizes that with a body of 435 Members here and 96 Members across the building it is absolutely impossible for anyone to be entirely familiar, and it is ridiculous for one to claim that with all of his multitudinous duties he can be thoroughly familiar, with all phases of everything that is happening here. Consequently, we must trust to the leadership and guidance of someone familiar with foreign affairs..."

11 299 U. S. 324.

12 67th Cong., 1st Sess. Hearings on H. R. 7359, Refunding Foreign Obligations, before the Committee on Ways and Means.

his request was denied. Instead, the World War Foreign Debt Commission with rigidly specified powers was created. The issue involved here was the settlement of money owed the United States and so was properly within the jurisdiction of Congress. It dealt with a precise matter to which the United States was a party.

The Court's remarks suggest another type of legislation, not wholly unrelated to that discussed above, which confers broad powers upon the President. In popular parlance these powers are referred to as emergency powers. A goodly portion of them stem from legislation enacted during World War I when Congress was least disposed to check the executive. The balance has found its way into the statute books through the course of more than a century. Like the neutrality legislation and other acts bearing more directly on foreign affairs, they may be invoked at the President's discretion although the discretion is circumscribed by the inclusion of the phrases " in time of war and national emergency " or simply " in time of war." Where debate has preceded the passage of such legislation, the emphasis has fallen upon the domestic character of the law. Legislators have not regarded the acts as bearing on foreign policy except insofar as they are part of the nation's defense. Almost none of the acts in itself would lend much support to the prosecution of a particular foreign policy.[13] Collectively, the powers they confer upon the President make an impressive array, supplementing those accruing to him from other sources. In recent years they have been the subject of increasing congressional attention.[14]

13 E. g., Act of October 6, 1917, 40 *Stat.* 394 (U. S. C., title 35, sec. 42), authorizing the Commissioner of Patents to order certain inventions kept secret and to withhold patent therefor "when the United States is at war." Act of February 4, 1887, 24 *Stat.* 380, as amended (U. S. C., title 10, sec. 1362), providing for preference to shipments of troops and material of war upon demand of the President "in time of war or threatened war."

14 76th Cong., 3rd Sess. S. Doc. 133. *Executive Powers under National Emergency. Ibid.* Speech of Senator Taft on the emergency powers of the President. November 3, 1939. *Cong. Record*, App., p. 713.

Congress, like a man near the bottom of a pyramid, can see only one side, at best two, and has only a limited gaze away from the structure; the President, standing on top, is able to take in a panoramic view around him and see down all sides. The Constitution alone did not create this presidential vantage point in foreign affairs. Nor has it been solely the product of legislation. To these two contributory sources must be added the principal one, that of presidential initiative. This is the shaft that supports the President. Unchallenged, or weakly challenged, precedents have slowly emerged as unchallengeable powers. What these accreted powers in foreign affairs are today has been summarized by Professor Corwin.[15]

An unlimited discretion in the President in the recognition of new governments and states; an undefined authority in sending special agents abroad, of dubious diplomatic status, to negotiate treaties or for other purposes; a similarly undefined power to enter into compacts with other governments without the participation of the Senate; the practically complete and exclusive discretion in the negotiation of more formal treaties, and in their final ratification; the practically complete and exclusive initiative in the official formulation of the nation's foreign policy.

In substantiation of this last statement one need only recall that the trite phrases so often used to describe American foreign policy—no entangling alliances, the Monroe Doctrine, the Open Door policy—were pronouncements of the executive, not the legislative, branch. To these may be added other utterances, perhaps less durable, but in their day equally important. Most recently, the exchange of American destroyers for naval bases in British possessions in this hemisphere was consummated by the President. The terms of the exchange were subsequently communicated to Congress " for its information." [16] Even

15 Edward S. Corwin, *The President's Control of Foreign Relations* (Princeton, 1917), pp. 205-206.

16 76th Cong., 3rd Sess. H. Doc. 943.

legislation, unequivocal in its language and purpose, may be the basis for the initiation of a policy not in harmony with the intentions of Congress. When Congress prohibited the use of American ships in transporting goods to belligerents in the 1939 neutrality act, it felt satisfied that a long step had been taken toward safeguarding American shipping. The act was barely a day old when the Maritime Commission gave conditional approval for the transfer of American ships to Panamanian registry. An indignant outburst on the part of many, including legislators who were staunch supporters of the bill like Congressman Bloom, killed the plan.[17]

It is not what the President *cannot* do because of legislative restrictions, but what he *can* do outside the framework of legislation, that poses a problem for those who, by legislation, seek to formulate foreign policy. The recognition of this problem has made Congress hesitant, even reluctant, to act.[18] Legislative reluctance is heightened by the postulate that the President's judgment is determined only by reference to the nation's best interests. The second paragraph of the adverse report on the McLemore resolution in 1916 expressed this thought.[19]

Under the practice and precedents in this country, the conduct of diplomatic negotiations has been left to the President and with this practice the committee does not feel it proper for the House of Representatives to interfere. We know that if the President reaches a point in any negotiations with foreign Governments at which he has exhausted his power in the premises he will in the usual way report all facts and circumstances to Congress for its consideration.

Treaties excepted, the inferior role of the House in foreign affairs is due to qualities inherent in its composition and organization. In our scale of political values the House stands below

17 *The New York Times*, November 9, 1939.

18 Note the Committee's discussion on the war powers of the President, *supra*, pp. 88-89.

19 64th Cong., 1st Sess. H. Rep. 793. This paragraph was written by Mr. Porter, a Republican member of the Committee. Minutes, C. F. A.

the Senate. Representatives aspire to a senatorial seat; the converse does not hold true.[20] Moreover, a senator is a definite article; he is *the* junior or senior senator from Nevada or from Georgia. Representatives, on the other hand, are indefinite articles—*a* representative from North Dakota or from New York. To refer to him as the representative from the Fourth District of Massachusetts makes him definite, but only emphasizes his obscurity. In short, senators belong to a more exclusive club with all the privileges that membership therein entails. In the expression of opinions which characterizes the democratic process senatorial judgments may have no more substantive value than those of representatives, but they certainly do have more news value. No doubt the skirmishes between the President and the Senate on treaties, of which that over the Versailles Treaty was among the most violent, have impressed upon the people the Senate's voice in foreign affairs. A senator is expected to be an expert on this subject; and few senators want to deny their public. The 1939 debate in the Senate on the neutrality measure was billed as the debate of the century. After the principals finished the first round, the seconds took over and sparred through several hundred pages of the *Congressional Record*. Yet the interest of the press, and presumably that of the country, did not lag. By holding the floor for most of the day a senator's views became news. Of course, the press followed the debates in the House; but except for a few national figures whose remarks received some extended publicity, the majority who spoke were lost in the summation of the day's proceedings.

There are other reasons, too, why this disparity prevails. The constituency of a representative is not only smaller but more homogeneous than that of a senator. His interests are strongly provincial. The fact that he must submit himself for the approval of the electorate with greater frequency makes it incum-

20 When the 76th Congress closed, twenty-nine senators had previously served in the House while only one representative had seen service in the Senate.

bent upon him to give closer attention to local matters. His political fences may not be as long as those of a senator but they have to be repaired more often. The people have been conditioned to look to the President for leadership in foreign affairs. This gives the President " a psychology factor ", to borrow a term from Mr. Laski. Without arguing the merits of this proposition so far as it pertains to the Senate, it is undoubtedly true that the people expect no strong convictions on foreign affairs from their representatives. I am not thinking here of questions like the tariff or immigration which may have a domestic, or sectional, appeal, but rather of those issues that are popularly called " political " and are closely identified with the executive. Representative Ludlow of Indiana attracted something like national attention when he asked his constituents to vote him up or down on the single issue of the war referendum of which he was the sponsor.

The House Rules recognize no distinction in the treatment of foreign affairs. All the artifices that ordinarily prevail are utilized. This means that party leaders and party discipline exert their influence. One enlightening, but inconspicuous, bit of evidence on this point is the consistency with which resolutions of inquiry pertaining to foreign affairs have been adversely reported. They are, as I pointed out elsewhere, a device of the minority to pinprick the executive's foreign policy. That they do not achieve their purpose is a testimony to the application of party organization and control.

The Rules of the House not only are more rigid, but they are more strictly enforced. The control of time is always a deterrent to lengthy expression or exchange of ideas. What passes for debate in the House is frequently nothing more than a series of short speeches. If the subject is one relatively unfamiliar to the members, it hardly pays to study intently to give a five-minute discourse. One can always beg off an insistent critic by refusing to yield in the few minutes allotted to him. This terseness compares unfavorably with the Senate where members must expect to have their remarks more carefully scrutinized and be prepared for a cross examination.

Perhaps this element of partisanship in the House is more striking because the Senate glories in what Woodrow Wilson termed " its pride of independence." It frequently has no more information upon which to proceed intelligently than has the House. But it makes a little information go a long way. It cannot be rushed by cracking the party whip; if anything, it becomes more truculent. If the fifteen years' struggle over American adherence to the World Court and the bitter debates on neutrality since 1935 prove anything on the respective positions of the House and Senate in foreign affairs, it is this: the Senate is less amenable to presidential leadership in foreign affairs than the House. Adherence to the Court, it will be recalled, was endorsed by both major parties, urged by every President since Wilson, and approved by an overwhelming majority in the House. The elections of 1936 and 1938 gave the electorate opportunities to register its disapproval of the neutrality policy urged upon the House by the President. It may be, as Wilson thought, that " the Senate is not so immediately sensitive to opinion," a result in part of the greater security its members enjoy. Yet both of these issues were before the country for a sufficient time to have permitted popular displeasure with the Senate's attitude to assert itself through successive elections. In none of the campaigns was either issue singled out for popular determination, and election results provide no clue as to how the country felt about the Court or neutrality.[21] National issues determined national elections only insofar as they were immediately applicable in local areas. It is not so important to

21 On the World Court, see Manley O. Hudson, " The United States Senate and the World Court," *Amer. Jour. of Inter. Law*, XXIX (April, 1935), pp. 301-307. During the hearings on the Lend-Lease bill in January, 1941, Secretary Hull observed: " I have almost talked my head off for about three or four years about the conditions abroad and what was developing. But most of our people have been engrossed in domestic affairs, unfortunately." Hearings, cited, p. 34.

argue whether the Senate or the House mirrors more accurately the country's views on foreign policy. What is important is that the Senate thinks it does, it has the power within its own organization to act as if it did, and the country interprets its conduct as evidence of the independence of the legislative power.[22]

The characteristics that mark the Senate and the House in their treatment of foreign affairs are, to a large degree, reflected in the committees within each House that handle that subject. The Senate Committee, comprising almost one-quarter of the Senate, is the most important to which a senator may aspire. The House Committee, with less than six percent of the representatives upon it, was long regarded as an ornamental committee whose members, the chairman included, were relatively obscure in the national scene.[23] Since 1935 legislation on foreign affairs has done much to bring the Committee into public and legislative prominence, although it is too early to predict that it will retain that position. Perhaps the most severe indictment that can be made against the House Committee is that its members have not developed into a body of experts, or even quasi-experts, who understand the complexities of foreign policy. I have no doubt that the usual demands made upon congressmen have served to divert the members from closer attention to their committee work. Nor does service in state and local offices, so frequently a prelude to service in the House, provide them with training for an understanding of international problems. The knowledge of foreign affairs that a member brings to the Committee is no greater than that attributed to Lord Dudley, Canning's foreign minister, of whom the

22 *Cf.* 70th Cong., 2nd Sess. (1928). H. Res. 264, introduced by Mr. Fish. "Resolved, That the House of Representatives desires to express its cordial approval of the said general pact for the renunciation of war and an earnest desire that the United States give it early ratification. Resolved further, That the House of Representatives expresses its willingness to participate in the formulation and enactment of legislation to effect the purpose of said general pact."

23 *Cf.* Perry Belmont, *An American Democrat,* cited, p. 216.

French said that he was entrusted with the care of foreign affairs " parceque ses affaires lui ont ètè toujours étrangères." [24]

The organization and control of the House are geared to the party system. Chairmen of committees, more than other members of the House, are conscious of their partisan obligations. In foreign affairs more than domestic, the greater hiatus between executive control and legislative incompetence reduces further the independence of the chairman.[25] The presumption upon which chairmen of the Foreign Affairs Committee appear to proceed may be put in this language: so long as the President's policy arouses no outbursts of criticism that reach back into their districts or those of a considerable number of their colleagues, it must be accepted that the President's policy meets the approval of the electorate. As between an aggressive President, possessing plenary powers, and a hypercritical Senate, exercising only a negative function, there is little choice but to follow the former. The principle of geographical distribution of committee assignments means that a group of representatives from scattered parts of the nation comprise the Committee. It takes an issue of the first magnitude to arouse the constituents in widely dispersed sections. So far as I have been able to determine, members of the Committee, as individuals, have not been plagued by pressure from their constituents. Their mail is no heavier than that of their colleagues who are not on the Committee. In the public view senators are regarded as the proper recipients of expressions on foreign affairs.

Commenting upon the failure of the House of Commons to display an interest in Lord Grey's foreign policy, Philip Morrell wrote, in 1912, that " if he (Grey) is reluctant to take the House of Commons into his confidence, the House of Commons has been equally reluctant to urge him to do so." [26] The

24 Cited by Algernon Cecil, " The Foreign Office," in the *Cambridge History of British Foreign Policy*, III, p. 563.

25 See *supra*, p. 102 f.

26 *Contemporary Review*, CII (November, 1912), p. 663.

same may be said of the attitude of Congress toward the President. During the last few years the President has made numerous calls upon Congress for legislation to strengthen the prosecution of his foreign policy. Almost without exception, each of the measures introduced has been debated along thinly disguised party lines. Opposition has centered around the enlargement of presidential powers resulting from its passage. The main check to this aggrandizement of power has been in the form of an imposition of a time limit, thereby assuring Congress the occasion at some future date to reexamine the desirability of continuing the legislation. One would have expected that at some time there would have been a strenuous effort made to debate the question of legislative collaboration with the executive in the making of foreign policy. Only two feeble attempts were made in this direction, neither of which mustered the support even of minority members.

In the special session of Congress in the fall of 1939, called by President Roosevelt to modify the neutrality law, Representative Rees (R., Kan.) introduced a joint resolution providing for the creation of a joint congressional committee of ten members, five named by the presiding officer of each body, " to consult and advise with the President respecting the present European situation with the view to obtaining information, to inform the Congress of developments, and to assist in formulating legislative policy." [27] The resolution made clear what Mr. Rees did not in his explanatory remarks, namely, that the sole purpose was to keep Congress abreast of world events and not to have it play a positive role in deciding how to meet their impact upon the United States. More far-reaching was the amendment to the neutrality bill offered by Senator Davis (R., Pa.) during the same session.[28] It called for a National Neu-

[27] 76th Cong., 2nd Sess. H. J. Res. 387; remarks in *Cong. Record*, October 2, 1939, p. 78. *Cf.* 76th Cong., 3rd Sess. H. Con. Res. 64 (Allen, Pa.), creating a joint committee to formulate a military policy for the United States.

[28] 76th Cong., 2nd Sess. *Cong. Record*, p. 911 f. October 26, 1939.

trality Commission of thirteen members. By party caucus the majority and the minority in each House were to choose two members each—a total of eight. Five cabinet members—the Secretaries of State, Treasury, War, Navy, and Commerce—comprised the balance of the Commission. Only the legislative members could vote except in the case of a tie when the cabinet officers, voting as a unit, could cast the deciding vote. In addition to determining when to issue and to revoke proclamations under the Neutrality Act, the Commission was to

advise and consult with the President with respect to, including the formulation of, the foreign policy of the United States, and the President is requested not to make public or authorize the making public of any official statement with respect to foreign policy of the United States without having first consulted with the Commission in connection therewith.

The fact that " the President is requested " indicates the limitations of the proposal. Under the guise of legislative participation in policy making, the amendment gave the minority a weight disproportionate to its representation in Congress. Yet no senator, apart from Senator Davis, spoke in its behalf and it was promptly voted down without a record vote.

The apathy of the Committee on Foreign Affairs toward securing a larger role in foreign policy is nothing more than a reflection of that which marks the House as a whole. Bearing somewhat obliquely on this attitude of the House is the serious consideration given to the war referendum (the Ludlow) amendment. No more vital control over foreign affairs rests with Congress than that pertaining to the declaration of war. Only by the slight margin of eleven votes did the House reject the plan to shift the responsibility for that decision from Congress to the electorate. If any moral can be drawn from the principle embodied in the resolution, it is that Congress lacked confidence in its own capacity to pass judgment upon a most important aspect of foreign policy.

Students of the democratic control of foreign policy have been more exercised by the subordinate role of Congress in foreign policy than has Congress itself. Although there is no unanimity among them on how best to achieve their objective, almost all of them see the necessity for fundamental readjustments in the relations between the executive and the legislative organs. The proposals include:

1. A constitutional amendment to permit the House to share in the treaty making process. President Wilson's difficulties with the Senate gave currency to this idea. Apart from the difficulty of initiating and securing the adoption of an amendment, most questions of policy are decided outside the realm of treaties.[29]

2. The presence of cabinet officers on the floor of Congress.[30] This could be done by amendments to the rules of each House. The interpellation of the Secretary of State would be either upon decisions already reached, in which case the House and Senate would have no voice in formulating policy, or upon decisions anticipated in the light of international events. In the latter instance, the debate would serve to inform the Secretary of the sense of each House—a weak argument when one considers that the hearings of committees and open debates serve much the same purpose. Moreover, a President intent upon acting as his own Secretary of State would be beyond the reach of Congress. The Secretary would stand before the legislature as an apologetic substitute for the real power in foreign policy.

3. A foreign relations cabinet which would include members of Congress, majority and minority. Dangerfield would assign to it the duty of defining the foreign policies of the United States. There is no obligation upon the President to follow the decisions of such a body. There is no reason to believe that the congressional members

29 Cf. Denna F. Fleming, The Treaty Veto of the American Senate (New York, 1930), p. 289 f. Also, I. M. Stone, "The House of Representatives and the Treaty-Making Power," Kentucky Law Journal, XVII (1929), pp. 216-257; Ralston Hayden, The Senate and Treaties, 1789-1817 (New York, 1920); W. Stull Holt, Treaties Defeated by the Senate (Baltimore, 1933).

30 Cf. Belmont, cited, chap. XXI. Also, Nicholas Murray Butler, Across the Busy Years (New York, 1940), II, p. 355 f.

of the same political faith as the President would offer any more effective opposition than they do under the present, less formal arrangement.[31]

4. A joint committee on foreign affairs " to maintain contacts with the President and the State Department, to study proposals and decisions made by them, and to keep the leaders and members of Congress constantly informed as to the steps being taken by the Executive." Such is Charles Beard's proposal. Attached to the committee would be a staff of experts to check the State Department's experts. How the committee's experts would acquire their information, controlled by the Department, is not explained.[32]

The basic changes necessary to put into operation any one of these plans constitute the greatest single obstacle to the acceptance of any of them. I have already pointed out that congressional interest in foreign affairs, like that of the public generally, depends upon the immediate state of international affairs. In times of quiet there is a complacency about, even an indifference to, the control of foreign policy. In periods of crisis there

31 Royden J. Dangerfield, *In Defense of the Senate* (Norman, Oklahoma, 1933), p. 321 f. Also, Quincy Wright, *Control of American Foreign Relations* (New York, 1922), p. 371 f. *Cf.* 70th Cong., 1st Sess. H. R. 13179, *To Provide for the Reorganization of the Department of State...*, introduced by Chairman Porter in April, 1928. Section 6 reads: " There is hereby created an Advisory Council in the Department of State, which shall be composed of the Secretary of State, who shall be the chairman thereof, and the Undersecretaries and Assistant Secretaries of State. The Council shall, upon the call of the Secretary of State, meet and consider questions relating to the foreign affairs of the United States. The Secretary *may* invite the chairmen and ranking minority members of the Committee on Foreign Relations of the Senate and the Committee on Foreign Affairs of the House of Representatives to participate in the meetings of such council." It need hardly be added that neither the President nor the Secretary of State needs legislative authorization to consult with such individuals as either may desire.

32 *The New York World Telegram,* September 27, 1939. *Cf.* 76th Cong., 3rd Sess. H. Con. Res. 65 (Rogers, R., Mass.), providing that the two congressional committees on foreign affairs " meet jointly and daily with the Secretary of State or his representatives in order to be advised by the most reliable and authoritative source of the exact development in Europe and Asia and to be prepared to take far-reaching steps for our national defense and our neutrality policy."

is no disposition to debate and initiate untried concepts of legislative collaboration with the executive.

Those who advocate a change have built their proposals upon certain assumptions. Among the most prominent is the notion that the President, enjoying plenary powers in foreign policy, is set off from Congress, especially the House, by a wide constitutional chasm. The history of the presidency, at least in the last forty years, shows that the gap has been spanned at many points. Congressional opposition to presidential policies is frequently interpreted as the opposition of an organ of government; rather, it is essentially a partisan opposition not unlike that offered to domestic issues. Nor is it correct to assume that Congress is more sensitive to public opinion than is the President. The methods of expressing and determining public opinion today give him a unique advantage over the more provincial contacts of the individual legislator.

If any of the proposals accomplished what was claimed for it—to give Congress a share in policy formulation—it would merit serious consideration. But none of them is able to get around the fact that in the selection of legislative representatives to sit with executive officers, the choice is made on the basis of party affiliation, that is, majority and minority members. The result is to erect a system that differs from that which presently exists only in form and not in substance. It is difficult to believe that, because the contacts between the executive and the legislature are put on a more formal basis, the influence of the President would be lessened or his position as party leader, with all the responsibilities that entails, would be altered. Basically, the proposals do nothing more than assure the President of advice. The execution of the decisions is still his task. Students of diplomatic history will readily recognize that the moment of execution may be more important than the contents of the note or statement. Nor do any of the plans take account of the constitutional powers entrusted to the President, powers which could be diffused only by amendment. The command of the army and navy may be used as a weapon of diplomacy as well as of war. Consistency would demand that the legislature share in the control of these services.

Unless one is prepared to advocate a complete redistribution of powers—constitutional as well as accretive—none of these plans offers much promise of improvement in legislative participation in foreign policy. It may be asked whether the contemporary practices of Congress are not evolving, slowly and somewhat unsteadily, toward greater participation. The more frequent recourse to hearings, both public and private, is only one indication. While each hearing is, of course, centered around a particular legislative proposal, it frequently serves as a point of departure to explore more fully related policies in the same general field. One need only cite again the several hearings on the neutrality measures. Hearings offer an opportunity, especially for the minority, for public expression as well as some degree of public education on foreign affairs. This is an advantage that would be lacking if a small legislative committee, even bipartisan in composition, met with the executive.

The technical content of modern legislation makes cabinet officers more dependent upon the assistance of departmental experts whose appearance before committees is regarded as both proper and necessary. Their presence before a full committee of each House assures that a larger number of congressmen will be appraised of the minutiae of legislation than if these experts imparted their knowledge only to a few. The argument that committees are too specialized, that they fail to integrate the many-sidedness of foreign policy, is important. Yet no Secretary of State would feel free to venture an opinion on naval policy or the workings of the Exchange Stabilization Fund; nor would a member of the Committee on Foreign Affairs deem it prudent to request that his Committee be kept informed on these matters or others outside its limited jurisdiction. There is no indication that Congress is ready to alter the committee system whatever its shortcomings. The vested interests are too strong. Proposals for reform must bear this in mind. A greater exchange of information between committees would seem highly desirable. It would even be appropriate to have ranking members of other committees present at hearings before the Foreign Affairs Committee to participate in the interrogation of witnesses in order that the complexities of the problem may be more fully explored; and, of course, other committees would return the courtesy. It would seem desirable that the Senate and House committees dealing with foreign affairs meet together, particularly when hearings on legislative proposals are held. The testimony offered by cabinet officers when the Lend-Lease bill was before the Senate Committee lost some of its effectiveness through repetition. Nor did the House Committee, on the other hand, have the benefit of the views of many of the individuals who testified before the Senate Committee. There is no evidence that either Committee is anxious to initiate such a procedure. Yet the result would be to give a more effective expression to the legislative viewpoint.

On the other side of the picture, the State Department is alert to the value of good relations with Congress. If Congress cannot always take positive steps in foreign policy, it can be an irritable critic and, at times, an obstructive element. To make for expeditious dealings with legislators, especially members of the committees having jurisdiction over foreign affairs, one of the assistant secretaries is charged with the duty of acting as a liaison officer between the Department and Congress. Finally, Secretary Hull has brought to the Department a unique comprehension of the legislators' viewpoint. His long experience in the House and the Senate has made him an unobtrusive link between the two powers of government. It is a quality that cannot be expressed in quantitative terms—one that critics cannot promise in the best conceived paper projects.

BIBLIOGRAPHICAL NOTE

The written materials upon which I have drawn are familiar to every student of American government. Most important, because the diverse views of members are reflected more accurately in them, are the Committee's printed hearings upon particular bills and resolutions. These vary in size and in value, but are the most intimate public records available. Along with other congressional publications, they are listed in the biennial *Document Catalog*. A measure reported to the House for its consideration is accompanied by a report containing a summary of the measure and the principal arguments for its passage. Members who do not agree with the report frequently secure the right to file a minority report. Some of the reports also include the views of the President and the State Department as set forth in correspondence to the chairman or to Congress. These reports form part of the collection of House reports which are numbered consecutively as they make their appearance and are bound together, usually in several volumes, for each Congress. Congressional debates on all bills and resolutions are found in the *Congressional Record*. At the end of each Congress the Committee on Foreign Affairs prints a *Calendar*, listing chronologically all bills and resolutions referred to it and the action taken on them.

Everyone undertaking a study of the functions of the House of Representatives and its committees owes a debt of gratitude to a former clerk of the House, Asher C. Hinds, for his encyclopedic work, *Precedents of the House of Representatives* (1907-1908), in eight volumes. Three supplementary volumes, edited by Representative Cannon, bring the work up to 1935. The sections on The Committee on Foreign Affairs, Inquiries of the Executive, and Prerogatives of the House as to Treaties proved extremely valuable as points of departure in examining these aspects of the Committee's functions.

More valuable for a study of the Committee were the unpublished materials retained in the Committee's possession or deposited in the Library of Congress. Dating from post-Civil War days are the large ledger-like volumes, one for each Congress, that hold the minutes of the meetings and cited in this work as *Minutes, C. F. A.* Until 1913 they are rather sterile, usually listing only the members present and the measures discussed. After that date they are more copious. Some of the clerks, able to take stenographic notes, made full entries of the discussion of business before the Committee. In other instances there are lengthy summaries of the day's proceedings.

Through the Sixtieth Congress the accumulation of correspondence, petitions, etc. received by the Committee is in the Library of Congress. The material for each Congress is deposited in a separate box. Beginning with the Sixty-first Congress there is a separate large red folder for each bill and resolution. Included within that folder are the correspondence, the manuscripts of hearings held, and any memoranda that may be brought to the Committee's attention. At the end of each Congress these folders are tied up in wrapping paper or put in large black file boxes which are stored in several rooms throughout the Capitol. Materials which I have taken from this source I have cited as *Files, C. F. A.*

INDEX